THE DRAMA OF THE LOST DISCIPLES

The Façade

BASILICA DI S. PUDENZIANA AT ROME

THE DRAMA OF
THE LOST DISCIPLES

BY

GEORGE F. JOWETT

THE COVENANT PUBLISHING COMPANY LIMITED
121 Low Etherley, Bishop Auckland, Co Durham DL14 0HA
United Kingdom
2009

First Edition	Dec 1961	3,000
Second Edition	Oct 1963	3,000
Third Edition	Jan 1966	2,000
Fourth Edition	Apr 1967	3,000
Fifth Edition	Nov 1968	3,000
Sixth Edition	Jan 1970	4,000
Seventh Edition	Jan 1972	4,000
Eighth Edition	Nov 1975	5,000
Ninth Edition	Oct 1978	2,000
Tenth Edition	Jan 1980	5,000
Eleventh Edition	Jul 1988	3,000
Twelfth Edition	Apr 1993	2,000
Thirteenth Edition	Nov 1996	3,000
Fourteenth Edition - 40th Anniversary	Dec 2001	3,000
Fifteenth Edition	Jun 2004	5,000
Sixteenth (USA) Edition	Nov 2009	5,000

ISBN-978-0-85205-042-2

Printed by Presto Printing Inc., P.O. Box 543, Conway, AR 72033

Cover photographs by John Battersby.

Front: The remains of the Nave arch of Glastonbury Abbey, seen through the east arch of St. Joseph's Chapel.

Back: The Chalice Well at the foot of the Tor at Glastonbury. The chalybeate spring water is reputed to have healing properties, and it is here some believe that King Lucius was baptized (see page 208 and note on page 214).

CONTENTS

ABOUT THE AUTHOR

George Fiusdale Jowett (1891-1969), came from a prominent literary family. He was born in England but moved to Canada at the age of nineteen where he began his research.

He founded a large publishing house in New York and Philadelphia. By the late 1930s he controlled five corporations with offices in Australia, New Zealand, Britain, Europe and the Far East.

He was Chairman of the Board of Planning and Development of the *St. Lawrence Seaway Project* – which was his last, among many, eminent positions in civic affairs – he also worked tirelessly for his community since it was destined to be flooded by the Seaway.

In his youth he became the international gymnastics champion in his age group and by the age of eighteen he had won world titles in boxing in feather, light, and welterweight divisions, which was remarkable since when he was nine-years-old his parents were told he would never walk again and was not expected to live past the age of fifteen, due to an accident he suffered when he was six months old.

He was founder of the *Jowett Institute For Physical Culture* in both Philadelphia and New York, and created a mail-order business writing numerous health and exercise booklets, one of which sold over 25 million copies.

In the year before he died he was honoured with the *Molson Trophy* in Montreal, distinguishing him as the man who had contributed more than anyone else to bodybuilding.

He is buried at St. Lawrence Seaway Union Cemetery. His gravestone reads, in part, "a humble man who carried his meritorious achievements with quiet dignity and thanksgiving."

INTRODUCTION

BY THE REV. ANSLEY RASH

IT was Edmund Burke who wrote, 'People will not look forward to posterity who never look backward to their ancestors', and it is certainly true to say that only a very real knowledge of what God has done for and through the British race in the days that are past can give confidence and courage with which to face the unknown in this era of crisis and tragedy. This is one of the major reasons for my satisfaction and pleasure in the privilege accorded to me of introducing this most interesting and instructive book to all those who are concerned with facts, not fancies.

So much rubbish has been written concerning Britain's pagan past and so many attempts have been made to destroy our justifiable pride in the very real achievement of our race that we welcome unreservedly one more book devoted to the purpose of informing our people of the glorious Christian heritage that was bequeathed to us in the first four centuries. Here the faith of Christ was firmly founded soon after the Passion and Resurrection of our Lord and here also the first Christian Church in all the world outside of Jerusalem was erected by the original disciple and followers of the Incarnate Word.

It is fashionable in these days for our leaders in Church and State to make the pilgrimage to Rome to seek economic security and ecclesiastical unity, but this book reminds us very forcibly that in those early days while the Roman Empire was still pagan, men braved the fury of the elements and the peril of the sword to journey to the Britannic Isles in order to proclaim the Gospel of love, light and liberty, and then as the Heralds of the Cross to bear it from Glastonbury and Iona, Bangor and Lindisfarne, to the far places of the earth, for Britain, not Rome, was then the Lighthouse of Europe.

The author of this book, a Canadian of British birth, a man of many parts and varied talents, has put us in his debt by reminding us once again of our glorious privilege and solemn responsibility as God's servants and witnesses. He has obviously spent a great deal of time in travel and research in order to collect and collate the wealth of valuable material here presented to the reader. With a well-arranged bibliography the book contains treasures both new and old and should without doubt appeal to all those who love and value the truth concerning our illustrious past. Observing all that God has wrought in the generations long ago, the reader will find faith strengthened and hope renewed for the future.

September 1961

CHAPTER 1

THE SCANDAL OF THE CROSS

O VER nineteen centuries ago in the Old City of Jerusalem, the
most power-packed drama in the history of mankind was
enacted when the Roman soldiery nailed Christ to the Cross, on
the Hill of Golgotha. With this ignominious death specially reserved for
the meanest criminals by the Romans, the powerful, fanatical Sadducean
leaders of the Sanhedrin and the Roman Procurator of the Province of
Palestine hoped they had rid themselves of the great disturbing religious
influence which, by their acts, clearly indicated they recognized as a
dangerous challenge to their authority.

From a material point of view the supreme sacrifice of Jesus might
have been the grand finale of His mission, ending in a futile gesture but
for the existence of one man. This man, but fleetingly mentioned in the
tragedy of the cross, passed out of scriptural mention under a mantle of
mystery in the fateful year of AD 36. From that year onward secular
history takes up the theme.

Ancient documents carefully preserved, and others recently
recovered from the dusty, long-forgotten archives referring to that
epochal year, record him as having been cast upon the seas with a few
faithful companions by their remorseless enemies, in an open, oarless
boat without sails, on an ebbing tide over which they drifted far from the
shores of their shadowed Judean homeland, to which they were never to
return.[1]

In order to grasp the significant, historical importance of this
particular person, and the considerable power he wielded, we must
retrace our footsteps and examine more closely the soul-stirring events
that began with the accursed kiss of Judas in the Garden of Gethsemane,
to the aftermath of the Crucifixion. In doing so one cannot help but
experience amazement at the revolting series of extra legal actions that
pursued the course from the arrest of Christ, to His death, indicated by
the bitter, bestial hatred of the corrupt ruling Priesthood of the Jewish
Sanhedrin.

On that dark night in the torch-lightened garden it did not need the
pointing finger of Judas, or his betraying kiss, to identify the Christ.

---

[1]Taylor, J. W. *Coming of the Saints* (London: Covenant Publishing Company) 1969 pp. 126-127.

Jesus forestalled the traitor by calmly walking to meet the guard, asking them if He was the one they sought. Undoubtedly, the soldiers knew Jesus by sight but the law required a civilian to make the identity in order for them to make the arrest.

For this historic act of treachery Judas was paid thirty pieces of silver by the Sanhedrin to betray his Master.

Contrary to popular belief the Roman guard did not make the arrest. It was executed by the priest's guard upon the authority of the Sanhedrin. The arrest was illegal. The Sanhedrin had not the authority to arrest a citizen. The power belonged exclusively to the Roman court which then ruled over Judea. It could only be carried out by the Roman guard on orders issued by Roman authority on a recognized complaint.

Jesus offered no resistance. Quietly He walked between the guards who had feared to lay hands on Him, through the darkened streets to the Temple of the Sanhedrin where its legislative members had been called to an emergency session at midnight for the sole purpose of trying Christ before its priestly court.

Here again we note an extraordinary breach of judicial process. The Roman law did not permit court hearings to be held after sunset. [2]

Even under an emergency measure no trial for life could be held after dark. Moreover, a trial for life was exclusively the prerogative of the Roman court, to be held only before the Roman Procurator. Yet we find Caiaphas, High Priest of the Sanhedrin, deliberately flouting the all-powerful Roman authority in a trial for life as late as midnight.

Off-hand, one is apt to obtain the impression that the Jews were a powerful people whom the Roman authority feared sufficiently to extend to them certain legal extenuations.

This was far from being the case. The Jews were subjects of the Roman State and looked upon with the contempt and scorn a dictatorship reserves for its meanest vassals.

The extra-legal practices of Caiaphas reveal two forms of circumstances which, even under casual investigation, appear quite evident.

It reveals the desperate position in which the Sanhedrin viewed the insecurity of their own situation by the popularity of Christ's teachings, or it indicates that Caiaphas possessed some damaging secret political knowledge whereby he dared to thwart retaliation by the Roman governor.

---

[2] Blackstone, *Commentaries on the Laws of England.* (Vols. I-IV 1765 – 1767)

THE SCANDAL OF THE CROSS

Into the crowded assembly of the Sanhedrin the tall, stately Christ was led to face His arch-enemies, Caiaphas and his father-in-law Annas who, as the reigning High Priests of Judaism, also represented the powerful, despotic Sadducean families, of which they were members. Never before, or since, has a court trial been charged with so much conflicting emotion. Hate, in all its seething virulence, spewed its evil venom upon the tense assemblage, a baleful challenge to any member who dared oppose the predetermined decision of the Sadducees. Malevolence was so potent that even at this late day one is readily convinced that any person who dared to stand for the defence of the prisoner must have known he was a doomed man.

Contrary to the common belief that Jesus was completely surrounded by enemies at that strange midnight trial, the light of recent findings proves it to have been very much otherwise.

That Jesus was encompassed by a vengeful, hostile group who sought His total extinction is substantiated, but the brilliant battle for the defence against the savage demands for destruction has, unfortunately, never been sufficiently reported. Today, we know the trial for life was fought out on the floor of the Sanhedrin with all the stormy violence of a bestial, prejudiced fury on one side and the granite uncompromising courage of the defence by men who knew that by the very act of their challenge they had signed and sealed their own death warrant.[3]

At this late date we who are Christians should bow our heads in reverent silence to the memory of that heroic group of defenders, unmentioned in history, who gave their all in a gallant attempt to save Christ from the agony of the cross.

The prosecution was led and conducted throughout by men whose vicious bigotry was all the more devastating by reason of their undeniable intelligence. Cruelly aided by those who bore false witness, a more suitable prosecution could not have been chosen.

Out of all this unreasonable prejudice it staggers the imagination to realize that the man then blazing with hatred who led the violent persecution of the Christians, within the next few years would be blazing with the zeal of Christ. The Bible names him first as Saul of Tarsus, but posterity was to remember him as the great Apostle to the Gentiles, St. Paul.

On this particular occasion we see the opposition potent with prejudice, slashing at Christ with their verbal darts, subtly fanning the

---

[3] cf. *Gospel of Nicodemus*, (Apocryphal New Testament) 5:6.

THE DRAMA OF THE LOST DISCIPLES

flame of antagonism against Him. On the other side, we see the champions of the defence striking back with rapier swiftness. The history of the Trial, as it has come down to us, shows that the defence fought back with all the resolute heroism of fearless warriors, invincible in the courage of their firm convictions.

The vindication of Christ must have been brilliant, a classic in legal annals, as proven by the amazing vote cast that night in the Sanhedrin. Dauntlessly, they carried their advocacy with an offensive vigour that overwhelmed the bigoted Prosecution. Emotions became unleashed in a tempestuous foment of conflicting opinions. In this confusion Caiaphas saw danger to his covert acts. Not to be thwarted, he cast prudence to the winds, causing a legal travesty that was not permitted in Jewish jurisprudence. He took the prosecution into his own hands, completely ignoring his prosecuting Counsel, and the Counsel for the Accused. Probably for the first time in Jewish legal history, Caiaphas personally conducted a vindictive cross-examination of the Prisoner, after all the evidence had been presented and the testimony of the opposing witnesses broken down by the superb resistance to their evidence.

Throughout the proceedings Jesus remained unperturbed, serene in His righteousness. He offered no defence to save Himself, on the grounds that that which is right needs no defence. He affirmed His status calmly before friend and foe, knowing beforehand He was destined to die.

The vote was cast and the triumphant defence established. The amazing fact is that out of the seventy-one legislative members of the Sanhedrin, forty voted for the dismissal of the case and the freedom of Jesus.

This was not to be. Foiled within the Sanhedrin, Caiaphas played a trump card which he knew could not be vetoed. He demanded that Jesus be tried before Pontius Pilate, the Roman Procurator of the Roman Province of Palestine, on the charge of treason.

It must not be thought that the classic defence alone swayed the vote of the Sanhedrin. What it did do was to pour courage into many hearts, inspiring them to stand by a religious conviction already instilled within them. Actually, for three years previous to this infamous trial by midnight, the Sanhedrin had been split on religious policy. Many had been the heated debates within the assembly, with the Sadducees clinging to an emasculated Judean faith into which they had injected their own corrupt personal policy. These were the old ultra conservatives led by Annas and Caiaphas. Ranged against them was the new Liberal Party who had openly declared for the new spiritual order. They could not win. The dice was loaded against them. The Sadducees controlled the wealthy ruling power in Jewry, with the exception of a single individual whose influence was so great it stretched beyond the boundaries of Jewry into the high places of Roman administration.[4]

He is the man who at this stage of events quietly moves into the scene. He was the power behind the throne who backed up the exhortations of the Liberal Party in the Sanhedrin, and the man who stood behind the defence of Jesus with his resourceful support on that fateful night.[5]

The only man who the Sadducees dared not oppose was Joseph, the great uncle of Jesus, known scripturally and in secular history as Joseph of Arimathea.[6]

To most people he is remembered as the rich man who kindly offered his private sepulchre for the burial of Christ; the man who boldly claimed the body of Jesus from Pilate, who, with Nicodemus took the body from the cross, providing the clean linens that enclosed the tortured, crucified form. In the scriptural record, at the most he appears but a transitory figure at the trial and the crucifixion, seldom mentioned, and then with no evident stress of importance, silently passing out of the scriptural picture four years after the passion of Christ.

In our own time Joseph of Arimathea is but slightly referred to, skimmed over as a person of little significance.

Why he has been indifferently by-passed, along with historic events covering that epochal period is both perplexing and surprising. The part he played in preserving The Word, and in paving the path for the proclamation of 'The Way' to the world, is as fascinating as it is inspiring. He was the protector of that valorous little band of disciples during the perilous years following the crucifixion, the indefatigable head of the Christian underground in Judea and the guardian of Christ's only earthly treasure – His mother.

---

[4] He is referred to as 'nobilis decurio' by Maelgwyn of Llandaff.

[5] *Gospel of Nicodemus* 11:5, etc.

[6] 'St. Joseph has the same word applied to him as to St. John the Evangelist – paranymphos – or attendant to the Blessed Virgin.' – Rev. L. Smithett Lewis, *St. Joseph of Arimathea at Glastonbury* (Cambridge: James Clarke & Co. Ltd) 1976 (quoting John of Glastonbury), p.67; also: '*Magna tabula Glastoniensis*', extracts concerning the history and saints of Glastonbury; 14th century, Bodleian Library, Oxford, refers to the Apostle John, then working in Ephesus, appointing St. Joseph of Arimathea as paranymphos.

Startling as it may appear to most Christians, and particularly to the Anglo-American world, the dominant role he performed in laying the true cornerstone of our Christian way of life should thrill our hearts with undying gratitude. His story is exclusively the story of Britain and, in consequence, America, and all Christian people wherever they may be.

In actuality, Joseph of Arimathea was the Apostle of Britain, the true Apostle first to set up Christ's standard on that sea-girt little isle, five hundred and sixty years before St. Augustine set foot on English soil. He, with twelve other disciples of Christ, erected in England the first Christian church above ground in the world, to the glory of God and His Son, Jesus Christ.

CHAPTER 2

THE NOBILIS DECURIO

JOSEPH of Arimathea was a man of refinement, well educated, and one who possessed many talents. He had extraordinary political and business ability and was reputed to be one of the wealthiest men in the world of that time. He was the Carnegie of his day, a metal magnate controlling the tin and lead industry which then was akin in importance to that of steel today.

Tin was the chief metal for the making of alloys and in great demand by the warring Romans.

Many authorities claim that Joseph's world control of tin and lead was due to his vast holdings in the famous, ancient tin mines of Britain.[7] This interest he had acquired and developed many years before Jesus was baptized by His cousin, John the Baptist, and before He began His brief but glorious mission.

The world's major portion of tin was mined in Cornwall, smelted into ingots and exported throughout the then known civilized world, chiefly in the ships of Joseph. He is reputed to have owned one of the largest private merchant shipping fleets afloat which traversed the world's sea lanes in the transportation of this precious metal.

The existence of the tin trade between Cornwall and Phoenicia is frequently referred to by classical writers, and is described at considerable length by Diodorus Siculus as well as Julius Caesar.

In the Latin Vulgate of the Gospel of *Mark* 15:43, and *Luke* 23:50, we find both referring to Joseph of Arimathea as 'Decurio'. This was the common term employed by the Romans to designate an official in charge of metal mines.

In St. Jerome's translation, Joseph's official title is given as 'Nobilis Decurio'. This would indicate that he held a prominent position in the Roman administration as a minister of mines. For a Jew to hold such high rank in the Roman State is rather surprising, and goes far to prove the remarkable characteristics of Joseph. We know he was an influential member of the Sanhedrin, the Jewish religious body that ruled Roman Jewry, and a legislative member of a provincial Roman senate. His financial and social standing can well be estimated when we consider he

---

[7] Lewis, L. S. *St. Joseph of Arimathea at Glastonbury*, pp. 51-52.

owned a palatial home in the holy city and a fine country residence just outside Jerusalem.

Several miles north of the ancient city he possessed another spacious estate at Arimathea, which is known today as Ramallah. It was located on the populous caravan route between Nazareth and Jerusalem. Everything known of him points to him as affluent and as a person of importance and influence within both the Jewish and Roman hierarchies.

According to the Talmud, Joseph was the younger brother of the father of the Virgin Mary. He was her uncle, and therefore a great uncle to Jesus. Chiefly from the secular reports we learn that Joseph was a married man and his son, Josephes, left a mark of distinction in British history.

During the lifetime of Jesus there constantly appears reference to his association with a relative at Jerusalem. Profane history is more positive on the matter, identifying the connection with Joseph. As we study the old records we find there is a valid reason for the close association of Jesus and his family with Joseph. It is quite obvious that the husband of Mary died while Jesus was young. Under Jewish law such a circumstance automatically appointed the next male kin of the husband, in this case Joseph, legal guardian of the family. This fact explains many things. History and tradition report Jesus, as a boy, frequently in the company of His uncle, particularly at the time of the religious feasts, and declare that Jesus made voyages to Britain with Joseph in his ships. Cornish traditions abound with this testimony and numerous ancient landmarks bear Hebrew names recording these visits.

Even during the short period of the ministry of Jesus there is definitely shown to exist a close affinity between them, far greater than one would expect from an ordinary guardianship. It was fatherly, loyal; with a mutual affection death could not sever.

We know that Joseph never forsook his nephew. He stood by Him as a bold, fearless defender at the notorious trial, and defied the Sanhedrin by going to Pilate and boldly claiming the body when all others feared to do so. His arms were the first to cradle the broken corpse when taken from the cross and place it in the tomb. After death he continued to protect the mutilated body of Jesus from the conspiring minds of the Sadducees. He risked his all, wealth, power and position in those crucial years fulfilling his obligation as guardian of Jesus and of the family of Mary. He loved Jesus dearly. The disciples spoke of Joseph with an affectionate regard. They wrote he was a 'just man', a 'good man', 'honourable', and 'a disciple of Jesus'. The latter clearly indicates that all through their association Joseph must have encouraged Jesus in His great work and that he was aware of the mystery of His birth and probably His destiny. All evidence proves that Joseph believed in the validity of all Jesus taught and ultimately suffered for.[8]

It is commonly taught that Jesus was poor and of obscure relatives. His relationship with the affluent Joseph of Arimathea proves otherwise. In His own right He was a property owner but long before He took up His mission He forsook all material wealth.

It should be remembered that Jesus was a true lineal descendant of the Shepherd King, David, and of Seth, son of Adam, who was the son of God.

---

[8] cf. Joseph's testimony, *Gospel of Nicodemus*, 9:5-11.

CHAPTER 3

WHO MOVED THE STONE AT THE TOMB?

DENIED the power of the vote Caiaphas lost no time in contacting Pilate, fully prepared to play his ace with the pressure of blackmail if Pilate hesitated to institute the charge of treason against Jesus. Under Roman law treason was a capital offence which, if proven, was punishable by death. Only the Roman Procurator could try such a case and only he could legally impose the death penalty. This Caiaphas demanded and silence was his price.

The High Priest possessed positive knowledge that Pontius Pilate had been an active party to a secret, futile plot to assassinate Tiberius Caesar.[9] Armed with this knowledge Caiaphas imposed his will on the Procurator, who trembled with fear of exposure, disgrace, and the threat to his life.

It is with certainty we can assume that Joseph pleaded with Pilate not to interfere in a new trial of Jesus. Joseph was unaware of the deadly secret Caiaphas held over the Spanish-born Procurator. Neither his pleadings nor his influence could prevail. Nor could the earnest supplication of Pilate's wife avail, who, disturbed by the potency of a dream the night before, begged of him to have nothing to do with the trial of 'that just man'.

Pilate deferred to his wife. He owed his exalted position to the social eminence his marriage had brought. His wife was Claudia Procula, the illegitimate daughter of Claudia, the third wife of Tiberius Caesar, and grand-daughter of Augustus Caesar. Pilate knew that the Emperor, against whom he had plotted, was very fond of his step-daughter and, being an astute politician, Pontius Pilate deferred to her every whim. For him to deny Claudia's urgent request is but to prove how serious Pilate considered the hold Caiaphas had on him. At heart Pilate was not in sympathy with the demands of the Sadducees. He found no foundation to their charges. Four times Jesus was pronounced innocent but Pilate, in his evasive gesture calling for a bowl of water to signify he washed his hands of the whole matter, acceded to the murderous demands of the Sanhedrin. Nevertheless, he permitted the Roman guard to carry out the tragic act historically known as 'The Scandal of the Cross'.

---

[9] Franzero, Carlo Maria *Memoirs of Pontius Pilate*. (Redman:1961)

The dream that tortured Pilate's wife on the previous night foretold disaster to him if he judged Jesus. The dream came true. Later Pontius Pilate committed suicide.[10]

From the beginning to the end the arrest and dual trial was a vicious frame-up, a betrayal, a travesty of justice. From that dark hour in the garden to the crucifixion, the plot was hurried to its conclusion. It had to be. The murmurings of the people had been growing louder, as evidenced at the final trial. Following the fatal verdict the whole city seethed with fear and unrest. Caiaphas and his fanatical collaborators had triumphed but the Romans held the lash and would not hesitate to use it unmercifully on the slightest provocation or interference. So greatly did terror prevail throughout Jerusalem that all known to have been associated with Jesus in even the slightest way fled into hiding.

Nine of the twelve disciples had fled the city directly after the arrest in the garden, leaving only three standing by. Judas was no longer numbered among the faithful. Only Peter, John and Nicodemus remained. Even though Peter had denied his Master he, with the beloved disciple John, had followed Jesus into the crowded court room of the Sanhedrin. There for the third time, Peter denied association with his Lord. After the fatal circumstances had arisen Peter, overwhelmed with self-torment and ashamed of his denials, despondently went into seclusion within the city. He did not witness the crucifixion. Of those present, the Scriptures refer by name only to John and Mary, the mother of Jesus, witnessing the tragedy at the foot of the cross, and the three women, Mary Magdalene, Mary the wife of Cleopas, and Salome who watched from a respectful distance.[11]

Wonderment is often evinced at the omission of the Bethany sisters, Martha and Mary, whom Jesus loved. The impression gathered is that they were not present. This does not seem conceivable. The name of Joseph is not mentioned but it seems safe to say they were all present. The record says, 'all the women who followed Him and others were mingled among the crowd'.

The speed with which Joseph called on Pilate after the demise indicates that he was present. Pilate appears to be surprised at hearing the swift news, asking those near him if it were true Jesus was dead.

---

[10] cf. Eusebius (c. 260–340) Bishop of Caesarea (modern Qisarya, Israel); author of a history of the Christian church to 324.

[11] 'But all those who were the acquaintance of Christ, stood at a distance, as did the women who had followed Jesus from Galilee, observing all these things' – *Gospel of Nicodemus* 8:11.

It is doubtful if the beloved John and the Blessed Mother witnessed the expiration on the cross. We are told that after Jesus committed His mother to the care of John, the disciple led her away to spare her the last dark hours of suffering.

Probably the average Christian of today fails to realize the extent of the physical and mental torture borne by the sensitive Jesus through this agonizing period. From the hour of the Last Supper to the time of His death, He had not touched food or drink. He had been 'third degreed' from the moment He stood in the torch-lit Sanhedrin, until after His trial before Pilate. Then followed the heckling, the crowning of thorns, and the reviling by His enemies who had placed the mocking sign on Him – 'King of the Jews'.

Following His condemnation to death He had been brutally flogged by His Roman executioners, His back slashed to ribbons. Even today it is conceded that the Roman flogging was the most cruel ever to be inflicted on a human being. This we can well believe as we scan the Roman records which attest to the fact that only one out of ten ever survived the ghastly scourging.

His suffering was intensified when the reviling Roman soldier pressed the bitter sponge of hyssop to His parched lips when He called for water as He hung on the cross.

All this He endured apart from the terrible torment He suffered as He slowly expired on the cross. Weighing all this as we must, we are not left in doubt that Jesus was as physically superb as He was mentally and spiritually.

According to both Jewish and Roman law, unless the body of an executed criminal be immediately claimed by the next of kin the body of the victim was cast into a common pit with others where all physical record of them was completely obliterated.

Why did not Mary, the mother of Jesus, as the immediate next of kin, claim the body of her beloved Son?

Perhaps John, fearing for the safety of Mary, restrained her, leaving it to Joseph, the family guardian, to make the request. We do know that Joseph was the one who personally went to Pilate and obtained the Procurator's official sanction to claim the body, remove it from the cross, and prepare it for burial in his private sepulchre which was within the garden of his estate.

You will likely agree that this was in order. But consider the circumstances.

A reign of terror continued to prevail within the city of Jerusalem. No follower of Christ was safe from the evil machinations of the Sanhedrin, who were then enjoying a Roman holiday in the persecution of the followers of 'The Way'. As already stated, all but two of the disciples had fled the city and gone into safe seclusion in fear of their lives. However, as we shall see, there was yet another, Nicodemus, who had not fled the city. But Joseph, the Roman senator, and the legislative member of the Sanhedrin, also a disciple, was the only close associate of Christ who dared to walk openly on the street without fear of molestation. Was he too powerful and prominent for either side to harm? Yet Joseph knew he was dealing with dynamite, and from the circumstances that followed it appears that Joseph did fear interference, not personally, but in his intentions.

Actually, why did he go to Pontius Pilate?

Why did he not claim the body in the ordinary way, according to custom?

Certainly, it was not a common occurrence to seek permission from the highest authority in the land in order to obtain the body of an executed criminal.

Why had he not sought permission from the Sanhedrin? They were inflexible in their rule that a body must be claimed and buried before sunset. Actually, under normal circumstances there was no need to go further than the Sanhedrin. Jesus was regarded as a Jew. Joseph was a Jew and a high ranking member of the Jewish Sanhedrin. There was only one reason why Joseph preferred to make the claim for the body to Pilate. He knew that the fanatical Sadducean Priesthood sought the total extinction of Jesus, even in death.

Annas and Caiaphas had succeeded in their diabolical, murderous scheme by having Jesus crucified as a common criminal.

Does it not stand to reason that they would seek to carry out the ignominy to its fullest extent?

Would they not have preferred that the body of Jesus be disposed of in the common criminal pit so that His extinction would be total and all memory steeped in shame?

Certainly, it would have been to the best interest of the Sanhedrin.

To have Jesus decently interred within a respectably known sepulchre was but to erect a martyr's tomb for the multitude to flock to in an ageless pilgrimage. That would have doomed the Sanhedrin more surely than anything else. Therefore, reason would indicate that the High

Priesthood were bent on interfering with the claim of the kin of the crucified Christ. With Mary, the Sanhedrin could interfere, but not with Joseph. He did not fear them and was determined to thwart them in their designs. The Scripture says he went 'boldly' before Pilate and successfully asserted the kin rights of his niece.

Between Caiaphas and Pilate there still existed an armed truce, but the latter played a skilful game. He played both sides to his own advantage. Pilate had already satisfied the Sanhedrin. No matter how they opposed him thereafter, at the moment they could not deny him the right of fulfilling this particular part of the law to which both the Jew and the Roman subscribed in the disposal of the body. Pilate needed Joseph's friendship and there was no easier way of securing it than by recognizing Joseph's claim to the murdered body of his favourite nephew.

By this act of interference, Joseph became a doubly marked man by the High Priesthood of Jewry.

Returning from his mission with Pilate, Joseph's acts are again shown to be hurried as though fearing interception. He returned to the scene of the tragedy followed by Nicodemus, who carried one hundred pounds of mixed spices with which to prepare the body, prior to burial. Premature darkness had set in following the phenomenal storm that broke loose upon the land as Jesus expired on the cross, rending in twain the curtain in the temple and scattering the spectators abroad. Only two remained: Mary Magdalene, and the wife of Cleopas, sister of the Blessed Mary. They watched as Joseph, with the help of Nicodemus, lowered the body from the cross, laid it on the ground and wrapped the mortal remains of Jesus in the burial linen which Joseph had personally provided. It was dark and time appeared precious. Again we are impressed with the evidence of hurriedness. Without any further preparation they carried the body to the sepulchre in the garden of Joseph and laid it within the tomb, while the two women who had followed, watched nearby.

Joseph and Nicodemus had too little time properly to anoint the body and dress it according to the custom in the linen shroud. Yet the surprising thing is that they sealed the entrance to the tomb with a 'great' stone.

Why? Did Joseph have other intentions?

Common sense alone tells us that Joseph would not have allowed the body of his beloved nephew to remain in the ghastly state it was when lowered from the cross, bloody, sweaty, grimy and torn.

Then what happened in between the few dark hours from the time the sealing stone was rolled to close the entrance to the tomb, and early dawn on the third day, when the second great drama took place – the disappearance of the body of Jesus from the sepulchre? We Christians accept without any reservations the biblical version of the disappearance, but it should be remembered that in those days there was no biblical version to go by; and Jesus was but barely known outside His native land. Not then was He the accepted Messiah; therefore, as we keep this in mind, we can better understand the impact, pro and con, this startling incident created among the populace, friend and foe.

The discovery was made on the sabbath dawn when Mary Magdalene, Mary the mother of James, and Salome appeared on the scene at the break of day, bringing with them spices with which to clean and anoint the body of Christ. Their intentions are evident. They knew the body had been hastily interred without the proper burial preparation. The two Marys had been witness to this. They had watched Joseph and Nicodemus take the body from the cross and hurriedly wrap it in the linens at the foot of the cross. They had followed the two men into the garden of Joseph, standing nearby, as the body was placed on the ledge within the tomb, and witnessed the sealing of the entrance to the tomb with the 'great' stone.

They were not likely to anoint the body twice within a few hours.

On approaching the tomb, the scriptural record tells us that the first experience of the three women was one of shock. They saw that the great stone was completely removed from the entrance. This shock was followed by another as the drama unfolded. To their astonishment they saw a young man dressed in white, seated in an unconcerned manner on the very ledge within the tomb on which the body of Christ had been laid.

From a study of the Marcan Manuscript, which relates the story with vivid realism, all evidence tends to prove that this particular young man was a complete stranger to the women and his attitude towards them was calm and unperturbed. He did not rush out to meet them excitedly. Before they had time to speak he told them Jesus was not there. The body was gone. They must go to Galilee, where they would meet Him. He told the stunned women the facts in the simple manner of one relating an incident he believed they should have known. But they did not know. Neither did they know the stranger within the tomb. All they were conscious of was that the body of their Lord was gone. Without questioning the stranger, the frightened women hastened back to the city, with Mary Magdalene, the youngest and most active of the three women, hurrying in advance to inform Peter and John of the startling news. Evidently the two disciples were just as ignorant and bewildered over the disappearance of the body, if not doubtful. We find them hastening to the tomb and, on arriving, investigating the interior. On entering the sepulchre John stooped to pick up the discarded linen that lay collapsed, but intact, supported only by the spices.

But where was the young stranger in white?

He was not there for the two disciples to interrogate.

Who was he? What was he doing there? Where had he gone? What did he know? Why was he never found?

History would give a great deal to know the answers to these puzzling questions. The records are silent.

Following the entombment the Sadducees, suspicious of the disciples, determined to prevent any possible tampering with the body. They requested Pilate to post a guard over the tomb, reminding him that Jesus had claimed that on the third day He would rise from the dead. They did not believe this and instead, considered it a ruse of the disciples to steal the body. Pilate flatly refused. He had already washed his hands of the matter and told them to arrange their own guard, which they did.

In this case where was the guard?

The tomb was unguarded when the three women had arrived.

Why had the guard left so early, and where was the change of guards?

Surely, the Sanhedrin, who had assumed full responsibility for posting the guard, would have taken every possible precaution. It was in their best interest to do so. To do otherwise was to invite the roused anger of the populace and of Pilate. They dare not have placed themselves in such an uncompromising position.

We can well believe that the Sadducees had nothing to do with the disappearance of the body. If they had caused the body to be removed they would never have unwrapped it, leaving the linen there. Neither would they have left the entrance to the tomb open. In their position there was no need for haste. The guard was theirs. Certainly, they would have concealed their crime by replacing the stone at the entrance, giving orders to the guard forbidding anyone entry.

Again, everything points to haste.

Much has been said, pro and con, in reference to the story of the guards, with the general assumption being that it was not true, but a whitewashed alibi of the Sanhedrin. Common opinion is that, even if the guard had fallen asleep at their post, a stone so large and heavy that sealed the tomb could never have been moved away without awakening them. If they had fallen asleep at their post of duty they would have been punished by death, as was the military custom of that time. In this, general opinion errs. It is generally assumed that the guard had to be Roman. If it were true the Roman penalty for dereliction of duty would undoubtedly have been imposed. But the guard belonged to the priestly Sanhedrin, whose discipline did not include the death penalty.

The story given by the priests' guards is most probable.

They admitted they had fallen asleep and, on awakening, were surprised to see that the huge stone had been rolled away. On further investigation they saw that the tomb was empty and straight away hurried to the Sanhedrin with the news. Caiaphas bribed them, giving them money to say that the disciples had stolen the body and to leave it to him to convince Pilate that such was the case. Nevertheless, they were deeply concerned over the disappearance and the Jewish record informs us that Caiaphas ordered Joseph to appear before the Sanhedrin for questioning. Another stormy scene occurred before the Assembly. Caiaphas openly accused Joseph of being the prime instigator of the plot and demanded to know where the body reposed. To all their questioning Joseph maintained a stony silence. He refused to talk, defiant in the knowledge that he was beyond their power to prosecute.

Why did they not interrogate Mary, the mother of Jesus, or Peter, John, or Nicodemus, whom the Sanhedrin knew were the only associates of Christ present in the city at that time? Why were the other women not questioned? Perhaps the Sanhedrin considered such simple people as they incapable of carrying out such a delicate operation. Perhaps the genuine agitation of the disciples, and of the women concerning the mystery, was enough to satisfy the priesthood that they had no knowledge of what had happened.

The difference between the members of the Sanhedrin and the disciples was that the Jewish priests insisted that the body of Jesus was stolen and secretly buried by Joseph or the disciples. The latter believed

Christ had risen according to His word, on the third day, to be the first-fruits of all who slept. Therefore, it matters not who moved the stone at the tomb.

Sorrow turned into triumph and an unquenchable zeal to preach the Gospel to all the world. Joseph of Arimathea, the great uncle of Jesus, was no longer guardian over His corporeal existence but over a greater treasure – Christ's sacred mission on earth. Henceforth he was to be the guardian of all the beloved against the arch-enemy, and ultimately their leader. He began to dedicate himself to his amazing destiny, which later was to make it possible for Peter and Paul to accomplish their great work in the service of the Lord. Joseph himself was to plant the roots of Christianity in fertile soil where it would flourish and never perish from off the earth.

CHAPTER 4

THE SAULIAN GESTAPO AND THE EXODUS AD 36

FOLLOWING the disappearance of the body and the Ascension of Christ, an evil, brooding passion for vengeance seized upon the ruling priesthood of the Sanhedrin. In secret conclave they plotted and planned a campaign of unremitting persecution against the followers of 'The Way'. Maliciously, they determined to exterminate all who failed to escape their bloody hands.

There is no greater hatred than in a divided house, or brother against brother. In the main, the victims of the Sanhedrin were of their own race. The hatred they bore for the followers of 'The Way' was far greater than the implacable hatred that had divided the kingdom of Israel before the captivity. At that time, the Ten Tribes under Ephraim had drawn north into Samaria, while the two tribes of Judah and Benjamin, with a few Levites, remained at Jerusalem. A wall of bitterness existed between them that was never removed. After each regained their freedom, the Ephraimites commenced their long march beyond the Euphrates, disappearing from scriptural history, to become known by other names.

Now, it was more than a bitterness. It was a blind, cruel, unreasonable, black hatred.

The 'Gestapo' the Sanhedrin formed was specially organized under the appointed leadership of the vengeful Saul. He wasted no time. He struck quickly and viciously. Followers of 'The Way' found in Jerusalem, be they Greek, Roman or Jew, were openly, or in secret alike struck down. No mercy was shown. The records of that time state the prisons were overcrowded with their victims.

The first notable victim Saul seized upon was the man whom he considered to be his inveterate foe, Stephen, the courageous leader of the Liberal Party who led the brilliant defence of Jesus on that fateful night in the court of the Sanhedrin. Along with Peter, John and others, Stephen had taken up the sceptre, defying the Sadducees by victoriously preaching the Word throughout the holy city. Thousands were daily converted and later, according to St. Luke, reached the spectacular number of three to five thousand daily. This testimony dissipates the idea that the Jews were unresponsive to the magic appeal of 'The Way'. The Jews were the first converts, a fact which further infuriated the corrupt Sadducean Priesthood.

Fate caught up quickly with Stephen. The Jewish minions of the Sanhedrin stoned him to death in the manner peculiar to the Jews, as Saul looked on. He perished by the gate that still bears his name. St. Stephen was the first martyr for Christ, AD 33.

So fierce was Saul's vindictive purge that he wrought havoc within the Church at Jerusalem. The boundaries of Judea could not confine him. Illegally, he trespassed far within Roman territory where he hounded the devotees without censure or interference from Roman administration. No doubt the Romans felt Saul was doing them a service, and a good job in ridding them of what they considered an undesirable religious pestilence.

Throughout this reign of terror Joseph remained the stalwart, fearless protector of the disciples and of the women. On every possible occasion he stood between them and their enemies, a veritable tower of strength. Saul's fury knew no bounds. Strive and scheme as they may, Joseph's position as an influential minister of mines in the Roman State defied the Saulian Gestapo from molesting his person, or those whom he defended. Nevertheless, it became a losing battle. Within four years after the death of Christ, AD 36, many of the devotees were scattered out of Jerusalem and Judea. There is little doubt that the ships of Joseph, co-ordinating with the Christian underworld, carried numerous of the faithful in safety to other lands. He spared neither his help nor his wealth in aiding all whom he could.

Callous as the Romans were with their own specific brand of brutality, even they were shocked by the ferocious atrocities of the Sanhedrin Gestapo. Out of this evil sprung the cause of their own ultimate doom. Later the Romans turned into a two-edged sword, becoming the rabid persecutors and executioners of both Jew and Christian. Saul was to meet a cruel death at their hands.

For the Judean Jews the culminating catastrophe occurred in the year AD 70, when Titus, son of the Roman Emperor Vespasian, massacred them at Jerusalem and put the ancient city to torch, levelling it to ashes, as Jesus had foretold. Those who escaped were scattered to the four corners of the world, despised and hated, forced to live in ghettoes, and never to return to Judea. The Christian persecution was to continue for centuries in an increasing, diabolic form. Tiberius proclaimed an edict, making it a capital offence to be a Christian. Claudius and other Roman Emperors repeated the edict. The Romans, noting with alarm the rise of Christianity, began to consider Christians a menace to their empiric safety; therefore a class of people to be exterminated. History proves with a mass of bloodstained evidence, how they strove their level best to crush the evangelistic movement. It was like striving to push back the waves of the sea with the palms of their hands. It was not to be. As prophecy proclaimed, and history has fulfilled, the cross was to triumph over the sword.

According to *Acts* 8:1-4, by AD 36 the Church of Jerusalem was scattered abroad. Even the Apostles were forced later to flee. This was the year of the epochal exile when the curtain descended darkly upon the lives and doings of so many of that illustrious band. Modern Christians are chiefly familiar with the New Testament record of the favoured few – Peter, Paul, Matthew, Mark, Luke and John, with passing reference to but a few others. What became of the rest of the original twelve Apostles, the seventy whom Christ first elected, then what of the later one hundred and twenty? They are the lost disciples on whom the scriptural record is as silent as the grave, particularly the two most outstanding characters, Joseph of Arimathea, and Mary, the mother of Jesus. The sacred pages close upon them in that fateful year of AD 36, leaving not a trace or a shadow of their mysterious passage into permanent exile.

Ponder the facts. Christ's mission lasted but three years. Four years later the Elect had fled into exile. The great crusade was ended in but six years. True, some disciples laboured later there in Judea, but the effects were transitory. Roman rule tightened down with a mailed fist on both Jew and Christian. Within thirty-five years the holy city was to be a rubble of ruins and thereafter largely occupied by the heathen and unbelievers. Christianity had its birth in Christ in the Holy Land, but not its growth that flourished to convert the world. This sprang to its full glory in another land. How could this happen? You may search the Scriptures in vain for record of Matthew, Mark, Luke and John ever being near this distant country. The journeys of Peter and Paul as described in the Bible do not seem to give any clue. Then who performed this monumental Christian evangelistic work?

Jesus Himself provides the answer as He denounces the Sadducean Jews, telling them that the glory shall be taken away from them and given to another.[12] Again, when He says He came not to the Jews, but to the lost sheep of the House of Israel.[13] He knew He would not convert

---

[12] *Matthew* 21:43
[13] *Matthew* 15:24.

the Sanhedrin and its following, so it had to be others – the lost sheep. Who were they? The answer lies in His commission to Paul, the converted Saul, whom he commands to go to the Gentiles. To what Gentiles did Paul go apart from the Romans? Or did Paul commission others of the illustrious band as missionaries? The answer has to be somewhere. The Romans did not Christianize the world. They were the greatest enemies of the Christian Gospel for over three hundred years after the death of Christ. Who crushed this Roman opposition so that Rome became Christian?

Many are the intriguing questions that can be asked, all of which would seem to deepen the mystery that revolves around those who can be truly called the Lost Disciples. We find the answers by studying ancient writings, the old martyrologies and menologies, the age-old parchments that have reposed in great libraries for many centuries, filed away, and for almost as many centuries, completely forgotten. These, and the works of eminent scholars who have explored the great scrolls, and deciphered the contents, reveal the astonishing facts. That is the object of this work, which at best can only quote briefly from the mass of data available. Where scriptural history ends secular history begins and in using the word 'history', we find greater faith and strength in understanding the original meaning of the word. As one great writer stated, 'There are Sermons in Stones'. Equally so, there is revelation in words.

The Bible was God's Book of history, the Word of God. In the Old Testament, history is given to us in prophecy, and in the New Testament demonstrated in fulfilment. Therefore, viewed in this light, the true explanation of the word 'history' as we employ the word is: 'Prophecy is history [His-Story] foretold, and history is prophecy fulfilled.' Fulfilment of His story began in the advent of Christ and will continue until the whole world accepts Him. Even we Christians have yet much to learn, but Jesus said it would become known unto us all as we are ready to receive.

All those who are inclined to consider the Gospel of Christ a mystical, intangible or incredible story founded on myth and superstition with no substance to His existence, will find solid evidence in tracing the footsteps of the Lost Disciples from the exodus of AD 36, when they passed out of biblical history into secular history, particularly the events concerning Joseph of Arimathea. While there are many learned minds dating from the era of Christ onward that provide the same record, there is a special advantage in quoting a more modern authority with the eminent ecclesiastical background of Cardinal Baronius, who is considered the most outstanding historian of the Roman Catholic Church. He was Curator of the famous Vatican library, a man of learning, and a reliable, facile writer. Quoting from his *Ecclesiastical Annals* referring to the exodus of the year AD 36, the mystery is solved as to the fate of Joseph of Arimathea and others who went into exile with him. He writes:

'In that year the party mentioned was exposed to the sea in a vessel without sails or oars. The vessel drifted finally to Marseilles and they were saved. From Marseilles Joseph and his company passed into Britain and after preaching the Gospel there, died.'

No doubt, this event in British history will come as a surprise to many Christians, but there is a mass of corroborative evidence to support this historic passage by many reliable Greek and Roman authorities, including affirmation in the *Jewish Encyclopaedia*, under 'Arles'.

The studious pronouncement made by Cardinal Baronius, derived from delving into the treasured archives of the Vatican at Rome, has proved to be as incontrovertible as it is revealing. To my mind, the Vatican would be the first to repudiate any testimony from their archives to support the priority claim of Christian Britain, if it were untrue.

The interesting part of the Baronius report is that the date coincides with that given in the Acts of the Apostles (*see Appendix*).

The expulsion of Joseph and his companions in an oarless boat without sails would be in keeping with the malicious design of the Sanhedrin. They dared not openly destroy him and, instead, conceived an ulterior method hoping their ingenious treachery would eventually consign Joseph and his companions to a watery grave. Little did they realize that, by this subtle act in ridding themselves of the outstanding champion of Christ, their very hope for destruction would be circumvented by an act of providence. Their perfidy made it possible for the forgotten Fathers of Christianity to congregate in a new land where they would be free of molestation.

The Saulian Gestapo had failed dismally and for the last time. It began to collapse completely when vengeful Saul, on the road to Damascus, was stricken blind. The incredible happened. Saul heard the voice of Christ speak to him and had his sight restored. He was

THE DRAMA OF THE LOST DISCIPLES

converted to the faith of 'The Way'. The news stunned the Sanhedrin, infuriating them beyond measure. Immediately, they ordered an all-out drive to seize Saul and kill him on sight, a reversal of circumstances. The hunter was hunted. He went into hiding appealing for aid from Christ's disciples. Their reluctance to save him is understandable. They were filled with suspicion as much as with surprise. Finally they complied, lowering him over the wall of the city with a rope,[14] making his escape in the company of the disciples. From then on he became famous as Paul. The rest is well known. He took up the cross with his great commission as given to him by His Redeemer, Christ, and with all his heart. Finally he gave his all to his Master, in martyrdom, leaving behind an unblemished record which marked him as St. Paul, the Apostle to the Gentiles.

[14] *Acts* 9:25.

32

CHAPTER 5

LET THERE BE LIGHT

W E have identified the sterling character of the Nobilis Decurio, his eminence in religious, political and commercial affairs in both the Jewish and Roman hierarchy, his intimate association with the family of Christ, and particularly the powerful influence he exercised in the last tragic days of Jesus, from the scene of the illegal trial for life to the time Joseph, with his companions, were banished from Judea, to their arrival at Marseilles, in Gaul. It will be helpful if we pause to consider the world of AD 36, before beginning the fascinating story of Joseph's landing in Britain with his companions and what followed.

Due to the historic discrepancies that commonly exist concerning this era, it is important that one becomes familiar, if but slightly, with the histories of the peoples of the various nations who played an active part in the Christian drama. We commonly find much confusion and misunderstanding caused by the random translation of names and places into the various languages that then prevailed. Historians do not quote, or even refer, to the language then spoken by the original Britons and Gauls. Reference is generally given piecemeal from the Greek or Latin, which had not the slightest affinity with the Cymric tongue.

Perhaps unwittingly, historians have been the worst offenders in erecting barriers to the truth, subscribing to the unsupportable belief that Britain, for centuries before and after AD 36, was an island populated by wild savages, painted barbarians completely devoid of culture and religious conscience. Nonchalantly, the reporters wrote off those majestic years as being steeped in myth, legend and folklore.

The strange distortion of ancient Britain is the most incredible paradox in history. One could be forgiven for thinking that certain academic minds had deliberately entered into a joint conspiracy to defame the history of those islands and their inhabitants. It is not as though the truth were hidden. They had but to read the classical histories of Rome, Greece and Gaul, as their course affected Britain, and compare notes with the early British Triads. It required but a mite of effort on their part to search the old church records and the stored tomes in the British Museum library and other libraries at hand, replete with concrete evidence contradicting the spurious writers. In addition, thousands of

Cymric Triads and monastic documents exist, particularly in the Vatican library, as well as the historic versions of the earliest British historians, Celtic and Saxon. A few enlightened historians did cast gleams of light on the truth, but it was darkened and made obscure by the mass of irresponsible literature foisted on the public.

Truth was lost in unbelievable error.

Strange as it may seem, it was the enemies of ardent Britain who wrote at length with candour the most faithful description of the early Britons, showing that they possessed an admirable culture, a patriarchal religion, and an epochal history that extended far beyond that of Rome. Modern writers also confirm their testimony.

E. O. Gordon, in *Prehistoric London*[15], states that the city of London (Llandin) was founded *circa* 1100 BC by Brutus of Troy, some three centuries before Rome.

The famed British archaeologist, Sir Flinders Petrie, discovered at Old Gaza gold ornaments and enamel ware of Celtic origin, dated 1500 BC, and in reverse found Egyptian beads at Stonehenge.

The art of enamelling is early identified with Britain as is the production of tin. The ancient Briton was the inventor of enamelling. He was so perfect in this craft that relics reposing in the British Museum, and the Glastonbury Museum, such as the famous Glastonbury bowl (over two thousand years old), and the beautiful Desborough mirror are as perfect as the day they were made. They are magnificent examples of "La Tène" art, as the Celtic design is named, their geometric beauty and excellence being beyond the ability of modem craftsmen to duplicate.

In *Early Britain*, by Jacquetta Hawkes[16], page 32, we read:

'These Yorkshire Celts, beyond all other groups, seem to have been responsible for establishing the tradition of La Tène art... Nearly all the finest pieces are luxuries reflecting the taste of warriors who enjoyed personal magnificence and the trapping out of their wives and homes. Brooches to fasten the Celtic cloak, bracelets, necklaces, pins, hand mirrors, harness fittings, bits and horse armour, helmets, sword scabbards and shields were among the chief vehicles of La Tène art. They show on the one hand strong plastic modelling, and on the other decorative design incised, in low relief, or picked out in coloured enamel. Both plastically and in the flat the Celtic work

---

[15] Gordon, E.O. *Prehistoric London* (London: Covenant Publishing Company) 1932 p.3
[16] Hawkes, J. *Early Britain* (London: William Collins) 1945

shows an extraordinary assurance, often a kind of wild delicacy, far surpassing its Greek prototypes. In these the finest artists achieved a marvellous control of balanced symmetry in the design and equally in its related spaces.'

S. E. Winbold, in *Britain BC*, writes:

'The Celtic curvilinear art, *circa* 300 BC and of which the famous Glastonbury bowl is a good example, reached its zenith of development in Britain.'

Roman testimony states that captive Britons taught the Romans the craft of enamelling.

Herodotus, father of profane history, *circa* 450 BC wrote[17] of the British Isles and its people, under the name of Cassiterides, remarking on their talent in the metal industry. Julius Caesar, following his campaign in Britain, 55 BC wrote[18] with admiration of their culture, their sterling character, ingenuity in commerce and craftsmanship. He refers in amazement to the number of populous cities, the architecture, universities of learning, the numerical population of England, and particularly to their religion with its belief in the immortality of the soul.

Ancient historians record the exploits of the Kimmerians-Kimmerii-Keltoi-Kelts, in their migrations through Europe into Britain. Modern historians refer to their passage and somehow leave and lose them on the European continent. Yet modern ethnologists have correctly charted their migrations from their ancient source in the East to their final destination in Gaul and Britain, which lands were uninhabited before their arrival. Archaeologists have uncovered their past from the Crimea to Britain as factually as they have substantiated the historic existence of Babylon and Chaldea.

Long before they were known as Kimmerians, the prophet Isaiah addressed himself plainly to the inhabitants of 'The Isles'.

Why historians have mutilated the facts, submerging in myth and mystery the antiquity of Britain, is a tragedy that baffles the mind.

While it is stated that the ancient Phoenician script is an ancestor of our own, philologists assert that the Keltic or Cymric tongue is the oldest living language. Its root words have a basic affinity with ancient

---

[17] *Book* 3:115.
[18] *Commentaries*, Book IV.

Hebrew. In making this statement it should be pointed out that the original tongue of the biblical characters had little association with modern Hebrew. The ancient language was devoid of vowels. Modern Hebrew was not formulated until the sixth century. To the modern Jew, the original Hebrew is a lost tongue.

In the Bible we read of Ezra bewailing the fact that his brethren could not understand their native language and, therefore, on their return to Jerusalem from the Babylonian captivity, 536 BC Ezra was obliged to read the law to them in the Assyrio-Chaldean language.

Modern Hebrew is like Greek and Latin, a classical language. The Jew of today reads and speaks in Yiddish, a conglomeration of several languages.

In the same manner as many modernists prate the dead, false theory of evolution, the prejudiced, and uninformed continue to regard the ancient British language as a mixture of several, regardless of philological contradiction.

Abundant proof exists today that the ancient language is still alive. It is frequently spoken in Wales, Cornwall, Ireland, Scotland, and in Brittany and Normandy. Available are many old Bibles written in the Celtic languages. One of the most prominent Scottish newspapers is published in the old tongue, and an adaptation of the Celtic is the official language of Eire.

It is interesting to know the important part the ancient language played in World War I. When the Allied Command could find no other method to prevent German Intelligence from deciphering the Allied wire messages, it was Lloyd George, Britain's wartime Prime Minister, who suggested that the ancient language, which he spoke fluently, be employed. Its use completely baffled German Intelligence, preventing further code interception. This could not have been possible if the Cymric tongue was garbled. It had to be grammatically organized and intelligible.

Even today, nothing is more distorted than the modern histories of world nations. They are either subject to political chauvinism, or glorified idolatry by super-patriots. The historic truth seems to be unpopular. Reporters seem to revel in biased national opinion, with an inclination to judge from the materialistic level of intelligence. Anything different is ignorant, medieval or prejudiced. They tend to describe their own native history according to their Party philosophy, ignoring its transition in name and language from the past. They fail to recognize the significant fact that language and geography is no criterion of race. There is change in everything. Language changes, so does the geographical habitation of people, but not race. To evaluate the history of any race we must recognize the progressive changes as they appear in language, religion, social custom, and their adaptation to geographical residence.

We must ever be on guard against the distorters, the irresponsible, the charlatan and the atheist. Their warped minds are motivated by bigotry, prejudice, intolerance, religious and racial hatred. They delight in destroying the champions of the truth. What they do not understand they scoffingly label as tradition. Actually, they do not understand the meaning of the word. To them it means a myth. Disraeli eloquently said: 'A tradition can neither be made nor destroyed.'

A tradition is a truth, though garnished with degrees of exaggeration in the passage of time from repetitive retelling. It can be clearly elucidated by separating the chaff from the wheat.

Through the common practice of generalizing we are prone to use terms loosely, which easily side-track us into forming faulty conclusions. Arising out of this habit we have come to generalize the meaning of the word 'Christian', insinuating that all followers of Jesus were known by that name from the beginning. In actual fact, the name 'Christian' had not then been coined. It was not created until years after His death. To the Judean, the Greek, and the Roman world, the early adherents to the new Gospel were known as 'Followers of The Way'. Jesus had said, 'I am The Way'. To all His devotees He was 'The Way'. In their devotions they referred to Christ and His spiritual philosophy as 'The Way'.

The title, 'Christian', is claimed to have originated at Antioch[19], following the enthusiastic reception given to the disciples who fled there in AD 36. It is nearer to the truth that the inhabitants of this ancient city referred to the converts as 'Little Christs', and, 'Little men of Christ'. These labels are by no means the correct interpretation of the name 'Christian'. The word is a composite of Greek and Hebrew. 'Christ' is the Greek word meaning 'consecrated', and 'ian' is from the Hebrew word 'am', meaning a person, or people. Therefore, the true meaning of the word 'Christian' and 'Christians' would be 'a consecrated person', or 'consecrated people'.

---

[19] *Acts* 11:26.

Early ecclesiastics and historians definitely state that the word is of British origin. Philologists also support its claim to British invention; created by the British priesthood, among whom the Christian movement gained its first and strongest impetus.

Substantiation is found in the statement by Sabellus, AD 250, who wrote: 'The word Christian was spoken for the first time in Britain, by those who first received The Word, from the Disciples of Christ.'

It is interesting to note that the Bethany group who landed in Britain, was never referred to by the British priesthood as Christians, nor even later when the name was in common usage. They were called 'Culdees', as were the other disciples who later followed the Josephian mission into Britain.

There are two interpretations given to the word 'Culdee', or 'Culdich', both words purely of the Celto-British language, the first meaning 'certain strangers', and the other as explained by Lewis Spence, who states that 'Culdee' is derived from 'Ceile-De', meaning, 'servant of the Lord'. In either case the meaning is appropriate.

This title, applied to Joseph of Arimathea and his companions, clearly indicates that they were considered as more than ordinary strangers. The name sets them apart as somebody special. In this case, since they arrived in Britain on a special mission with a special message, we can fairly accept the title meant to identify them as 'certain strangers, servants of the Lord'.

In the ancient British Triads, Joseph and his twelve companions are all referred to as Culdees, as also are Paul, Peter, Lazarus, Simon Zelotes, Aristobulus and others. This is important. The name, was not known outside Britain and therefore could only have been assigned to those who actually had dwelt among the British Cymri. The name was never applied to any disciple not associated with the early British missions. Even though Gaul was Celtic, the name was never employed there. In later years the name Culdee took on an added significance, emphasizing the fact that the Culdee Christian Church was the original Church of Christ on earth. It became a title applied to the church, and to its High Priests, persisting for centuries in parts of Britain, after the name had died out elsewhere in favour of the more popular name, Christian. Culdees are recorded in church documents as officiating at St. Peter's, York, until AD 936. And, according to the Rev. Raine, the Canons of York were called Culdees as late as the reign of Henry II. In Ireland a whole county was named Culdee, declared with emphasis when reference was heard at a court hearing in the seventeenth century, as to its laws. The name Culdee, and Culdich, clung tenaciously to the Scottish Church, and its prelates, much longer than elsewhere.

Campbell writes in his poem *Reullura*:

'The pure Culdees
were Alby's [Albion] earliest priests of God,
ere yet an island of her seas
by foot of Saxon monk was trod.'

In the days of Christ the popular language of the East was Greek, more so than Roman. Aramaic and Hebrew were chiefly confined to the Judeans. Jesus was, in all probability, fluent in Aramaic, Hebrew, Greek and Latin. And, if what we are told is factual, He was also versed in the Celtic language. The cultured people of the Roman province of Palestine were conversant with Greek, Hebrew and Latin.

The Septuagint translation of the Old Testament was written in Greek at Alexandria, 285 BC. It is interesting to note that this work was compiled by seventy Jewish scholars, and not Greek, as was generally supposed.

Centuries before Christ, the Greek language was well known to the ancient British, from commercial association with the Phoenicians, Greek tin traders and sailors. Julius Caesar tells us that the Druids employed the Greek script in all their commercial transactions.[20] At this particular period of British history, the island was more commonly referred to by its industry than by its British name. Known as the Cassiterides, meaning 'Tin Island', it was for many centuries the only country in the world where tin was mined and refined. Aristotle, 350 BC, is one of the first writers to name Britain, the 'Tin Islands'. Herodotus uses the name earlier, *circa* 450 BC (*Book* 3: 115).

Julius Caesar writes of his visit to the famous Spanish tin mine at Talavera, 50 BC. Many centuries before tin was discovered at Talavera the tin trade flourished in Britain. In fact, Spanish history tells of a close association with Cornwall and it appears that the Spanish Government sought the skilled miners of Cornwall, to instruct them in obtaining the wolfram and in constructing the mines. Many Cornish names appear in Talaveran tin mining history of men who were instructors, superintendents, overseers and foremen and experts in assaying the rock.

---

[20] *Gallic War*, vi, 13.

Proof of British superiority in the tin industry and its affluent world-wide trade is referred to by Herodotus 450 BC, Pytheas 353 BC, Aristotle 350 BC, Polybius 150 BC, Diodorus Siculus, Posidonius and others, most of whom wrote long before the Christian era. Each deals at length with the British tin industry in Cornwall and Devon, explaining the paths of transportation from Britain, overland and by sea to the various ports on the Mediterranean and elsewhere in the known world of that time.

The ancient ships of biblical Tarshish were the first navigators to transport tin and lead from Britain to the nations of the empiric world. Their navy controlled the seas and later became known in history as the Phoenicians. The tin that garnished the splendour of the Palace of Solomon, 1005 BC, was mined and smelted into ingots at Cornwall and thence shipped by the Phoenicians to Palestine.

Sir E.S. Creasy, the eminent British historian, in his *History of England*, writes: 'The British mines mainly supplied the glorious adornment of Solomon's temple.'

For many years the Phoenicians held a monopoly on the transportation of British tin over the sea lanes. They guarded their secret jealously. It is well known that when followed by other seacraft, seeking to learn the source of their trade, their mariners would deliberately strike a false course, and in extremity would purposely wreck their vessel. This sacrifice was reimbursed out of the Phoenician treasury. For confirmation of this it is interesting to quote Strabo, who died AD 25:

'Anciently the Phoenicians alone, from Cadis, engrossed this market, hiding the navigation from all others. When the Romans followed the course of a vessel that they might discover the situation, the jealous pilot wilfully stranded the ship, misleading those who were tracing him to the same destruction. Escaping from shipwreck, he was indemnified for his losses out of the public treasury.'

The Phoenicians of Carthage were more successful. Anxious to share in the trade of Cadis, an expedition under Hamilco passed the Straits about 450 BC, and sailing to the north, discovered the Tin Island.

Ptolemy and Polybius, vigorously support Diodorus, writing of the friendliness of the people of Cornwall and of Dammonia, which was the name then applied to Devon. These locales were where the tin mining chiefly existed. In the making of bronze, tin was the main alloy. Thus it

LET THERE BE LIGHT

can be safely said that the Bronze Age had its inception in Britain. Knowledge of this fact alone is sufficient to refute all malicious insinuation that the ancient Britons were barbarian.

By necessity, to excel in mining and smelting tin and lead, to be proficient in casting metal, and expert in enamelling, a people must be intelligent in the science of mineralogy and metallurgy.

The world-wide demand for these precious metals beat a sea lane to Britain's shores, bringing its inhabitants in close contact with the ancient powers. Consequently, it is quite understandable why the British, with the foundation of their own language steeped in ancient Hebrew, and their knowledge of Greek, could be responsible for coining the word 'Christian'. Also, we can understand why many of the oldest landmarks in this area of Britain abound in Hebrew names.

The association of Joseph of Arimathea with the tin industry in Cornwall is positive. Fragments of poems and miners' songs, handed down through the centuries, make frequent reference to Joseph. It has long been customary for the miners to shout when they worked, 'Joseph was a tin man,' 'Joseph was in the tin trade.'

These were their chief trade slogans which identified Joseph as a prominent person in the British tin industry.

At the time of our story, the islanders were known racially as Kelts, derived from their historical racial name Kimmerian-Kimmerii-Kymry-Keltoi-Kelt. The letter 'C' began to substitute the letter 'K' in spelling the name, but the pronunciation is the same. Even in those remote times the name Kelt took on a different enunciation and spelling, arising out of native patois. Then, as today, we find the descendants of this ancient people in England and Wales referred to as Celts, the inhabitants of Hibernia – Ireland – as Kelts, Gaels, in Scotland and the people of Gaul, now France, as Gauls – Gallic. Ethnically they are all the same people. The meaning of the word in each case is 'stranger', indicating that a Celt, Kelt, Gael or a Gaul was a stranger to the land in which they dwelt, not an aborigine as some would have us suppose. It is important to note, though they were strangers to the land, they were its first settlers, securing their new homeland in peace, and not with the sword, since there were no people to conquer.

They were truly colonizing strangers in a virgin land.

We know they were strangers to Britain and Gaul, though very ancient, but, like a silver thread woven in a dark woof we can trace their wanderings as one people from their original homeland beyond the

Euphrates river, for over three thousand years BC to their new domicile in the Mystic Isles, and in Gaul.

François Guizot, the authoritative French historian in his *Histoire de la Civilisation en France,* writes: 'The Gauls, or Celts, had the honour of giving their name FIRST to this land.'

The name of the Gaul persisted until about the middle of the fifth century, when the Gothic Franks, under the leadership of Meroveus, invaded, and settled the land, displacing the Gaul in numbers and in name.

The national name 'France' is derived from the tribal name of Frank, meaning 'Freeman'. Yet, the Gaul left his impress on the land in his co-British name in the first province he founded. Today it is still known by its original ancient name – Brittany.

At one time the Continent had been land-locked with Britain, until a natural upheaval caused the present separation. Evidently for a considerable length of time the separation was not too widely marked. In the ancient Druidic Triads we read of a Gaulish bishop, walking over the divide across a plank as he journeyed from Gaul to pay the annual tithe to the mother Druidic Church in Britain.

Despite the washing of the lands by the seas for many centuries, the distance between Dover and Calais today is only twenty-four miles.

Separated, the island became geographically known as Britain, and the nearby Continental section as Gaul.

CHAPTER 6

THE GLORY IN THE NAME

AFTER the Kimmerians had settled in the Isles of the West they were known to the rest of the world by another name. The name held no affinity with their racial title by which ancient ethnologists identified them. In many respects the name was more of a sobriquet which they appeared willingly to accept.

They became referred to as British.

Why were they so named?

What was so different about the Kimmerii, or their way of life, that actuated other nations to christen them with this strange surname that was ever to identify them before the world, both ancient and modern, even to the subjection of their racial name?

Ancient chroniclers leave no doubt that it was the religious beliefs and customs of the Kimmerians that set them markedly apart from all other faiths. It was diametrically opposed to all other religions of that time. They believed in One Invisible God, and the coming of a Messiah. They had no graven images, abhorring the sight of idols. They always worshipped in the open, facing the east. They had a passionate belief in the immortality of life, to such an extent that both friend and foe claimed this belief made them fearless warriors, disdainful of death.[21]

The religious ritual that appeared to make the greatest impression on the foreign historians was their custom of carrying a replica of the Ark of the Covenant before them in all religious observances, as did their forefathers in old Judea. For centuries, as the Kymri passed through foreign lands in migratory waves on their march to the Isles of the West, the chroniclers noted that this custom was never omitted.[22]

It was this ritual that gave birth to their British surname.

The name British is derived from the ancient Hebrew language, with which the old Cymric language was contemporaneous. Formed from two words, 'B'rith' meaning 'covenant', and 'ish' meaning a man or a woman. Joined as one word the meaning is apparent: 'British' means a 'covenant man or woman'. The ancient word 'ain' attached to

---

[21] Caesar on the Gauls; Aristotle on the Celts.
[22] Dobson, C.C. *The Mystery of the Fate of the Ark of the Covenant* (London: Williams & Norgate) 1939

43

the word 'B'rith', signifies 'land', therefore the interpretation of the word 'Britain', as then and still employed, is 'Covenant Land'.

Unknowingly, the ancients named the Keltoi rightly. They were, and still are, the original adherents of the Covenant Law. With the later adoption of Christianity, and the name Christian, a startling new interpretation presented itself. The 'Covenant People' became the 'Consecrated People', living in the 'Covenant Land'. This carries the implication that by the vicarious atonement the British were consecrated in the Covenant Law and initiated to be the advance guard of Christianity, to evangelize the world in the name of Jesus Christ.

From a close study of their religious beliefs everything points to the fact that the Kimmerians held fast to the patriarchal faith of the Old Testament. Many eminent scholars point out the great similarity between the ancient Hebrew patriarchal faith and the Druidic of Britain.

Sir Norman Lockyer, in *Stonehenge and Other British Stone Monuments* (p. 252), writes: 'I confess I am amazed at the similarities we have come across.'

Edward Davies, in *Mythology and Rites of the British Druids* (Pref., p. 7), states: 'I must confess that I have not been the first in representing the Druidical as having had some connection with the patriarchal religion.'

W.M. Stukeley, in his book *Abury* (Pref., p. 1), affirms after a close study of the evidence: 'I plainly discerned the religion professed by the ancient Britons was the simple patriarchal faith.'

Earlier testimony also affirms. Procopius of Caesarea, in his *History of the Wars* (AD 530), says: 'Jesus Taran, Bel – One only God. All Druids acknowledge One Lord God alone' (*De Gothicis*, bk. 3).

Julius Caesar wrote, 54 BC: "The Druids make the immortality of the soul the basis of all their teaching, holding it to be the principal incentive and reason for a virtuous life' (*Gallic War*, VI, 14).

It is a curious fact that the British title was never conferred on their Keltic kinsmen in Gaul, Ireland and Scotland. Historically the people of Gaul were even referred to as Gauls – Gallic and the land known as Gaul-Gallica, and Galatia, until the coming of the Franks. It is believed that the biblical version of the Epistle to the Galatians was addressed to the Gauls of Galatia.[23] The inhabitants of Hibernia (Ireland) and Caledonia (Scotland) retained both their geographical and original racial name. The peoples of what is now England and Wales actually never

---

[23] Bishop Lightfoot on *Galatians*.

lost either. The land was always Britain and the inhabitants were documented as British Celts. The Irish perpetuated the name Kelt but the Scottish, while known to be Kelts, were called Gaels. One immediately recognized the similarity between the name Gaul and Gael – Gallic and Gaelic. Incidentally, the Gaels were the original inhabitants of Iberia. After centuries of domicile in Iberia, a large host migrated into Caledonia (Scotland), making way for the constant flow of Kelts from the Continent, to Iberia (or Hibernia), who retained the Irish title.

Even though this distinction in names has always persisted, the affinity between them was recognized. The islands were always referred to as the Brittanic Isles even in ancient times … Not until the reign of James I, when the Irish and Scottish began to be blended into a central Parliament, were the islands known as the British Isles and the United Kingdom. Of later date is the name Great Britain.

This may appear confusing to some who more commonly speak of the people of Britain as English and Welsh, and the race as Anglo-Saxon. The national name English was never shared, or employed to designate, the other inhabitants of the Isles. To this day they each retain their Celtic clan title of Welsh, Irish and Scottish, in spite of the fact that they all shared the title of British citizens.

The name Britain continued to name England and Wales, long after the arrival of the Anglo-Saxons in AD 426. Not until the invading Normans began to be domestically absorbed by the British Kelts and Saxons did the Anglican title obtain ascendancy. From the lesser used name Angle the national name took form to label the land and its people, England. Strange as it may appear on first thought, yet there are no misnomers in the various names and titles. Racially the Kelts, Anglo-Saxons and Normans were but separate tribal branches of the same Keltic race. This also includes the Danes, who had invaded Britain in AD 787. Ethnologically the whole Keltic race is composed of the Keltic-Saxon-Scandinavian stock. Historically the arrival of the Danes, Saxons and Normans are referred to as invasions, but actually it was a converging of the one race into their predestined homeland, which to them and to the world became their Motherland, Britain. Together they have grown in stature, wearing the British title like a badge, in honour and with glory.

The fact that the British name was singularly identified with the people of England and Wales is more curious than mysterious. As the history of ancient Britain unfolds before us we can understand the reason more clearly. Irrevocably they were bound together by the ties of language and religion. Cymric was their mother tongue and each practised the Druidic religion. Britain was the central headquarters of Druidism, to which all paid tithe. It was by far the most populous and by its commerce and industry was world renowned. What London is to Great Britain today, Ottawa to Canada, and Washington to the United States, so was Britain to the whole Keltic race. Largely, this was the reason for other nations identifying the British name with England. From the religious point, of view, out of which the British name arose, this island was entitled by priority to the title. England was the first of the British Isles to be inhabited. Before the Kelts arrived in significant numbers, from circa 2000 BC, it was a virgin land almost devoid of human habitation. Druidism was nationally organized under the capable leadership of Hu Gadarn, circa 1800 BC, the period given for the erection of Stonehenge, which is also ascribed to Hu Gadarn. He was contemporaneous with Abraham. Like Abraham, Hu Gadarn was the chief patriarch of the people, known as Hu the Mighty.

Looking backward over the many centuries we see the deep significance for this Isle being named Britain and its people British. We see destiny motivating these people in their course; a greater will than their own subconsciously directing them to a predestined land where, as Jeremiah had prophesied, they would 'plant the seed'. The climax was reached with the arrival of Joseph of Arimathea and the Bethany group. From then on the meaning of the word Motherland became apparent. England is the only country in history to be naturally known as the Motherland. The long centuries had prepared it for its Christian destiny. From its womb the Christian cause was born, cradled, and carried to the world.

We know that the Kelts were by commandment and custom not given to committing anything religious to writing. Neither were they permitted to build altars with the use of metal, or nails. They were the true people of the biblical 'Stone Kingdom'.

A traditional custom that indelibly bound the Kelts with the old patriarchal faith was the building of altars wherever they rested on their trek to the Isles, a religious custom as marked as the carrying of the Ark of the Covenant before them. Today their passage across the world into the Isles can be clearly traced by the relics of the altars they raised in stone, enduring memorials to their great pilgrimage.

This custom outlasted the ritual of the Ark, which was abandoned with the acceptance of Jesus Christ. It lingers today and, as then, only among the Keltic-Saxon people. In our times the custom of erecting these memorials to some great historic event is chiefly practised by the Scottish and the Canadians. They comprise pyramids of stones piled to a peak and are known as cairns. This is the Keltic name for the word used in the Bible, 'heaps', 'stones of witness'.

The first stone altar in the biblical record was erected by Jacob, after his significant dream of the ascending ladder between heaven and earth, known to all Christians as Jacob's Ladder. He built it as a witness to his contact and covenant with God on that occasion. Ever after the erection of such altars, or cairns, became a religious custom of the wandering Hebrews and Keltoi, as they passed through strange lands; a declaration and a witness to their belief and faith in the covenant with the One and Only Invisible God.

Despite the evolution of names that identified the people finally named British, the names have always been synonymous with their heritage and religion. The name Kymri originated from King Omri, founder of Samaria, the capital of Israel. The Assyrians called their Israelite captives Beth-Omri, Beth Kymri and People of the Ghomri, after their king. The Greeks called them Kimmerioi. The Welsh are the only people today retaining the ancient title as the people of the Cymri.

In the British Museum can be seen the famous Black Obelisk of Shalmaneser II. This important relic bears reference to the captivity, and to all kings subject to the King of Assyria. Amongst these rulers so subject was Jehu, called the 'son of Omri', king of Israel. The obelisk is a series of twenty small reliefs with long inscriptions. The second relief depicts 'the son of Omri' on his knees, paying tribute in gold and silver in obeisance to the Assyrian ruler.[24]

In Keltic the word Kymri is still pronounced with the vowel sound, K'Omri, and easily became Kymri from which Kimmerii, Kimmerians, Keltoi, Keltic and Cymri have evolved. Crimea, by which that land is still known, is a corruption of Cimmeri. Vast cemeteries have been disclosed in the Crimea in recent years producing numerous monuments identifying the Kymry in name, religion, and character with that area where they remained centuries before marching on. It is interesting to know that the Welsh are the only members of the Keltic race that

---

[24] cf. *A Guide to the Babylonian and Assyrian Antiquities* (British Museum), p. 46.

retained throughout time to the present the original name Kymri. Today it is usually spelt Cymri, and their ancient language Cymric. The Welsh have perpetuated their ancient racial characteristics more than any member of the great Celtic-Saxon-Scandinavian race. The people of ancient England later became more Saxon in type. This could be due to the vast influx of Engles, Frisians, Jutes and Saxons that settled in the land following their invasion. Of these the Engles or Angles and Saxons were by far the most numerous. However, each acted according to their native disposition. All of them originated from the northern kingdom of Samaria, where they were first led by Ephraim.

It should be remembered that the Ephraimites were the legal inheritors of the title Israel and not Judah, or the Jews. In the Bible the southern kingdom at Jerusalem and the northern kingdom of Samaria are always addressed separately under different names, Judah and Israel. Even God in His instructions refers to them as such: 'Judah was His sanctuary and Israel His dominion' (*Psalm* 114:2). Consequently, as to be expected, the Ephraimites continued to govern according to the patriarchal law. Originally, Judah was part of the priestly sect, with the Levites, the latter being the true dispensers of religious jurisdiction who were divided between Judah and Israel, in service. Among the Kelts are the descendants of the priestly group that served Ephraim, or Israel, which is manifested throughout the ages by their deep religious disposition. They also represented the professional class – scientists, doctors, lawyers, etc. which we find so vigorously demonstrated in ancient Britain, in religion, industry and commerce. The Ephraimites were the true warrior tribe of Israel, the Defenders of the Faith, as they are today. The Levites were not permitted to bear arms or serve in war; neither were the Druids. Nevertheless, the Keltoi were famed as valiant warriors. This was because there were enough of the warrior Ephraimite clan among them to protect the Priesthood and associates in the professions. It has been stated that the major warrior legions of the Ephraimites were the last to leave Samaria, protecting the westward trek of their brethren. This could be true. History shows that even though the Kymri were engaged in conflict during their passage they did not experience one fraction of the combat as fought by the Ephraimites.

The question arises: how do we connect the Saxons with the Ephraimites and as brethren of the Kelts?

It is aptly said that the Bible is the truest history book ever written, to which the writer subscribes. Within Scripture we find the clues which

THE GLORY IN THE NAME

modern scientists, particularly the detectives of science, the archaeologists, have proved to be real.

When Isaac was born, God made a strange statement to Abram. He said: 'In all that Sarah hath said unto thee, hearken unto her voice; for in Isaac shall thy seed be called' (*Genesis* 21:12). Nowhere in the biblical record are God's people so known. Theologians either evaded the explanation, or were blind to the meaning and to other statements later given by the prophets and by our Lord on the matter. Isaiah and Jeremiah not only strongly emphasized the fact but gave positive clues to their identity. Jesus said He had come to 'the lost sheep' – Ephraim. He told the Jews their inheritance was to be taken away from them and given to another. Jesus could only give such an inheritance to God's own people, since from the beginning they were bound within the Covenant Law to carry out God's purpose on earth through the Christ. His strongest commission He gave to St. Paul, to go to the Gentiles who would receive Him. While St. Paul went to the Gentiles, more directly and positively he went to the people of Britain and ordained the first Christian Bishop in Britain, in the name of Jesus.

Jesus had said that the old law was finished in His sacrifice. He came to fulfil the Law – the Covenant between God and man. Until the British Druidic church and its peoples were consecrated in 'The Way', they were as Gentiles. But of all the peoples of the earth the only existing faith that was prepared beforehand to accept Christ, and the only people to know His name, and to speak it before Christ was born, were the British Druids.

Christ knew to whom He was addressing Himself. St. Paul knew to whom he was specifically directed, as we shall show by historic fact. Joseph of Arimathea, from longer and closer association with Jesus, knew, and to these people both these great Apostles went.

The Christian elect were to be known in the name of Isaac.

Are they so known? Most certainly they are, and the name is Saxon.

Equally as the excavated monuments and artefacts from the Royal Cemeteries of the Crimea have positively identified the Kymri by actual name, so have the ancient historians documented the evolution of the Saxon name from Isaac in their records.

Let us check farther back in history. These important facts are necessary to prove God's course and purpose, as later demonstrated by Joseph of Arimathea and St. Paul.

The name Semite is derived from Shem, who was the son of Noah, and of whom it is said in *Genesis* 9:26, 'Blessed be the Lord God of Shem.' From Shem is descended the special seed elected to be the chosen race. Until the exodus of Abraham from Chaldea the Covenant People were known as Shemites. Under Abraham they became known as Hebrews. This term derives from Eber, who was a descendant of Shem. The word Hebrew does not specifically designate a race. It means 'colonist or colonizer, applied in the same manner as it was once associated with the Americans and Canadians. Like the Americans and Canadians, the people were spoken of as colonists until they were nationalized. Nationalization of the Covenant People was acquired under the dying Jacob, grandson of Abraham, and the son of Isaac. Then they became a nation formed of twelve tribes to be so known by the Will of God as Israel, meaning 'Ruling with God'. Later, when the tribes revolted under Ephraim, the son of Joseph, they became divided into two kingdoms, that of the north and of the south, being known as Judah and Israel. Both went into captivity. A fragment of Judah returned to Jerusalem but Israel, as Ephraimites, never returned nor was ever again mentioned in scriptural history. During this long existence from Shem to the vanishing Ephraimites the name Jew never occurred in history and was unknown to the Shemites, Hebrews, Israelites or Ephraimites. Nevertheless it is true that some of the Jews who later sprang from the remnant of Judah that returned to the Holy City after the Babylonian captivity are Shemites, or Semites, as we now use the name, and they were part of Israel, but only a fragment. In fact they had become so mixed from inter-marriage with other peoples during their captivity, it is doubtful how clear their native claim to Israel could be. However, they are recognized as part of Israel, but only in the same manner as we would say all Pennsylvanians are Americans and all Ontarions are Canadians, but all Americans and Canadians are not Pennsylvanians or Ontarions. Consequently it is a serious misnomer to consider the Jews of today as the only surviving Semites or Israelites. The major portion of both Judah and Ephraim had long passed out of their original homeland to be known by other names, some of which have already been explained.

Now we come to the mysterious promise of God to Sarah, 'In Isaac shall thy seed be called' (*Genesis* 21:12). The prophets had said they would dwell afar off and be known by another name, one representing their racial heritage. On being questioned by the people through whose

50

lands they passed, the Israelites (Ephraimites, and the many of Judah who had joined up with them in their march) explained that they were the Sons of Isaac.

The ethnological chart shows that they divided into two groups, each taking a different route that was ultimately to lead them into the Isles of the West – Britain. The Kymri we have already established but the warrior Ephraimites became more markedly referred to as Sons of Isaac. In writing this name it took on different variations according to language but the pronunciation was the same, leaving no doubt as to their identity. Ancient documents and monuments refer to them as I-Saccasuns, I-Sak-suna, Sakasuna, Saksens and finally Saxons. It is true, historically, they are also known collectively as Scythians, but it must be remembered it was not the name by which the amalgamated tribes called themselves but the name applied to them by the Greeks. For about seven hundred years they lived in the districts known to the Greeks as Scythia, to the Romans as Dacia (now Romania), and Thrace. Just as the Kymri of Britain assumed the name British, so did the old Ephraimite Israelites elect to be known as Saxons, the name which both concealed and revealed the name of Isaac.

The Anglo-Saxons were the chief and most powerful among the associated tribes, hence the accepted leaders. As Saxons, on the invitation of the British chieftain Vortigern, they first entered Britain.

After the Saxon settlement in Britain, observers of other nations would have noticed what they might have termed a strange breach of Saxon policy. They began to intermarry with the British Kelts.

Whether or not the fair, blue-eyed Saxons and the darker Kelts realized their racial affinity, mutually they blended together.

In all their migratory wanderings the Keltic and Saxon peoples steadfastly refused to intermix, or intermarry with the people of other races. To do so was a serious tribal offence recognized by both. In this they were more loyal to the patriarchal law than were their brethren of Judah during their Babylonian captivity. As prophesied, for this overt act this section of Judah was to be branded by 'the shew of their countenance'. This is markedly shown, even today, in their descendants by the Hittite cast of black hair and the hooked nose.

Not only did they refuse to intermix. They were true to the ancient command to 'dwell together'. History informs us whenever they began their next migratory step they left few behind, emptying the land. Contrary to the custom of other people who either left behind the aged, the too young and the infirm, or slew them, the Kymri and the Saxon tribes took all with them. This was more particularly related of the Anglo-Saxons, whose migrations were more numerous and longer spaced in reaching the eventual 'Homeland'. This fact is historically stated in the mass migration of the Saxon peoples into Britain. Dr. Latham writes in his *Ethnology of the British Islands:*

'Throughout the whole length and breadth of Germany there is not one village, hamlet or family which can show definite signs of descent from the Continental ancestors of the Anglo-Saxons of England.'

Professor Sayce writes:

'All the branches that flowed into Britain are branches of the self-same stock. Not a single pure Saxon is to be found in any village, town or city of Germany. We once came there, but came out again in our wanderings to these British Islands.'

That they all were kinsmen, Briton-Kelt, Gaels, Anglo-Saxons, Jutes, Frisians, Danes and Normans is emphasized by Freeman in *The Norman Conquest*: 'It is difficult to realize the fact that our nation which now exists is not really a mixed race in the sense which popular language implies.'

Professor Huxley, writing of the political tumult in Ireland in 1870, when agitators tried to make racial difference an issue, wrote: 'If what I have to say in a matter of science weighs with any man who has political power, I ask him to believe that the arguments about the difference between the Anglo-Saxons and the Celts are a mere sham and delusion.'

In referring to the characteristic of the Kelt, like the Saxon, to 'dwell alone', he states that during the Roman occupation of Britain, Roman and Kelt led a separate life from each other. And when the Romans withdrew permanently from Britain AD 410, the population was as substantially Celtic as they had found it.

In the name of Isaac the promised Seed of God was to be found. As I-Sax-Sons, they became Israelites, to be lost, punished for their sin in worshipping the golden calf, scattered throughout the nations, but 'like corn winnowed in a sieve' would finally be gathered together into a place appointed by God Himself (2 *Samuel* 7:10) where they would settle and move no more, and where no weapon formed against them should prosper (*Isaiah* 54:17).

The validity of these facts cannot be overlooked, nor the other ancient custom among them of keeping the Sabbath.

In *Exodus* 31 we read to whom the command to observe the Sabbath was given:

'Wherefore the children of Israel shall keep the sabbath, to observe the sabbath throughout their generations, for a perpetual covenant' (v. 16). 'It is a sign between Me and the children of Israel for ever' (v. 17).

The Anglo-Saxon race were and are the only people to observe this sign. In the past, when foreigners were questioned as to what impressed them most about English and American customs they replied, 'Your English Sunday.' While all places were wide open in foreign lands, in Britain and America the Sabbath was observed. Even at the great Paris Exhibition only the British and United States sections were closed on Sunday.

Voltaire, the extraordinary intellectual infidel, said: 'Whether Englishmen know it or not, it is the English Sunday which makes England what England is.'

This is equally true of America, and the British Commonwealth of nations.

Dr. Ryle, Bishop of Liverpool, said:

'I assert without hesitation that the only countries on the face of the globe in which you will find true observance of the Sabbath are Great Britain, the Commonwealth nations and America. No other nations can possibly be said to fulfil this sign.'[25]

However, the warning is sounded in the announcement that when we begin to forsake the Lord's Day, which all Anglo-Saxon people have been doing in various degrees over the years, our prosperity will depart from us.

A few years ago a foreigner visiting England made the remark in the Press: 'You have in England something which we have always longed to

---

[25] *Isaiah* 58:13-14

have, and never could attain – Sunday – and you are losing it almost without a protest.'

America has always been the greatest desecrator of the Sabbath, more so than the other Anglo-Saxon nations. We all should heed the warning.

England derived its name from the Engles (Angles). The meaning of the name is again significant. Engles means 'God-Men'. This name was not conferred upon them because of any special righteousness but because instead of worshipping idols of stone, as others did, they worshipped God. The idolaters called them God-Men – Engles (Angles).

The story is told that one day, when Pope Gregory was walking along the streets of Rome, he encountered a group of Roman soldiers with several British (Yorkshire) captive children. He paused in wonderment, enamoured by their unusual countenance: golden hair, blue eyes and fair skin, something he had never seen before. He asked the soldiers who they were. On being told they were Engles, from Engle-land, he remarked on their beauty, replying, 'They are well named. They look like angels.' From this encounter it is claimed Pope Gregory became persuaded of himself to send Augustine to Britain on his mission.

The religious habits, customs and characteristics that so definitely marked the Kymri and the Saxons from the rest of the peoples of the earth cannot be charged to mere coincidence with the ancient patriarchal law. They are too deeply significant. Regardless of how the Keltic-Saxon people may have deviated from full adherence to the Law, in their wanderings, the Covenants were the core of their spiritual life, directing their material policies. The Covenant-meaning name, British, would never have been conferred upon them by other peoples if they had not been more than duly impressed by their religious observances. As one studies the Druidic Triads, a greater association with the Covenant Law is shown with startling clarity. Considering these Hebraic religious customs and the acquisition of interpretative names, one can readily realize how simply and effectively the wedding between the old Druidic religion and the new Covenant of 'The Way' took place, providing a fertile field and a safe sanctuary for Joseph of Arimathea and his companions.

This was not an accident. It was the beginning of the new destiny long before prophesied, which was brought to birth in the great sacrifice of Jesus Christ, our Saviour.

There are still people who insist that the British story is a superstitious myth without foundation, just as they continue to debate that the Bible is untrue. They are as mentally fogbound as the Victorian historians who could not understand how, why or where there could be any connection between the ancient British and the continental races, and less with the prophecies and people of the Bible. Unfortunately at that time the historic past was not so well revealed to them as archaeology has disclosed it in modem times.

Even as the amazing discoveries in the caves of the Dead Sea, during the years 1955-56, have brought to the light of day thousands of stored documents secreted therein by the Essenes, substantiating the books of the Bible in every instance, equally so, during the last twenty-five years, archaeologists have supplied the modern ethnologist and historian with indisputable evidence to vindicate the historic age-old story of the people of Britain.

The Essenes were the most cultured and learned religious order existing before the birth of Christ, free of the contamination of power politics, or orthodox religion. They were the greatest truth seekers of their time. Most of the discovered documents were written before Christ and much after His advent. Every day translators are disclosing material that has long puzzled theologians concerning both the Old and New Testaments. Much of this testimony proves the historic validity of the facts given herein. Archaeologists unearthing monuments, tablets, coins and various other artefacts name and trace the Covenant Peoples of our story from their ancient birthplace to the Isles of the West and the British and Americans to their place in modern history.

Crushed beyond revival are the diatribes of the atheists and the mocking voices of the Higher Critics of Germany. Authority has been stripped from the irresponsible historians.

It is not so well known that H. G. Wells' *Outline of History*, that sold by the million copies, was most severely criticized by an angry group of scientists and scholars who dubbed Wells' work as 'a gross mass of mediaeval historic error'. Wells was obliged to abridge the next edition. Although he corrected a number of his flagrant errors he was unable to make a complete correction without rewriting the whole work, which he did not do.

The devil is ever alert to use the infidel mind and careless writers to divert all whom he can from the truth.

In the end truth always wins.

There is ever a fascination to be found in a name. It seldom fails to intrigue the mind, creating a curious desire to learn what it may mean and how it was derived. In names, as shown herein, invariably is found the key that unlocks the door to an age-old mystery. No names can equal the drama of Kymri, Saxon and British, and of them all the name British is the most enthralling name in all history.

CHAPTER 7

GALLIC TESTIMONY

THE religious spirit of the Gaul diminished with the coming of the Franks but the fire never flickered in Britain. It flamed like a volcano, fiery in its evangelism and bursting forth fiercely at foreign interference. Even when resting, its complacency was deceptive as the Nazis found out in World War II. To strike at her Christian institutions and sacred edifices is to pierce her heart, causing her people to fight back with that invincible fury that has always astonished the world, as it finally shattered her enemies.

Long before the arrival of the Bethany castaways at Marseilles, Guizot informs us that the south of France was known as the Province Viennoise, populated by Gauls, Phoenicians and Greeks, 'with the Gauls most populous everywhere'. The significance of this is quite important. The Phoenicians and the Greeks had a long association with the south of France, particularly the Phoenicians, who were the leading mariners before the Grecian seafaring ascendancy. The ancient port of Marseilles was the chief port of call for both in the comings and goings in the transportation of tin and lead from Britain. Over the centuries a common friendship had developed between them and the Gauls; consequently it is understandable how Phoenician and Grecian colonies came to be founded in Gaul. Marseilles is reputed to be the oldest city in France and its oldest seaport. It was a port long before either settled there but it was the Greeks who developed the port to its peak of prominence and gave it the name it bears. However, we should never lose sight of the fact that the port had its first association with the biblical ships of Tarshish, commanded by the Danites, of the tribe of Dan. They were the first great sea power in history and the first to know intimately the inhabitants of Britain, and to trade with them. The Phoenicians and Greeks were very largely Danites.

At the time of our story the port of Marseilles was familiar with the ships of Joseph. To the Gallic populace his name was well known as are the names of Carnegie, Schwab and Bethlehem Steel to us today. Therefore, it can be well assumed that Joseph had many influential friends at Marseilles, who would gladly welcome him amongst them.

Among the Gauls there existed a deep receptivity for the persecuted followers of 'The Way'. Between the Gauls and the Judean advocates of

Christ there was mutual sympathy. The Gauls were Druidic, and their faith held sway over all Gaul, which explains more than anything else why the land was a safe haven for Joseph and the Bethany family, as well as the many other converts who had previously found refuge there, after a safe escape from Judea in the ships of Joseph.

Those who have been indoctrinated by the false stories describing the Druidic religion may pause in consternation. The malevolent infamy heaped upon the Druidic priesthood, their religion, with the practice of human sacrifice, is just as untruthful, vicious and vile as the other distortions stigmatizing the ancient Britons. On close examination it will be found that those who uttered the vindictive maledictions stand out in Roman history as the dictators of the Roman Triumvirate. Their bestial hatred for everything that was British and Christian deliberately promoted the insidious propaganda to defame the people they could neither coerce nor subdue. In our own time, among others, none other than the eminent archaeologist Sir Flinders Petrie, on examination of the ground around and under the altar at Stonehenge, completely exploded the infamous accusations. He found only the fossilized bones of sheep and goats which more firmly established the affinity with the patriarchal faith of the East. In each case the sacrificial burnt offerings were as stated in the biblical record.

The influence Druidism had upon the rest of the ancient world, and its peaceful and ready reception of the Christian faith, proves its noble structure. Hume, the high-ranking British historian acknowledged for his impartiality and the lack of bias in his reporting, wrote: 'No religion has ever swayed the minds of men like the Druidic'.

It prepared the way for Christianity by its solid acceptance of 'The Way'. But for Druidism Christianity might never have flourished. It drove the first nails into the Christian platform that held it fast through all its early stresses, giving it the vigour to endure for all posterity.

The Roman persecutors, despising Druidic opposition, intensified their malignancy with the British conversion to Christianity. The Emperors Augustus, Tiberius and the Claudian and Diocletian decrees made acceptance of Druidic and Christian faith a capital offence, punishable by death. Some have claimed that this persecution by Rome drove both the religions together to form the solid phalanx of Christianity. This is far from being the case. It has been already pointed out how the ancient Kymry were bonded in the ancient patriarchal faith even before they arrived in Britain. Organized by Hu Gadarn (Hugh the

Mighty) the faith took on the name of Druid, a word some claim derived from the Keltic word 'Dreus', meaning 'an oak', arising out of the custom of worshipping in the open within the famous oak groves of the island. A more likely derivation is from 'Druthin' – a 'Servant of Truth'. The motto of the Druids was 'The Truth against the World'. A casual study of the Triads emphasized the old Hebrew faith with positive clarification. The British Mother Druidic Church continued to teach the immortality of the soul, the omniscience of One God and the coming of the Messiah. They were aware of the prophesied vicarious atonement and, extraordinary as it may seem, the actual name of Jesus was familiar to them long before the advent of Christ. They were the only people to know it and say it, a fact that has astounded students of theology. From this it can clearly be seen that there existed a mutual understanding between the Druid and the converted Judean on religious principles that readily opened the door to general acceptance of 'The Way'. From this we can believe it was no accident whereby the refugee followers of 'The Way' found a natural haven in Gaul, and their apostolic leaders a safer sanctuary in Britain.

At that period in history Britain was the only free country in the world. Gaul had received its baptism of Roman persecution long before the Caesars turned their attention upon the British. It was the constant aid given the Gaulish brethren by the warriors of Britain which brought about the invasion of the Isles. The first attack, led by Julius Caesar, 55 BC was purely a punitive expedition against the Britons for thwarting his arms in Gaul. Contrary to general opinion that Caesar's attack was a conquest, it was a dismal failure. Within two weeks his forces were routed and pulled back into Gaul. On his return to Rome Caesar was openly ridiculed by Pompey's Party in the Triumvirate. His famous legend, 'Veni, Vidi, Vici' ('I came, I saw, I conquered') was satirized by the pens of the Roman élite. They wrote in rebuke, 'I came, I saw, but failed to stay'. Over the ten years that followed, to 43 BC the mightiest armed forces of Rome, led by its ablest generals, fought to establish a foothold in Britain. In this Caesar failed to penetrate farther than a few miles inland.

It was not until the reign of Hadrian, AD 120, that Britain was incorporated (*by treaty – not conquest*) within the Roman dominions, as described by Aelius Spartianus in *Vita Hadriani*. By this treaty the Britons retained their kings, lands, laws and rights, accepting a Roman nucleus of the army for the defence of the realm.

Surely no one can misconstrue this conquest or support the belief that naked barbarians could defy and defeat the Roman legions, during those ten years led by its Emperors and greatest generals.

The invasions were repelled by the famed British Pendragon, Caswallen, who reigned for seven years after the invasion.

For Gaul it was not to last. They lacked the security of the seas which protected the British Isles. Unhappily Gaul, later to be known as France, was destined to be the world crossroads of continental invasion, and on its soil, up to our own time, some of the bloodiest battles in all history have been fought. Until the coming of the Franks, the Visigoths, Ostrogoths and Vandals, the Gauls for centuries were to carry on the great evangelizing work of Christianity, laying the foundation of the Church by the great leaders who stemmed from Britain, with carefully formed plans. It was to be immortalized with the presence and great work of Philip, Lazarus, Mary Magdalene and the other Marys, each of whom left an enduring mark in the name of their Saviour.[26] As the story of Joseph of Arimathea is brought forth to the light of day, so are those others, who laboured under his instruction, lifted out of the obscure darkness of the past to thrill us with their devotion and sacrifice.

The record shows that Joseph frequently journeyed to Gaul to confer with the disciples, particularly with Philip, who had arrived at Marseilles ahead of Joseph, and was awaiting him and the Bethany family.

It must not be forgotten that Joseph, by his tin mining interests in Cornwall and Devon, had a long association with the British. Consequently the comings and goings of his ships most certainly would have kept the British up to date with world happenings, and also with Gaul.

Long before Joseph arrived in Britain, the scandal of the cross was known to them and had become a cause of grave concern to the Druidic Church. By similarity of patriarchal faith and knowledge of prophecy, the Druidic prelates recognized in the death of Christ the fulfilment of prophecy. The swiftness with which the Druidic delegates journeyed to Gaul to meet Joseph shows how concerned they were to obtain first-hand information. Contrary to the fallacious story of later historians, there was no argument, civil or religious, no bloodshed. It was an open acceptance that elected Joseph of Arimathea to the head of the Christ-converted British Church.

---

[26] cf. J. W. Taylor, *The Coming of the Saints.*

From then on the Druidic name and the old religion in Britain and Gaul began to be superseded by the Christian name, which the British created to identify the accepted Christ faith, formerly known as 'The Way'.

The miraculous safe arrival of Joseph and his companions at Marseilles, and thence to Britain, surely was the Will of God working out His inscrutable purpose gradually to fulfil the prophetic words of Jesus, to come to the lost sheep of Israel. From that time commenced the organization of the Christian clan, the marshalling of their forces into determined action. Thus began the epochal drama that was to change imperial destiny and lead the peoples of the world to a better way of life. Yet, before this was to be fully achieved, millions were to wade their way through unbelievable tragedy, defying tyranny in its basest and most terrifying form, wholesale massacre and fiendish torture, suffering the brutalities of the Coliseum, the horrors of the fetid prison of the Mamertine, and the dreadful scourging wars in which the British were to make the most colossal sacrifice in blood and life known to history.

CHAPTER 8

ST. PHILIP CONSECRATES JOSEPH OF ARIMATHEA IN FRANCE

IT is not difficult to visualize the joyous meeting that took place between old, tried and trusted friends when the Bethany group arrived at Marseilles. Every record scrutinized points to the closeness that banded the disciples and followers of 'The Way' to Joseph. In him they possessed an intelligent, intrepid leader, a born organizer with the cold, calm reasoning of the shrewd, successful business mind; truly a much-needed asset to guide them in those crucial years. Throughout his lifetime he was to continue to be their salvation against the new and rising storm of Roman persecution that was soon to be loosed upon all followers of 'The Way', with a murderous fury that overshadows the brutalities of Hitler and Stalin. He was to be the means of raising the first Christian army to battle for Christ on the shores and fields of Britain that sent the bestial Romans reeling on their heels.

Joseph was ever the unseen power behind the throne, as he had been on that black night in the Sanhedrin and the following four years in Judea. All rallied around him eager to begin proclaiming the Word to the world.

How many of the disciples were with him during his short stay in Gaul it is difficult to say. It is amazing how nonchalantly the records deal with this important matter. Various existing records agree in part with the Baronius record,[27] naming among the occupants of the castaway boat Mary Magdalene, Martha, the handmaiden Marcella, Lazarus whom Jesus raised from the dead, and Maximin the man whose sight Jesus restored. Then non-committaly the report read, 'and others'. Other records state that Philip, and James accompanied Joseph. Others report that Mary, the wife of Cleopas, and Mary, the mother of Jesus, were occupants of the boat. That there were many congregated at this time is obvious by the manner in which the various names appear in the early Gallic church records. It is well known that a great number of converts had preceded Joseph to Marseilles. Banded together they formed a godly company of eager, enthusiastic workers in the Christian vineyard.

---

[27] Baronius, Cardinal Caesar *Annales Ecclesiastici*, (Ecclesiastical Annals) vol. 1, p. 327, quoting *Acts of Magdalen* and other manuscripts.

Philip, one of the original twelve Apostles, was certainly present. There is a wealth of uncontroversial testimony asserting his commission in Gaul, all of which alike state that he received and consecrated Joseph, preparatory to his embarkation and appointment as the Apostle to Britain.

Some have misconstrued this act of consecration as an act of conversion to the Christ Way of Life, chiefly because Joseph's name is not mentioned as being one of the seventy elected by Jesus on His second appearance. In fact few names are mentioned and none of the later one hundred and twenty. They overlook the facts of the biblical record which states that during the last tragic days of Jesus the Apostles at Jerusalem referred to Joseph, being a disciple of Christ. This pronouncement antedates the enlistment of the two later elect groups of disciples; therefore it was not necessary for Joseph, to be named among them. His devotion to Jesus, and the apostolic reference show that he was one of the early disciples of Christ.

In order to be properly ordained to an apostolic appointment it was necessary for the consecration to be performed by the laying on of hands by one of the original Apostles. Strange as it may seem, thrice within thirty years Philip performs this special consecration for Joseph, the third time for a very peculiar reason that will be related in its order.

St. Philip is referred to in the early Gallic church as the Apostle of Gaul. Undoubtedly he was the first acknowledged Apostle to Gaul but, as we shall later see, the unceasing evangelizing effort in Gaul stemmed from Britain, with Lazarus in particular dominating the Gallic scene during his short lifetime.[28] Due to Philip's apostolic authority it might be more correctly said that while in Gaul he was the accepted head of the Gallic Christian Church.

The biblical and the secular records show that he did not remain constantly in Gaul. There is frequent record of his being in other lands, in the company of other Apostles and disciples. Scriptural literature ceases to mention him circa AD 60. Evidently he returned to Gaul at various intervals. Many of the early writers particularly report Philip being in Gaul AD 65, emphasizing the fact that it was in this year that he consecrated Joseph, for the third time. Philip did not die in Gaul nor were his martyred remains buried there. He was crucified at Hierapolis at an advanced age. Two notable church authorities report his death.

Isidore, Archbishop of Seville, AD 600-636 in his *Historia*, writes:

[28] Taylor, J.W. *The Coming of the Saints*, pp. 238-240.

'Philip of the city Bethsaida, whence also came Peter, preached Christ to the Gauls, and brought barbarous and neighbouring nations, seated in darkness and close to the swelling ocean to the light of knowledge and port of faith. Afterwards he was stoned and crucified and died in Hierapolis, a city of Phrygia, and having been buried with his corpse upright along with his daughters rests there'.

The *Dictionary of Christian Biography* refers to Isidore as 'undoubtedly the greatest man of his time in the Church of Spain. A voluminous writer of great learning'.

The eminent Cardinal Baronius, in his *Ecclesiastical Annals*, writes:

'Philip the fifth in order is said to have adorned Upper Asia with the Gospel, and at length at Hierapolis at the age of 87 to have undergone martyrdom, which also John Chrysostom hands down, and they say that the same man travelled over part of Scythia, and for some time preached the Gospel along with Bartholomew. In Isidore one reads that Philip even imbued the Gauls with the Christian faith, which also in the Breviary of Toledo of the school of Isidore is read.'

Julian, Archbishop of Toledo, AD 680-690, whom Dr. William Smith in his biographical work states was 'the last eminent Churchman of West Gothic Spain, and next to Isidore of Seville, perhaps the most eminent', along with the Venerable Bede, AD 673, declare that Philip was assigned to Gaul. The talented Archbishop Ussher also asserts: 'St. Philip preached Christ to the Gauls.' Further testimony is found in the MS. *Martyrology of Hieronymus*.

Finally, to substantiate Philip's mission and presence in Gaul, I quote Freculphus, Bishop of Lisieux, France, AD 825-851:

'Philip of the City of Bethsaida whence also came Peter, of whom in the Gospels and Acts of the Apostles praiseworthy mention is often made, whose daughters also were outstanding prophetesses, and of wonderful sanctity and perpetual virginity, as ecclesiastical history narrates, preached Christ to the Gauls.'

At this time it is quite in place to discuss the recently revived belief that the Epistle to the Galatians was addressed, as the ancient writers claim, to the inhabitants of Gaul, and not the small colony of Gauls in Asia, particularly since the testimony is related by various authoritative writers discussing Philip's mission in Gaul in the same breath. This evidence is quite important to consider, substantiating the great Christian evangelizing effort in Gaul and supporting the mass of evidence associating Britain with Gaul in those dramatic years.

Cardinal Baronius writes:

'We have said in our notes to the Roman Martyrology that, "to the Galatians" must be corrected in the place of "to the Gauls".'

St. Epiphanius, AD 315-407, wrote:

'The ministry of the divine word having been entrusted to St. Luke, he exercised it by passing into Dalmatia, into Gaul, into Italy, into Macedonia, but principally into Gaul, so that St. Paul assures him in his epistles about some of his disciples – "Crescens", said he, "is in Gaul." In it must not be read in Galatia as some have falsely thought, but in Gaul.'[29]

Pere Longueval remarks that this sentiment was so general in the East that Theodoret, who read 'in Galatia', did not fail to understand 'Gaul' because as a matter of fact the Greeks gave this name to Gaul, and the Galatians had only thus been named because they were a colony of Gauls (*Memoire de l'Apostolat de St. Mansuet* [*vide* p. 83], par l'Abbé Guillaume, p. II).

No better authority may be quoted in discussing this matter than the learned Rev. Lionel Smithett Lewis, MA, late Vicar of Glastonbury, considered the foremost church historian of our times. The Rev. Lewis writes:[30]

'Perhaps it may be permitted to point out that Edouard de Bazelaire supports this view of Crescens being in Gaul, and not in Galatia. He traces St. Paul about the year 63 along the Aurelian Way from

---

[29] 'Crescens to Galatia'; 2 *Timothy* 4:10.
[30] Lewis, L. S. *St. Joseph of Arimathea at Glastonbury*, pp. 114-115

Rome to Arles in France [*Predication du Christianisme dans les Gaules,* t. IX, p. 198]. He names his three companions: St. Luke who had just written the Acts; Trophimus whom he left at Arles; Crescens whom he had sent to Vienne [Gaul].'

'De Bazelaire goes on to say: "On his return he retook Trophimus with him, and was not able to keep him as far as Rome, for he wrote (St. Paul) from there to Timothy, 'Hasten and come and join me as soon as possible. Crescens is in the Gauls. I have left Trophimus sick at Millet' [Miletus]." The Abbé Maxime Latou, referring to Trophimus being in Gaul says, "In 417 the Pope Zosimus recognized in the Church of Arles the right of being Metropolitan over all the district of Narbonne because Trophimus its first Bishop had been for the Gauls the source of life whence flowed the streams of faith."'

The Rev. Lewis also states,

'All this goes to prove that Gaul was known as Galatia , and their chronicling St. Paul's and his companions' journey does not in the least mean that they deny St. Philip's. For the same M. Edouard de Bazelaire quotes M. Chateaubriand as saying, "Peter sent missionaries into Italy, *in the Gauls*, and on the coast of Africa." The part that St. Peter played is duly emphasized by many illustrious Roman historians. And without St. Peter in the least exercising any primacy, this ardent and potent man might well have influenced his compatriot from Bethsaida [St. Philip].'

'It is quite important to know that the Churches of Vienne and Mayence in Gaul claim Crescens as their founder. This goes far to corroborate that Galatia in 2 *Timothy* 4:10, means Gaul, and not its colony Galatia in Asia, and that Isidore meant to say that St. Philip preached to the Gauls, and not to the Galatians of Asia.'

'We have seen that the *Recognitions of Clement* (2nd century) stated that St. Clement of Rome, going to Caesarea, found St. Joseph of Arimathea there with St. Peter, Lazarus, the Holy Women and others, a quite likely place for the start of the voyage of St. Joseph and the Bethany Family and others to Marseilles. Caesarea was the home of St. Philip in the Bible story. Afterwards tradition [supported by secular records] brings him to France, whence he sent St. Joseph to Britain. William of Malmesbury, quoting Freculphus, calls Joseph, St. Philip's "dearest friend". They must have been in close association. Tradition brings the Holy Women and St. Joseph to France. All the way up the Rhone Valley, as we have seen, from Marseilles to Morlaix, we find constant memories of the occupants of that boat without oars and sails. From Morlaix in Brittany it is a short step to Cornwall in Britain. The route from Marseilles must have been known well to St. Joseph. It was that of his fellow traders, seeking ore. From Cornwall an ancient road led to the mines of Mendip, remains of which exist. Arviragus's reception of St. Joseph, though unconverted, suggests a very possible previous acquaintance. Testimony from the Early Fathers and varied branches of the Church show that the Church was here in earliest days.'

In discussing reference to the Gauls of France and the Gauls of Asia, Archbishop Ussher sternly rebukes contemporaneous writers for creating the misunderstanding through their inaptitude to examine the ancient documents and compare the records. As we have seen from the few quotations provided, apostolic reference is indicated to the Gauls of France, and not the Gauls of Asia. The presence of St. Philip is established in Gaul and as being his first allotted mission. Other Apostles are mentioned working in Gaul, some of whom we shall see journeyed with Joseph of Arimathea to Britain. St. Clement throws historic light on the illustrious gathering at Caesarea, about the time of this exodus, which tends to support the statement by many that Philip, as the dearest friend of Joseph, with James, was an occupant in the castaway boat along with the Holy Women and others. It is on record that St. Philip baptized Josephes,[31] the son of Joseph and later, when Joseph revisited Gaul, Philip sent Josephes to Britain with his father and ten other disciples. Evidently, the Saints arrived in Britain in groups. It is ultimately stated that one hundred and sixty had been sent to Britain at various intervals by St. Philip to serve Joseph in his evangelizing mission.[32]

---

[31] *Magna Tabula Glastoniensis*
[32] From early manuscript quoted by John of Glastonbury, William of Malmesbury and Capgrave.

Joseph did not linger long in Gaul. A British Druidic delegation of Bishops arrived at Marseilles to greet him and extend an enthusiastic invitation to Joseph, urging him to return to Britain with them and there teach the Christ Gospel. This magnanimous invitation was enlarged upon by the Druidic emissaries of the British Prince Arviragus, offering Joseph lands, a safe haven and protection against Roman molestation. Arviragus was Prince of the noble Silures of Britain, in the Dukedom of Cornwall. He was the son of King Cunobelinus, the Cymbeline of Shakespeare, and cousin to the renowned British warrior-patriot, Caradoc, whom the Romans named Caractacus. Together they represented the Royal Silurian dynasty, the most powerful warrior kingdom in Britain, from whom the Tudor kings and queens of England had their descent.

The invitation was gladly accepted and Joseph made ready to embark for Britain, with his specially elected companions immediately after his dearest friend, St. Philip, had performed the consecration in the year AD 36. From then on Joseph of Arimathea becomes known in history as 'the Apostle to Britain'.

Undoubtedly Joseph was attracted to the Sacred Isle for other reasons apart from welcoming the opportunity of proclaiming 'The Way' to the British populace. We are informed that Arviragus and Joseph were well known to each other long prior to the invitation; consequently we can well believe he had acquired many influential friends in the south of Britain during the years he had administered his mining interests in Cornwall and Devon. He would be as well known to the common folk as he was to the aristocracy. In one sense it would be a homecoming to the uncle of Jesus. On the other hand, the land held for him many tender memories which he would hold most precious.

In the traditions of Cornwall, Devon, Somerset, Wiltshire and Wales, it has ever been believed and definitely claimed, that Jesus as a boy accompanied His great uncle to Britain on at least one of his many seafaring trips; then later, as a young man. During those silent years preceding His ministry it is avowed that Jesus, after leaving India, journeyed to Britain and there founded a retreat, building a wattle altar to the glory of God.

The ancient wise men of India assert that He had dwelt among them. It is mentioned in the Vishnu Purana that Jesus had visited the Himalayan Kingdom of Nepal. Moreover, the religious teachers of India were familiar with the Isles of Britain. Wilford states that the books of old India describe them as 'The Sacred Isles of the West'. One of the books refers to 'Britashtan, the seat of religious learning'. They employed the term used by Isaiah and others: 'Isles of the West', 'Isles of the Sea.' The British Isles are the only islands lying to the far west of Palestine.

Centuries after Joseph's time, St. Augustine confirms the tradition of the wattle altar built by Jesus in a letter to the Pope,[33] stating that the altar then existed. Consequently we can believe the records in the ancient Triads that the altar was standing when Joseph, with his twelve companions, arrived in Britain. We can well understand why Joseph made this sacred spot his destination, settling by its site, and there building the first Christian church above ground in all the world, to the glory of God in the name of Jesus and continuing the dedication to Mary, the mother of Jesus.

Who were the twelve companions of Joseph that embarked with him from Gaul to Britain?

This is a question one may ask with eager interest. It holds a fascination all of its own which becomes exciting as we ponder over the names of the men and women so closely associated with Jesus during His earthly ministry. Our interest is increased as we realize that all of them are lost to the biblical record following the exodus of AD 36. Truly they are the lost disciples destined to write Christian history with their lives in letters of blood, fire and gold.

Because the personalities of Peter, Paul, Matthew, Mark, Luke and John so greatly dominate the scriptural spotlight and illumine the historic scene, one cannot help but feel thrilled as we meet again the beloved of Christ, long lost to the sacred record and, of all places, on the shores of the Sacred Isle – historic Christian Britain.

Here is the list of them, the Champions of Christ as selected by St. Philip and St. Joseph, following the latter's consecration in Gaul.

Cardinal Baronius, in his great work, quotes from Mistral, in Mireio, and another ancient document in the Vatican Library. He names them one by one, and by the names all Christians know them best.

---

[33] *Epistolae ad Gregoriam Papam.*

St. Mary, wife of Cleopas	St. Mary Magdalene
St. Martha	Marcella, the Bethany sisters' maid
St. Lazarus	St. Maximin
St. Eutropius	St. Martial
St. Salome	St. Trophimus
St. Clean	St. Sidonius (Restitutus)
St. Saturninus	St. Joseph of Arimathea

All the records refer to Joseph and twelve companions. Here are listed fourteen, including Joseph. Marcella, the handmaiden to the Holy women, is the only one not bearing the title Saint, consequently she is not considered as one of the missionary band. Probably Marcella went along in her old capacity of handmaiden to the Bethany sisters. Many other writers insist there was another member to this party not recorded in the Mistral report – Mary, the mother of Jesus. Along with tradition, a great deal of extant documentary testimony substantiates the presence of the Christ Mother being with Joseph, he having been appointed by St. John as 'paranymphos' to the Blessed Virgin Mary. Being 'paranymphos' she had to be with him, and we know Mary remained in Joseph's safe keeping until her death.

What tender memories these illustrious names conjure in the mind!

What tales of tragic experiences they brought with them to relate to the sympathetic Druidic priesthood!

Here were the people most closely associated with Jesus in the drama of the cross: Joseph, the fearless, tender guardian who embraced the torn body in his arms; the suffering mother whom John led away from the final agony; the women who had discovered the deserted tomb; Lazarus,whom Jesus raised from the dead to walk out of the sepulchre into the Glory and follow Christ; and Restitutus, now known as St. Sidonius, whose eyes had never seen the light of day until Jesus touched them ... whose first vision was the Light of the World.

Is there any wonder that the little isle of Britain became commonly spoken of as 'the most hallowed ground on earth,' 'The Sacred Isle', 'The Motherland'?

CHAPTER 9

JOSEPH BECOMES THE APOSTLE OF BRITAIN AND ARRIVES ON THE SACRED ISLE OF AVALON

TAKING their farewell of Philip and the faithful in Gaul, Joseph and the Bethany group of missionaries set sail for Britain in company with the Druidic delegation. Reaching its shores the illustrious band sailed up the waterway of the west, the Severn Sea, until they came within sight of a lofty green hill, as Dean Alford writes, 'most like to Tabor's Holy Mount', known to this day as Glastonbury Tor. They made their way up the estuary of the Brue and the Parrett, arriving at a cluster of islands about twelve miles inland from the coast. The most inspiring of these was the 'Sacred Isle of Avalon', its shores sheltered in apple orchards.

The isle derived its name from Aval, Celtic for Apple, which was the sacred fruit of the Druids, the emblem of fertility. Thus its name applied a special symbolic significance to the spot destined to become the Mecca of Christendom.

This was the manner of arrival of the Saints in Britain.

On this fruitful Isle of Avalon Joseph of Arimathea and his dedicated companions were met by another assemblage of the friendly British Druidic priesthood, King Guiderius and his brother Arviragus, Prince of the royal Silures of Britain, and an entourage of nobles. The first act of Arviragus was to present to Joseph, as a perpetual gift, free of tax, twelve hides of land, a hide for each disciple, each hide representing 160 acres, a sum total of 1,920 acres.

This was the first charter given to any land to be dedicated in the name of Jesus Christ, defining them as the Hallowed Acres of Christendom, AD 36. It was the first of many charters this historic sacred spot was to receive, during its sacred existence, from the kings and queens of Britain. We find these charters officially recorded in the British Royal archives; many are extant today, and over one thousand years later we find in remarkable detail record of the original charter embodied in the *Domesday Book*, on recognition of William I, first Norman king of England, AD 1066.

Throughout the reigns of the British sovereigns these charters were the means of settling state, political and religious disputes in refusing to recognize Papal authority,[34] proclaiming Britain's seniority to unbroken apostolic succession through its Bishops, dating from St. Joseph, the Apostle to Britain, appointed and consecrated by the Apostle St. Philip and, as we shall see, on orders arising from St. Paul, the Apostle to the Gentiles. Incidentally, the British claim of seniority was never denied by the Vatican Popes and was affirmed by Papal statement as late as 1936.

With the chartered gift of land to the Josephian Mission, Arviragus promised his protection. With his brother he led the first army in battle against Roman Christian persecution as Defender of the Faith, AD 43. King Lucius, AD 156, grandson of Arviragus, who renewed and enlarged the charter, was baptized many years earlier at Winchester by St. Timotheus,[35] his uncle, who then proclaimed him 'Defender of the Faith'. At this time Roman Catholicism was not founded. It remained for the intrepid Queen Elizabeth, lineal descendant of Arviragus, to make the worldshaking declaration for the Reformation, when challenging the threats of the combined forces of France, Spain and Rome, by Pope Pius V, AD 1570, to subject Britain to Roman Catholicism. In her famous address from the throne she rebuked and denounced Papal authority. Alluding to the charters, she pronounced Britain's priority in the Christian Church. She made it a royal decree for the sovereigns of England on their coronation officially to take oath as the 'Defender of the Faith'.[36] Personally she declared, as her ancient ancestors had done, that only Christ was the Head of the Church. Ever since, on their coronation, the sovereigns of Britain have taken this oath, as did the present Queen of the British Commonwealth, Elizabeth II, on her succession to the British Throne, AD 1953. On this occasion the Roman Catholic Church petitioned for this oath to be omitted. It was stoutly refused, stating the British Kingdom was the Defender of the true Christian Cause with Christ at its Head.

It is stated that following their disembarkation the travellers made their way up the hill where it is reputed that Joseph, weary from his travel, stopped to rest, thrusting his staff into the ground. Tradition tells us that the staff became part of the earth, taking root, and in time blossomed. Historically it is known as the 'Holy Thorn'. From ancient times it is referred to as a phenomenon of nature, being the only thorn

---

[34] Ussher, *Britannicarum Ecclesiarum Antiquitates*, ch. 2.
[35] Morgan, R.W. *St. Paul in Britain*, (Oxford and London: Parker) 1861 p. 182.
[36] The title was conferred on Henry VIII and confirmed by Parliament in 1544.

tree in the world to bloom at Christmas time and in May. It endured throughout the centuries as a perpetual, living monument to the landing of Britain's Saintly Disciples of Christ, and a reminder of the birth of Jesus in far-away Bethlehem.

To this day this spot bears the name it received in Joseph's time – 'Weary All Hill'.

For centuries the phenomenon of the blooming thorn was looked upon as a miracle by the early devout Christians of Britain and, as one could expect, the Holy Thorn provided critical opportunity to the nineteenth-century scoffers. Modern science shows their ignorance. Tree experts affirm it is not only possible, but a natural process, under favourable conditions, for such a staff formed from the limb of a tree to take root and develop into a live, thriving tree. The strange blooming propensity of the thorn tree at Christmas, as well as in May, is something different, but one we can accept as an Act of God to remind us of the fulfilment of Divine prophecy.

The Holy Thorn continued to be world famous for its strange blossoming habit until the regime of Oliver Cromwell, AD 1649. During these years it was cut down by a fanatical Puritan, when the Cromwellian desecration of holy places by his blind, bigoted followers was in operation. But the sacred phenomenon did not die. Its scion, already planted, lived to thrive and bloom as had the mother thorn tree. It can be seen today, a healthy, fertile tree, blooming gloriously at the same appointed seasons, in the hallowed churchyard of St. John, at Glastonbury, where the noble ruins of the Mother Church of Christendom stand. Nowhere in the world is there another similar tree enacting the same blossoming phenomenon. Its lovely snow-white petals spread out like a beacon in the midst of dead nature, its immaculate beauty looking skyward and mutely proclaiming that God still reigns in the heavens. Other shoots taken from this tree, and grafted to wild stock, bloom in the same manner.

Within a mile of the Sacred Isle of Avalon was another smaller island known as Ynys Witrin, or Glass Island, a name some claim derived from the pure glassy waters that once surrounded it. Archaeologists provide the more probable answer. Excavations have revealed that it was once a busy site of the glass industry for which the ancient Britons were famous. Later the Saxons named it Glastonbury by which name it has continued to be known. During the Saxon period the famed Isles ceased to exist. The monks drained the land, making where the islands once stood a dry plain, though it is yet below water level and swampy in wet weather.

Today as you wander among the noble ruins of the glorious old Abbey, you cannot escape the feeling of entrancement that touches your heart as you realize you are standing in the centre of the hallowed twelve hides of land which the Silurian prince deeded to St. Joseph and his twelve companions. The beauty of the scene in this quiet little English town of Glastonbury encircled by verdant meadows, all part of the dedicated 1,920 acres of Christendom, makes it difficult to get down to reality and comprehend the fact that one is walking on the same holy ground on which they trod; where they communed together, including Mary, the mother of Jesus; the beautiful Mary Magdalene; the Bethany sisters whom Christ loved; their brother Lazarus; Peter and Paul, Philip and James, Trophimus, Mary Cleopas and Mary Salome, Aristobulus, the father-in-law of Peter, and Simon Zelotes, among a multitude of others, and where tradition asserts that Jesus built His wattle chapel, where He talked with God. Here countless pilgrims from all parts of the world made their vows. Here illustrious converts were confirmed and went forth into the world to preach the Word and die gruesome deaths for the Christian cause. Here, for over a thousand years, mighty kings bowed in reverence and were buried with the elect in Christ, within God's Acre. You see embedded in the walls the ancient weather-worn stone which has mystified so many, causing centuries of controversy, mutely bearing the two sacred names, 'Jesus – Maria', first hewn and placed within the outer wall of the original stone church by the hands of the faithful Saints. You see the ruined Altar of St. Joseph of Arimathea and just across the way the ancient cemetery which contains more famous characters and more dramatic history than all the cemeteries in the world put together.

These magnificent ruins of Glastonbury Abbey are the remains of the beautiful church erected over the very spot where the great uncle of Jesus and our Lord's own disciples built their first altar in a church of wattle, thatched with reed, as was the custom of that time. This was the first Christian Church erected above ground to the glory of God and His Son Jesus, dedicated to the Blessed Mary, His mother.

Wattle was the common building material of the ancient Britons, used in the construction of their homes, just as cabins of log and mud and houses of sod were commonly built in the colonizing years of America and Canada. Therefore Joseph and his companions, in building the First Church of Christ of wattle, did not employ unusual or inferior materials for the purpose, but only that which was then of the common order. We find proof of this in the book *The Church in These Islands before Augustine*, written by the Rev. G. F. Brown, a former Bishop of Bristol. Herein the Rev. Brown refers to the excavations of Arthur Bulleid, L.R.C.P., F.S.A., at Godney Marsh, in 1892:

'This wattle church survived till after the Norman invasion when it was burned by accident. Wattle work is very perishable material and of all things of the kind, the least likely would seem to be that we in the nineteenth century should, in confirmation of the story, discover at Glastonbury an almost endless amount of British wattle work. Yet this is exactly what happened. In the low ground, now occupying the place of the impenetrable marshes which gave the name of the Isle of Avalon to the higher ground, the eye of the local antiquary had long marked a mass of dome-shaped hillocks, some of them of very considerable diameter, and about seventy in number, clustered together in what is now a large field, a mile and a quarter from Glastonbury. Peat had formed itself in the long course of time, and its preservative qualities had kept safe for our eyes that which it had enclosed and covered. The hillocks proved to be the remains of British houses burned with fire. They were set on ground made solid in the midst of the waters, with causeways for approach from the land. The faces of the solid ground and the sides of the causeways are revetted with wattle work. There is wattle all over, strong and very well made. The wattle when first uncovered is as good to all appearances as the day it was made. The houses of the Britons at Glastonbury, as a matter of fact, as long tradition tells us, and their church were made of wattles.'

Soon after Joseph and his apostolic company had settled in Avalon painstakingly they began to build their wattle church. It was sixty feet in length and twenty-six feet wide, following the pattern of the Tabernacle. The task was completed between AD 38 and 39. To those who followed after every particle of clay and every reed was held sacred. To protect it from dissolution it was encased in lead and over it St. Paulinus, AD 630, erected the beautiful chapel of St. Mary's. It remained intact until the year AD 1184, when the great fire gutted the whole Abbey to the ground and with it perished the structure of the first Christian Church above ground.

The pattern of the wattle church was the model employed in the architecture of all the early British churches and perpetuated in many up to the present time. Within that humble wattle church the first Christian instructions were given and the first prayers and chants of praise to the glory of God and to His Son Jesus rang forth over the Island. Sanctuary at last! Safe and free from the persecution of the Sanhedrin and the tyranny of pagan Rome, those faithful, fervent hearts taught the Gospel of Love and Truth in all its original Christian beauty and humble simplicity. Protected by the valiant armed might of the invincible Silures, before whom the might of Rome was to tremble and crumble, the Apostle of Britain and his noble companions dedicated their lives and efforts in fulfilling the Word of God, through the teachings of the crucified Jesus, in the quiet, restful sunlight of the English vales.

British peoples the world over, Americans whose roots are British, and Christians wherever they may be, should take a heart-throbbing pride in this monumental event. No wonder England is known as the Motherland to the world. Hers is the womb of Christianity, out of which has sprung the world's most humane democracies. Proudly they proclaim the source. America and Britain are the only two nations that permit another flag to fly above their own national standard and that flag is the Flag of Christ – the Church Flag, more commonly known as the Flag of St. George. By this act they proclaim to the rest of the world that they acknowledge Christ and the Law of God.

Back of the little wattle church rose the great Tor, which was a Druidic Gorsedd, or 'High Place of Worship', a hand-piled mound of earth vaster in its dimensions than the Pyramid of Egypt. To this day the terraces that wind around the Gorsedd to its summit can be traced. On such eminences the Druids had their astronomical observatories from which they studied the heavens. In this knowledge, Greek and Roman alike extolled the Druids as the greatest teachers of this complicated science.

There are many who maintain that the reason for the heartfelt, friendly welcome extended to the Josephian Mission was because the Druids, simultaneously with the wise men of Persia, had discovered in the heavens the Star of Prophecy, which heralded the long-expected 'Day Spring' that was to lighten the world with the new dispensation - the glory of 'The Star' that should rise out of Jacob.

This could be so – prophecy has a strange way of revealing itself – in which case, to the Druidic priesthood, the discovery was but the revelation of the great event which they knew, equally with the Israelites of old, was to happen. The astounding fact is that whereas the Sadducean Judeans were never familiar with the name of the Messiah, His name was known to the British long before the memorable event transpired on Golgotha's Hill. It was a name familiar on the lips of every Briton.[37] The indisputable fact is that the Druids proclaimed the name first to the world. A translation from a reading in the ancient Celtic Triads is:

'The Lord our God is One.
Lift up your heads, O ye gates, and be
ye lift up, ye everlasting doors, and the
King of Glory shall come in.
Who is the King of Glory? The Lord Yesu;
He is the King of Glory.'

How the Druidic Priesthood knew the consecrated name so long beforehand is indeed a mystery in itself. The name 'Yesu' was incorporated in the Druidic Trinity as the Godhead. In Britain the name Jesus never assumed its Greek or Latin form. It was always the pure Celtic 'Yesu'. It never changed.

The more researchers study the Celtic Druidic religion the more astonished are they with its similarity with that of old Israel. They taught it as a gospel of peace more faithfully than did their brethren in Israel. Wars, hatreds, persecution and family separation had never divided them as it had the Israelites of Judea. To the members of the Arimathean Mission the British environment must have appeared as a true haven of happiness after all their bitter experiences.

To the Druids the advent of the Josephian Culdees was but a confirmation of the Atonement. They did not need to take up the Cross. It was already with them, a familiar symbol in their religious rituals. The early British Christians never employed the Latin Cross. Their Cross combined the Druidic symbol with the Cross. Even today, the Celtic Cross appears on the peaks and spires of many Anglican churches throughout the world. The Druidic circle embracing the Cross is the

---

[37] cf. Procopius, *De Gothici*, bk. 3.

symbol of eternity. The Cross is the symbol of victory over the grave, through the salvation bought by the vicarious atonement.

The merging of the British Druidic church with Christianity was a normal procedure, peacefully performed. Those who state that Christianity was bitterly opposed by the Druids speak falsely. Nowhere in the Celtic records is there any mention of opposition. The Druidic Archbishops recognized that the old order was fulfilled according to prophecy, and with the coming of Christ and His atonement the new dispensation had arrived. In this light of understanding Druids and Judean Apostles marched forward together firmly wedded in the name of Christ. It was never marred with the persecution, bloodshed and martyrdom that accompanied the teaching of the Christ Gospel in Rome. The former President of the United States, Franklin Roosevelt, truly said, 'All histories should be rewritten in truth.' School history books still erroneously teach that the Augustan Mission, sent by (Pope) Gregory, AD 596, marked the introduction of Christianity into Britain. Actually it is the date of the first attempt to introduce the Papacy into Britain. Therein lies both error and confusion.

The Vatican has always been more emphatic in correcting this mistake than have the Protestant denominations. Baronius and Alford, the two foremost historians of the Vatican, each referring to ancient documents in the Vatican Library, affirm St. Joseph as the Apostle of Britain and the first to introduce Christian teachings in the Island. The Popes also have substantiated this statement.

In 1931 Pope Pius XI received at the Vatican the visiting English Roman Catholic Mayors of Bath, Colchester and Dorchester, along with a hundred and fifty members of The Friends of Italy Society. In his address to them the Pope said that St. Paul, not Pope Gregory, first introduced Christianity into Britain.

This statement is quoted from the report made in the London *Morning Post*, March 27th, 1931.

The Pope spoke the truth; in fact St. Paul was authoritatively the first to deliver the Message from Rome, though actually his appointed representative, Aristobulus, preceded him. The important point to remember here is that St. Joseph did not go to Britain from Rome. He went direct from Palestine, via Marseilles, and preceded St. Paul in Britain by twenty years.

At the Ecclesiastical Councils of the Roman Catholic Church the religious representatives of each country were accorded honour of place at the Council, in the order that each had received Christianity. Due to the bitter envy some of the countries bore towards the British they vigorously sought to dispute Britain's precedence in priority but on each occasion Britain's position was defended by Vatican authority.

Theodore Martin, of Lovan, writes of these disputes in Disputoilis super Dignitatem Anglis it Gallioe in Concilio Constantiano, AD 1517:

'Three times the antiquity of the British Church was affirmed in Ecclesiastical Councils. 1. The Council of Pisa, AD 1417; 2. Council of Constance, AD 1419; 3. Council of Siena, AD 1423. It was stated that the British Church took precedence of all other Churches, being founded by Joseph of Arimathea, immediately after the Passion of Christ.'

The erudite Bishop Ussher writes in *Brittannicarum Ecclesiarum Antiquitates:*

'The British National Church was founded in AD 36, 160 years before heathen Rome confessed Christianity.'

The founding of Christianity in Britain by the Josephian Mission was truly the beginning of the British national Church. Conversion spread rapidly through the Isles. It is recorded, AD 48, that Conor Macnessa, King of Ulster, sent his priests to Avalon to commit the Christian law and its teachings into writing, which they named 'The Celestial Judgments'.[38] However, it was not until AD 156 that Britain, by the royal edict of King Lucius, officially proclaimed the Christian Church to be the national Church of Britain, at Winchester, then the royal capital of Britain.

Quoting from *Augustinicio Mission*, AD 597, it reads:

'Britain officially proclaimed Christian by King Lucius, at National Council at Winchester, AD 156.'

Winchester was the ancient capital of Britain where its kings were crowned for over fifteen hundred years. It was founded 500 BC.

---

[38] Lewis, *St. Joseph of Arimathea at Glastonbury*; also Irish Tourist Bureau *Old History of Ulster*.

There is no lack of evidence among the earliest writers, many of whom were citizens of nations hostile to Britain. Confirmation of the facts by them and by prelates of a powerful religion opposed to the British Church, cannot be denied on any pretext.

St. Clement of Rome, AD 30-100, refers to the disciples in Britain in *The Epistle to the Corinthians.*

As we turn the pages of the *Demonstratio Evangelica* by Eusebius, of Caesarea, we read the potent passage:

'The Apostles passed beyond the ocean to the Isles called the Brittanic Isles.'

Tertullian of Carthage, AD 208, tells us that in his time the Christian Church 'extended to all the boundaries of Gaul, and parts of Britain inaccessible to the Romans but subject to Christ'.

Sabellius, AD 250, writes this important passage:

'Christianity was privately confessed elsewhere, but the *first* nation that proclaimed it as their religion and *called it Christian*, after the name of Christ, was Britain.' (*Author's italics.*)

Origen, in the third century, wrote:

'The power of our Lord is with those who in Britain are separated from our coasts.'

The famed and benevolent St. Jerome, AD 378, writes:

'From India to Britain all nations resound with the death and resurrection of Christ.'

Arnobius, AD 400, adds his trenchant message, writing:

'So swiftly runs the Word of God that within the space of a few years His Word is concealed neither from the Indians in the East, nor from the Britons in the West.'

Chrysostom, the venerable Patriarch of Constantinople, AD 402, potently pens in his *Sermo De Utilit*:

'The British Isles which are beyond the sea, and which lie in the ocean, have received virtue of the Word. Churches are there found and altars erected. ... Though thou shouldst go to the ocean, to the British Isles, there thou shouldst hear all men everywhere discoursing matters out of the Scriptures, with another voice indeed, but not another faith, with a different tongue, but the same judgment.'

In later years the confirmation continues undenied and unabated.

Polydore Vergil, an eminent Roman Catholic divine, who wrote during the denunciations and quarrels between the Pope and Henry VIII of England: 'Britain partly through Joseph of Arimathea, partly through Fugatus and Damianus, was of all kingdoms the first to receive the Gospel.'

Another Roman Catholic leader, the Rev. Robert Parsons, definitely states in his book *The Three Conversions of England*: 'The Christian religion began in Britain.'

Sir Henry Spelman, the eminent scholar, writes in his *Concilia*:

'We have abundant evidence that this Britain of ours received the faith, and that from the disciples of Christ Himself, soon after the Crucifixion.'

And the famed Taliesin, AD 500-540, one of Britain's greatest scholars, Celtic Arch Druid and Prince Bard, forthrightly declares that though the Gospel teaching was new to the rest of the world it was always known to the Celtic British. He writes: 'Christ, the word from the beginning, was from the first our teacher, and we never lost His teachings. Christianity was a new thing in Asia, but there never was a time when the Druids of Britain held not its Doctrines.'

Gildas, AD 520, Britain's foremost early historian, wrote in his *De Exidio Brittanniae*: 'We certainly know that Christ, the True Son, afforded His Light, the knowledge of His precepts to our Island in the last year of Tiberius Caesar.'

He also wrote the following most important statement: 'Joseph introduced Christianity into Britain in the last year of the reign of Tiberius.'

Tiberius was the Roman Emperor against whom Pontius Pilate plotted, with others, the secret knowledge of which Caiaphas had used to compel Pilate to carry out the evil will of the Sadducean Sanhedrin to crucify Jesus. Tiberius reigned for twenty-two years. The crucifixion of Christ took place in the seventeenth year of his reign, AD 30, according to the reckoning of their time, and AD 31 according to our present reckoning. The last year of Tiberius's reign being his twenty-second, would be, according to the respective calendars, AD 36 and 37. Thus the general agreement that the Gospel was transplanted to Britain within five years of the Passion is in accord with the dates recorded.

To all this is added absolute confirmation that Joseph of Arimathea was the one who first brought Christianity to Britain and was the first and truly appointed Apostle to and of the British.

Probably the statements quoted herein will appear revelatory to many, particularly those saturated with the unreliable, impotent theories of school-book historians. The references are beyond dispute and are only a fraction of the mass available. They substantiate the fact that Joseph and the Arimathean Mission in Britain was known the world over, and in all cases accurately reported long before the Roman Catholic Church was founded at Rome. Later, when the Vatican had become established, Popes, prelates and historians of the Roman Catholic See freely confirmed the record.

From the dates given it will be seen that many of the authorities quoted, both secular and ecclesiastical, lived before and during the epochal period of our story. Others quoted lived close enough to the era to be familiar with Britain and its inhabitants. The ever-rising mass of confirmation from the turn of this century to the present time is proof of the zealous research of scholars and scientists in reaffirming the ancient truth and lifting the curtain of error and misinformation which unqualified and indifferent writers of the last century had clouded with the unstable dogma of myth and legend. Undoubtedly they acted under the influence of atheism which staggered religious belief during the Victorian era, and to a certain extent still lingers to mislead too many. The vicious invectives of the Higher Critics of Germany are squelched along with the fraudulent distortions of Darwin's treatise of evolution by Henrich Haerlik, pseudo-scientist, nakedly exposed by the German Institute of Science and the Lutheran Church, along with the destructive interpretation of socialism by Karl Marx, from which Communism sprang. Communism gave the old propaganda a new dress but it was the same villain, deliberately distorting the true principles of the Western Democracies.

The Britons of our Lord's time were no more barbarian, or 'painted savages', than are the modern English-speaking nations 'war-mad barbarians', as the Soviet press describes us. Educationally the Celtic British ranked among the highest to be found anywhere. Each city had its university apart from the special Druidic seats of learning. In AD 110 Ptolemy states that there existed fifty-six large cities. Marcianus says there were fifty-nine, and Chrysostom wrote, with the acceptance of the new order of 'The Way', a greater impetus was given to the erection of seats of learning. To this great work the converted British Prince Arviragus, then a young unmarried man, along with the rest of the royal Silurian families in England and Wales, gave the fulness of their support.

Quoting from the ancient British Chronicles, we obtain an interesting picture of the conversion of Arviragus by Joseph:

'Joseph converted this King Arviragus
By his prechying to know ye laws divine
And baptized him as write hath Nennius
The chronicler in Brytain tongue full fyne
And to Christian laws made hym inclyne
And gave him then a shield of silver white
A crosse and long, and overthwart full perfete
These armes were used throughout all Brytain
For a common syne, each man to know his nacion
And thus his armes by Joseph Creacion
Full longafore Saint George was generate.
Were worshipt here of mykell elder date.'[39]

It is interesting to note in this verse that Joseph, on the conversion of Arviragus, gave him as a sign for all nations to know, 'the long cross' as his coat of arms, then customarily worn on the shield of the chieftain. This is the first record of the cross officially becoming the symbol of a king. The reason is plain. It was given to King Arviragus as a sign and declaration that he was the elected Christian king, and of added interest, given as the writer states long before St. George, the Patron Saint of

---

[39] Hardynge's *Chronicle.* 1465

England, was born. This symbol, representing the Flag of St. George and known as such today, was inherited from Arviragus. Its religious significance is still dominant, being the accepted Church flag of the present Protestant Church. Since the time of Arviragus it has always been the Christian flag of the British Church. Protestantism had nothing to do with it. Actually it is a mistake to name all Christian denominations separate from the Roman Catholic Church Protestants. The name arose out of other religious sects appearing later in Britain, which protested against the ritualism of the original British Church. In fact the name applies to the religious sects still holding to the Christian faith, who are known today as the Free Churches, meaning free of ritualism of any kind. Up to and during the reign of Queen Elizabeth I, there was only one religion in Britain. Throughout the Isles it was known as the British Church and so known to the rest of the world. It was also known as the Holy Catholic Church and never Roman Catholic. When Elizabeth and her Parliament struck back at the powerful forces of the Papal States, France, Spain and Rome, the Papal See was so determinedly denounced that a cleavage was created that left no doubt in the minds of people for all time to come that the British Church, as at the beginning, had no association with the Roman Catholic hierarchy. Both the British Church and the State determined on a reformation within the British Church to exclude anything and everything that bore any comparison with the Roman Catholic Church in Liturgy and in ritual. Certain Roman innovations had crept into the British Church over the years. The order to reform began, returning to the original concept. Therefore it was not a protest, creating Protestantism, it was as the historic act declares a cleansing reformation of the British Church. Since then the separation has been positive. The British Church was still the national religion of the Isles. Shortly after, the religion began to take on its own native national title, becoming the Church of England, the Church of Wales, the Church of Scotland, and the Church of Ireland, all holding the same communion, all designating themselves as Holy Catholics as separate from Roman Catholics. The word 'Catholic' means 'universal'; thus Holy Catholic means a universal, holy, Christian Church, with Christ alone being the sole Head of the Church. The Roman Catholic Church designates itself as the universal Christian Church of the Romans, with the Pope as its head. This the British Church would never recognize. In the United States of America, prior to the Revolution, the established Church was the Church of England.

Following the Revolution, the name was changed to the Episcopal Church of America of the Anglican Communion.

It is still so known, maintaining the original service and communion of the Mother Church. The German Lutheran Church service also observes a great similarity. All the named churches are Episcopalian, meaning a church government by bishops. In this manner the original Christian Church was created by the Apostles, who appointed Bishops to govern the Christian Church. The present Mother British Church is the only Christian Church that has maintained an unbroken apostolic succession of Bishops from the beginning, with all the named Episcopal Churches sharing in this distinction. Protestantism is claimed by many to have arisen with the protests of Martin Luther against the abuses of the Roman Catholic Church. In this case the word could be applied, for at that time Germany had long been part of the Holy Roman Empire, with the Emperor of Germany the appointed representative of the Pope. Britain was never part of this Empire and never nationally under the domination of the Vatican. It was from the beginning to this day – British – the Church of the Covenant People.

Christianity was founded in Britain AD 36. The first Christian Church above ground was erected AD 38-39. The Roman Catholic hierarchy was founded *circa* AD 350, after Constantine, and not until centuries later was the Papal title created. Until then, the head of the Roman Catholic Church was still a Bishop. The title of Pope, or universal Bishop, was first given to the Bishop of Rome by the wicked Emperor Phocas, in the year AD 607. This he did to spite Bishop Ciriacus of Constantinople, who had justly excommunicated him for his having caused the assassination of his predecessor, Emperor Mauritus. Gregory I, then Bishop of Rome, refused the title but his successor, Boniface III, first assumed the title of Pope.

Jesus did not appoint Peter to the headship of the Apostles and expressly forbade any such notion, as stated in *Luke* 22:24-26; *Ephesians* 1:22-23; *Colossians* 1:18; and 1 *Corinthians* 3:11.

Returning to the history of the cross as the Christian symbol of Royal heraldry and given to Arviragus by Joseph, the cross on the shield up to the present time has remained the special symbol of the sovereigns of Britain. In later times the Lion was superimposed on the shield, as shown today. The Lion was the emblem of Judah, Keeper of the Sanctuary but, as Christ said, it would be taken away from them and given to another who would keep the Law. This symbol appearing on the British Royal Arms, with the cross, is significant. The cross denotes that the British were the first to accept Christ and by keeping the Law inherited the Kingdom of God taken from the nation of the Jews.

Arviragus was to carry the banner of the Cross through the most bitterly fought battles between the Britons and the Romans. In spite of the fact that the early Christian and Roman records abound with the name and warrior fame of Arviragus, he is entirely lost to the later histories. His fame is overshadowed by his famous cousin Caractacus. In spite of this, Arviragus was the most powerful representative of the royal house of the Silures and the most famous Christian warrior in history, not excepting his illustrious descendant, the Emperor Constantine.

The royal boundaries of the Silures were divided into two sections. Arviragus ruled over the southern part of England and Caradoc, or Caractacus, over Cambria, the region that is now Wales. Each was king in his special domain but in time of war they united under a Pendragon or Commander-in-Chief, agreed upon by the people. At that time they represented the most powerful warrior clan in Britain. Arviragus ruled as Pendragon, while his cousin Caractacus was captive in Rome, conducting the war against the Empire for years[40] in Britain in a manner that gained for him immortal fame exceeding that of Caractacus.

Juvenal, the Roman writer, in his works clearly indicates how greatly the Romans feared Arviragus, stating that his name trembled on the lips of every Roman, and that no better news could be received at Rome than the fall of this Royal Christian Silurian. He writes, asking: 'Hath our great enemy Arviragus, the car borne British King, dropped from his battle throne?'

Edmund Spencer adds his tribute: 'Was never king more highly magnifyde nor dread of Romans was than Arviragus.'

Despite the fact that the Romans were the implacable foe of the British, and sought by every means at their command in their vicious hatred to exterminate the Christian faith at its source, they held the British warriors in high esteem, holding that their religion was the reason for their fearlessness in battle and disdain of death.

Julius Caesar wrote, *circa* 54 BC: 'They make the immortality of the soul the basis of all their teaching, holding it to be the principal incentive and reason for a virtuous life. Believing in the immortality of the soul they were careless of death.'[41]

---

[40] Tacitus, *Annals*, bk. 5, ch. 28
[41] *Gallic War*, ch.1 sec.1.

Lucanus, AD 38, writes in *Pharsalia* that the Britons' indifference to death was the result of their religious beliefs, and Pomponius Mela, AD 41, in his works, describes the British warrior in astonishment. He also ascribes the extraordinary bravery of the Britons to their religious doctrine, based on the immortality of the soul.

Such was the invincible spirit of the ancient Britons who formed a living wall around the sacred boundaries of Avalon in the domain of Arviragus. No Roman army ever pierced it. These were the lands which Roman writers referred to as 'territory inaccessible to the Roman where Christ is taught'.

Behind this heroic warrior wall of protection Joseph and the disciples of Christ were safe from harm, free to preach and teach the glorious faith on the Sacred Isle of Avalon. To the Britons this was hallowed ground and they died willingly to preserve the first planting of the Christian Way, so that it might thrive and blossom to bless the whole world.

There was to be a second separate planting of the Christ Seed in Britain about twenty years after Joseph's arrival. Independent of the Josephian Mission it was also to be sponsored by the Royal Silurian House, in Wales, by the father and family of Caractacus, under the commission of St. Paul. It originated at Rome, where this same family were to be the divinely ordained instruments of St. Paul in developing his great mission as directed by Christ. After contact with them he declares it in his statement, 'I turn henceforth to the Gentiles.'

This Royal British family at Rome were to provide the Christian story with its greatest romance, its greatest drama, and its most terrible tragedy.

They were destined to be the first martyrs to suffer for Christ in the Gentile Church and millions more were to follow later.

Believe it or not, the British have paid the greatest blood sacrifice in all history in the defence and for the preservation of the Christian Church, more so than all other nations put together. The underground cemeteries of Rome, the Catacombs, are packed with their tortured, murdered bodies – men, women and children. The soil of Britain is saturated with their blood, eternal testimony to their undying faith.

Knowing that Christ died for them, they were fearless in dying for Christ.

CHAPTER 10

EDICT OF EMPEROR CLAUDIUS, AD 42: 'EXTERMINATE CHRISTIAN BRITAIN'[42]

THE past is so remote it seems inconceivable and perhaps insignificant to the indifferent Christians of today, basking in luxury and the comfort of security, that it is nearly two thousand years ago when as the first armed challenge of a powerful world-conquering nation it was officially decreed to destroy Christianity at its core by the extermination of the Island British.

It was ten years after the Scandal of the Cross had taken place and less than six years since Joseph, the Nobilis Decurio, had proclaimed the Christ Way throughout Britain from his sanctuary on the Isle of Avalon.

The Holy Crusade had spread so rapidly from Avalon to beyond the seas that Rome was disturbed it could no longer ignore the challenge to its own pagan policies and imperial security.

In the year AD 42 Claudius, Emperor of the Romans, issued the fateful decree to destroy Christian Britain, man, woman and child, and its great institutions and burn its libraries. To this purpose Claudius equipped the largest and most efficient army ever sent by Rome to conquer a foe and led by its most able generals.

In this edict, Claudius proclaimed in the Roman Senate that acceptance of the Druidic[43] or Christian faith was a capital offence, punishable by death by the sword, the torture chamber, or to be cast to the devouring lions in the arena of the Coliseum. It is interesting to note that this ruling also included 'any person descended from David'. This meant the Jew, making no exceptions as to whether he be a converted Jew or one holding to the orthodox Judean faith. This indeed was a paradox. While the converted Jew embraced Gentile followers of 'The Way' as brethren, regardless of race, and died with them with equal courage, the orthodox Jew perishing in the arena by the side of the Christian, never relented in his bitter hatred. With his dying breath he spat on the Christian in malevolent scorn.

In this peculiar manner British Christian and Jew now had one thing in common, the penalty of death.

---

[42] O'Reilly, *The Martyrs of the Coliseum.*
[43] Suetonius

The Romans had not previously held any special enmity to the British. Actually, and perhaps grudgingly, they had held the Briton in respect. Association in commerce and culture had drawn them together for centuries and it was not uncommon for the children of the nobility on both sides to seek education in the institutions of each. It was the impetus the British had given to the new Christian faith that had cast the Roman die.

The Romans had always despised the Jew, and oppressed though the Jews were under Roman domination, they hated the Roman with a burning vehemence which they displayed on the slightest pretext. They would never willingly break bread with a Roman, nor share their home, and on the street would not allow their clothing to touch that of their enemy. When flogged, the unforgiving Jews would spit out vile epithets at their torturers as they writhed or died in agony. The Romans could never understand why the Jewish religion could incite such hatred against members of other faiths, nor could they understand the disdainful contempt the Jews held for women. From the time of Abraham the marital life of the Hebrews was polygamous. While one woman would be named the wife, and be head of the household, yet Abraham had several concubines, sometimes referred to as handmaidens. At the time of our Lord it is stated that marital conditions among the Jews were at their lowest ebb. Women were regarded as mere chattels. Divorce was prevalent and declared at will without resort to law, with seldom any provision made for the divorced woman. It is recorded that it was common for a Jew to consort with several women to the knowledge of his so-called legal wife. It amused and angered the Romans to note the hypocritical, puritanical attitude of the Jewish male toward adultery. A woman, be it one of his own consorts or not, was apt to be stoned to death if found guilty of adultery. The suspicion of it would cause her to be branded. The Jewish brand of adultery was to cause the woman to wear her hair in braids to be reviled and shunned by both Jewish sexes. There was no forgiveness in the Jewish male heart. Realizing these conditions at the time of our Lord, we can better understand the significance of the test the cohorts of the Sanhedrin put to Jesus when they led before Him the adulteress to be judged. Under the circumstances our hearts can swell with pride at the courage of Jesus and the magnificent manner in which He made the decision by writing in the sand with His finger, 'He that is without sin among you, let him first cast a stone at her.' With these words Jesus challenged each and every man present to prove his right to stone the woman to death. They slunk away. It was Jesus who set women free from this male bondage. He freely forgave the adulteress and simply told her to sin no more.

Contrary to common belief the Romans, though granted to be licentious, abhorred divorce. The wealthy Romans had many consorts, including the Emperors, but the wife held a sacred place as the head of the house which could not be disputed. Consorts were the common practice of the Romans, which found little ill-favour in the eyes of the legal wife. For centuries a divorce could not be obtained. The first record of a Roman divorce occurred five hundred and twenty years after the founding of the Roman dynasty. It was obtained by Spurius Carvilius Rugo on the grounds of sterility. The act so shocked the people that Rugo was shunned by all and so completely disgraced that he was obliged to leave Rome. Even though divorce was not recognized long before Christianity entered Rome, we can understand the attitude of the Roman Catholic Church towards divorce, being so embedded in the original Roman law. The attitude of the British Holy Catholic Church, the Anglican Church, stems from the words of Jesus.

All this added to the Roman hatred of the Jew. Now a new hatred had developed, manifested in the Claudian Edict which accused them of being responsible for the Advent of Christ and for the rise of the new faith which had found its first converts among the people of Judea.

The efforts of the Sanhedrin to eradicate 'The Way', in the calumny of the Cross and the terrifying persecution of the Followers by the Saulian Gestapo, was completely overlooked by the Roman Senate or ignored.

Further to seek to inflame the populace against Christian and Jew, the Romans were the first to create the false slander that Christian and Jew alike practised human sacrifice in their religion. They knew better. They knew that the burnt offerings of Judean and Druid were animals, chiefly sheep, goats and doves. The Romans spread the ridiculous propaganda that the Jews devoured Gentile babies. Communist distortions of the truth and insinuating fabrications are not new. They are merely imitating the vile trickery of the Romans of Caesar's time.

Probably because the Jews were unorganized and not militant like the British, the Roman campaign of extermination was not so widespread, less determined, and never as constant. The Jews were driven into ghettoes, where they could do no harm. The British were a dominating problem. They were a warrior nation skilled in the art of warfare on land and on sea. They were guided by intelligent rulers and commanders, all of whom were steeped in the invincibility of the spirit created by the passion in their faith that declared all men should be free. One of the earliest battle hymns of the Britons was 'Britons never shall be slaves'.

The overwhelming rise of Christianity in populous Britain and Gaul was viewed with grave consternation at Rome. Britain was the seeding-ground where an ever-flowing stream of neophytes were tutored and converted by Apostles and disciples of Christ and sent out into other lands to teach the Gospel. This the Romans declared had to be stopped. To them, as to all dictatorships, might alone was right. Nevertheless, from past experience with British military ability they had good reason to fear this stubborn, valorous race, now inspired with the zeal of Christ. Forewarned, Rome built the mightiest army in its history to enforce the Claudian Edict to destroy Britain.

The decree of Claudius was inspired by fear and with sadistic intentions. Rome believed from the experience of her other conquests that only violent persecutors would terrify the Briton into ultimate submission.

How wrongly they judged their opponents they were soon to learn.

Defamers of ancient Britain should turn back the pages of history and read the works of Geoffrey of Monmouth, who describes how in the year 390 BC Belinus and Brennus, sons of the most famed British King Dunwal, assaulted and captured Rome with a British army. And from 113 to 101 BC European observers affirm that the Cimbri-Keltoi of Britain were the terror of Rome and could have brought that Empire under their own subjection if they had so desired. They point out with emphasis that British aggressions were not inspired by wars of conquest but were punitive expeditions arising out of Roman depredation against their Gaulish brethren.

Looking back on the pages of those bloodstained years the heart recoils in horror at the savagery, murder, massacre, rape and destruction inflicted upon the inhabitants and the land of the Sacred Isle.

The Romans, who had ground so many nations under their despotic heel, looked upon all other nations with scorn as inferiors, labelling every enemy as barbarian, no matter how magnificent their culture. The records attest to the indisputable fact that the Romans of all people were the most barbarous and brutal in history.

The people of the Christian democracies still shrink in horror at the blood-chilling viciousness of the Communistic purges. The soul faints before the terrifying pictures of the vile concentration camps, the gas ovens and the fiendish modes of torture inflicted upon the Jews, other peoples, and the Allied war prisoners by the diabolic Nazis. It makes one feel as though the Devil himself had scraped the bottom of his foul satanic barrel. But vile as it all was, the Nazis, the Japanese and the Reds could have learned more dreadful forms of torture by studying the methods of Roman persecution during the pagan centuries.

The slaughter of the British Kelts was not confined to the short but too-long period of War II. It endured from the time of the Claudian invasion, AD 42, to the close of the horrible, infamous Diocletian savagery of AD 320, nearly three hundred years. Where was the invincibility of the great Roman Caesars?

Numerous as were the lives ravished in the Russian, Nazi, and Japanese purges and incredible tortures, the loss of life is small compared with the total sacrifice of British lives given entirely in the Cause of Christ during those three hundred years. Strange as it may seem, though Gaul was at various times invaded by the Romans and suffered great loss of life, no massed campaign was ever directed against them and never on religious grounds. Britain alone was the chief culprit and against them the vengeance of the bestial Roman knew no bounds. Britain is the only nation in history ever attacked by the full might of another powerful people in an effort to purge Christianity off the face of the earth. Rome sent her very best against the British legions. As they failed to subdue the British, Rome recalled many brilliant generals who had gained fame for the double-headed eagle in other foreign conquests, as she determinedly sought to wipe out one defeat after another to her armies.

From the Claudian to the Diocletian persecution, extermination of Britain and all that was Christian was a Roman obsession. How satanic it was can be estimated in the brutal act which touched off the Diocletian campaign. The finest warrior battalions in the Roman army were the famed Gaulish Legions. On the order of Maximian, co-ruler with Diocletian, the Christian Gaulish veterans were slaughtered to a man in cold blood. His hatred of the Christian is stated to have exceeded that of Diocletian and to satiate it he butchered his finest soldiers.

The martyrologies state that during the first two hundred years of Christianity over six million Christians were entombed within the catacombs of Rome – murdered. How many more were buried within the other unexplored catacombs is difficult to say. The total number would be appalling. It is claimed that if the passages of the catacombs of Rome were measured end to end they would extend to a length of 550 miles, from the city of Rome into the Swiss Alps. It seems almost incredible that while only about one million Christians today walk the streets of Rome, under their feet are over six million mutilated bodies which had testified for Christ.

Let free men and women wherever they may be today, take stock of the price their Christian ancestors paid to obtain and make secure the freedom which they now enjoy. The ancient Britons appear to have better realized than does the present-day shirking Christian that Christianity sets men free and freedom can only be maintained in preserving the Christian faith. The present democracies of the English-speaking world owe all they have or ever will have to their Christian ancestors.

Let us remember that, when it seemed as though Christianity was crushed on the Continent by the murderous Diocletian persecution, it was a British king with an army of Christian British warriors who crossed the seas and smashed the Diocletian-Maximian armies with defeat so catastrophic they never rose again. That British victory ended for all time Roman Christian persecution. Following the victory this British king marched his army of Christian warriors into Rome and there declared Rome Christian. From thence dates Roman national acceptance of Christianity.

It was not Peter who nationally Christianized Rome but Constantine, the great-grandson of Arviragus, and son of the famous Empress Helena, a British princess.

Surely we cannot afford to forget.

CHAPTER 11

JESUS OR JUPITER?

THE Commander-in-Chief selected by the Emperor Claudius to carry out his edict was none other than the famous Aulus Plautius, called the Scipio of his day. He stands in Roman history as one of the most brilliant commanders and conquerors in her military record. He arrived in the area of Britain, we now know as England, AD 43, making his headquarters at Chichester.

Plautius lost no time in sending his veteran Legions into action, directing his campaign to the south against the Silurians, thus cutting off the powerful Brigantes in the remote north, who were the Yorkshire Celts. Both armies clashed with appalling violence and in this first conflict the Romans, probably underestimating the quality of their opponents, were forced to retreat. In the various battles that followed, to his surprise the Roman General realized he was confronted with a military intelligence that matched his own and an army of warriors, though greatly outnumbered, were undaunted and fought back with a fearless ferocity which had never before been encountered by the veteran soldiery of Rome.

For the first time the Romans found they were not opposing a race of people who could be terrorized by numbers or brutalities. To their dismay, as reported by Tacitus and like the Nazis in World War II, they found that destruction of the British sacred altars increased their anger, making them blind to odds and circumstances. The more destructive and brutal the Roman persecution the more determinedly did the Briton strike back.

At the onset the British Silurian army was led by Guiderius, the elder brother of Arviragus who was second in command. Guiderius had succeeded his father to the kingdom of the Silures. Arviragus, as Prince, ruled over his Dukedom of Cornwall. In the second battle with the Romans Guiderius was killed in action. Arviragus succeeded his slain brother in command of the army and to the kingdom of the Silures. At this time the second branch of the Silurian kingdom lying farther south in what now is Wales, had not entered the conflict. Caradoc, King of the Welsh Silures, was first cousin to Arviragus, a much older man and an experienced military leader. A few years before this record his father, known as 'the Good King Bran', had abdicated his throne voluntarily in favour of his son Caradoc. Bran was a deeply religious person and had resigned his kingship to become Arch Druid of Siluria. He and his family had accepted the new faith and some of the members of the family had been already converted and baptized by Joseph by the laying on of hands, but Bran and Caradoc had not received this final act of conversion. Now as the conflict between Roman and Briton increased in vigour and territorial scope, Caradoc realized the seriousness of the situation, particularly since the death of his cousin Guiderius. It was agreed that a more concerted and determined military action was needed against the Romans. Arviragus, by necessity, was only substituting in command for his slain brother. It was law among the British that the supreme leader of the army, especially when more than one clan was involved, could only be appointed by general acclamation of the people, the military council and the Arch Druids. The election to such a command was known by the official title of Pendragon, meaning Commander-in-Chief. By popular election Caradoc, better known in history by the name the Romans gave him – Caractacus – was created Pendragon.

Caractacus, as we shall now call him, was a man of great vigour, intelligent, versed in the arts of politics and warfare. As is to be expected, being raised in a religious household, he had deep religious convictions. He had received his education chiefly in the British universities and partly at Rome. He was an able administrator, of noble mien and outstanding stature. His countenance was described by Roman writers as 'bold and honourable'. Such was the man who was elected Pendragon to conduct the war against the invading Romans. He began the continuation of the strife with all his natural energy. Out of this bitter conflict his outstanding military genius, his indomitable character and invincible courage carved for him an immortal name in history that was never to perish in British and Roman annals. In them he stands out as one of the greatest examples of all that is grand and noble. A magnificent patriotic representative of the unconquerable valour of his race. Feared by the foe, it is said that Roman mothers used his name to quiet their children. His military merit won the unstinted admiration of the enemy who named him 'the Scourge of the Romans'.

Historically his achievements are well known, but not so well the reasons for them. Modern historians in dealing with the Roman invasions completely ignore the reason for the great Roman invasion of Britain. Never once do they mention the Edict of Claudius, or explain that it was a war of religious extermination, designed to crush Christianity at its source. Evidently they were totally ignorant of the true reason. They could easily have been enlightened by reading the Roman records of that time. They write off the nine years of ceaseless warfare between Roman and Briton, led by Caractacus and Arviragus against the greatest Roman generals, as though it was of no significance. They give the impression that the British armies were driven like wild sheep before the Roman Legions. Surely it takes but little imagination from even a casual perusal of this campaign to realize that it would not take nine years for the Roman Empire to subdue opponents who were merely 'wild, painted barbarians'. By this time Rome had conquered all the world except Britain. They had defeated mighty armies skilled in warfare and led by brilliant kings and generals. The conquered nations they had enslaved in Africa, Asia and Europe testify to their despotic brutality. The same Roman generals who had accomplished these conquests led the Roman army in Britain and failed, one after the other.

With such a far-flung Empire to protect the Roman emperors could not afford to keep their greatest army and best commanders in Britain for nine years. Less could they afford the decimation of their veteran Legions in useless combat. The enormous loss of lives on both sides sustained in many of the battles in Britain, according to the records, were larger than the loss in most of the battles in World War I and World War II. Such losses do not indicate a leisurely Roman campaign in Britain. In some of the battles several of the greatest Roman generals were engaged in conducting battle strategy at the one time.[44] This was an experience of Roman generalship never before called for.

In World Wars I and II, when the full forces of the Allies were engaged, their numbers greatly outnumbered the enemy. It was the absolute reverse in the British-Roman, Claudian campaign. Common sense shows there could only be one reason for this long conflict. The Romans had met their match in military genius and in man-to-man combat a warrior ferocity that outmatched their tough veterans. The fierce, fearless spirit of the British soldiery appalled the Romans. Their bravery and disdain of death shocked them. The great Agricola, engaged in the British campaign, stated that it would be no disgrace if he fell in battle among so brave a people.

---

[44] Tacitus, *Agricola*. ch.14 and 17.

This had to be more than a defence of the shores which could have been readily ended by coming to terms with the Romans. It was a battle against extermination of all the Briton held dear and, as Winston Churchill promised the Nazis, would happen again. They fought on the sands, on the fields, in the streets and the lanes and by-ways, to very death.

On these fields the Cross of Christ was unfurled as given to Arviragus by St. Joseph, so 'all nations should see', for the first time in military history. This alone proclaimed what the British were fighting for: defence of their new faith, Christianity, the Gospel of Jesus, with the freedom it gave to all who believed in Him.

Caractacus is given official credit as being the first general to lead a Christian army in battle in defence of the faith. As Pendragon of the British, elected by them in open council, this is true. But it was Guiderius and Arviragus who led the first battle against the Romans. It was they who first stopped Aulus Plautius in his tracks. Guiderius was the first British king to fall for Christ. Before Caractacus was elected Pendragon the British battalions had marched towards the foe flying the coat of arms bequeathed to Arviragus by Joseph, on their battle standards and painted on their war shields and this, long before St. George was born.

Fearlessly they met the full force of unconquered Rome and defeated them. This is the imperishable record of the valiant British in the Claudian nine-year war. Throughout the entire campaign Arviragus fought as the right-hand man of the Pendragon, Caractacus and for years after when Caractacus no longer led the British forces against the plundering, murdering Romans, he conducted the conflict. Though the Romans destroyed every altar in their path, not once were they able to pierce through to their objective, the Isle of Avalon, the Sanctuary of Christendom. St. Joseph and his Bethany companions were never molested nor was their shrine ever violated by Roman intrusion.

No better picture can be obtained of the relentless manner in which this war was fought, with victory swinging from one side to the other, than by reading the reports of the foremost Roman writers, Tacitus, Martial, Juvenal and others. The story chronicled by the pens of the enemy gives more substance to the truth than if it were written by our own. With ungrudging admiration they tell how the Silurian warriors, led by Caractacus, Arviragus and the Arch Priests, swept onward in irresistible waves over the bodies of their dead and dying comrades with a battling savagery that appalled the hardened, war-scarred veterans of the Roman Legions. Their fierce outcries of defiance rang over the din and clash of sword and shield. For the first time the Romans met women warriors fighting side by side with their men in righteous combat. Tacitus states that their long-flowing flaxen hair and blazing blue eyes were a terrifying sight to behold.[45] For the first time the Roman soldiery heard the amazing motto of the ancient Druidic priesthood transferred into a clarion Christian battle cry: 'Y gwir erbyn y Byd', meaning 'The Truth Against the World'. No finer battle cry was ever employed with equal truth. It has never died. It has lived through the ages and today it is the motto of the Druidical Order in Wales.

Truly the British stood alone against the world, fought alone and died alone, even as they did in the most hazardous early years of the last two world wars, battling for the Great Truth and the preservation of its principles of freedom, in the name of their accepted Saviour, Jesus Christ.

Tacitus, the Roman historian, writing of the Claudian campaign that lasted for nine years, except for one brief six months' pause, dismally wrote that, although Rome hurled at the British the greatest army in her history, it failed to prevail against the military genius of Caractacus and the reckless fierceness of the British warrior. Many drawn battles were fought and the famed Legions of Rome frequently suffered defeat with terrible slaughter. On occasions when the British suffered severe reverses Tacitus said, 'The fierce ardour of the British increased.'

After two years of ceaseless warfare Claudius, recognizing the futility of the struggle and the terrible drainage on his finest Legions, took advantage of a reverse against Caractacus, at Brandon Camp, AD 45, to seek peace through an armistice. A six month truce was declared in which Caractacus and Arviragus were invited to Rome to discuss the possibilities for peace. The facts that followed prove that Claudius went to great lengths to come to satisfactory terms with the obstinate British leaders.

Hoping to clinch the peace the Emperor Claudius offered to Arviragus, in marriage, his daughter, Venus Julia. And, amazing as it appears, they were married in Rome during the truce period, AD 45.[46]

---

[45] Tacitus, *Annals*, 14:30.
[46] Venus Julia, named after Venus, mother of Aeneas, and of the Julian family, therefore of Trojan stock.

Here we have the strange instance of a Christian British king becoming the son-in-law of the pagan Roman Emperor Claudius, who had sworn to exterminate Christianity and Britain.

Surely one is justified in asking would the Emperor of a nation, then the most powerful in the world, high in culture and intellectual pursuits, have sacrificed his natural daughter in marriage to be the wife of a 'crude barbarian', just for the sake of peace? Impossible. There had to be some other valid reason and, as we shall see as time moves on, the unseen Hand of God was writing the script. The circumstances refute the later pernicious propaganda of the Christian-hating Romans who in their benighted prejudice sought to label their most noble foe – barbarian.

It is inconceivable.

This marriage was but the beginning of other similar strange circumstances that were swiftly to arise. They were to have a tremendous influence on the Christian movement in Rome, with the British dominating the entire scene. For sheer drama and stirring romance these incidents have no equal in the pages of history.

During the six months' truce while Caractacus and Arviragus were at Rome discussing peace terms and the latter was getting married, Aulus Plautius, the Roman commander, remained in Britain maintaining the truce on behalf of Rome. During this interval another strange alliance took place in Britain. Gladys (Celtic for Princess), the sister of the British war lord Caractacus, was united in marriage to the Roman Commander-in-Chief, Aulus Plautius! Again we witness the amazing spectacle of a member of the Silurian royal family, a Christian, married to a Roman pagan.

Gladys had been personally converted by Joseph of Arimathea, together with her niece Eurgain, Guiderius, Arviragus and other members of the British aristocracy. Like her father, the ex-King and present Arch Druid, she was devoutly religious, completing her religious instruction at Avalon and in association with the Bethany women. Considering all this, one is immediately intrigued by this unusual situation. It is made more exciting as we realize that her brother and husband were wartime opponents.

The marriage of Gladys and Plautius is brought into the Roman limelight by Tacitus in his *Annals*,[47] wherein he relates with humour the peculiar circumstances and results of a Roman trial in which Gladys, the

---

[47] Tacitus, *Annals*, 13:32.

wife of Plautius, is accused of being Christian. On her marriage Gladys took the name of Pomponia, according to Roman custom, which was the name of the Plautium clan. Later the name Graecina was added, so that she is thereafter known as Pomponia Graecina Plautius. The added name was a distinctive academic honour conferred upon her in recognition of her extraordinary scholarship in Greek.

As we shall see, the truce fell through and hostilities were resumed between the British and Romans. Following the marriage of the Roman Commander Aulus Plautius, to the British Princess, it appears as though the Emperor Claudius distrusted leaving further operation of the war in Britain to Plautius. He is recalled to Rome, AD 47, though honourably relieved of his command. Reference to these events and the trial of Gladys is well covered by Tacitus, as will be noted from the following quoted text:

'Pomponia Graecina, a woman of illustrious birth, and the wife of Plautius, who, on his return from Britain, entered the city with the pomp of an ovation, was accused of embracing the rites of a foreign superstition. The matter was referred to the jurisdiction of her husband. Plautius, in conformity to ancient usage, called together a number of her relations, and in her presence, sat in judgment on the conduct of his wife. He pronounced her innocent.'

From our point of view, the method of the trial provides a humorous situation.

It was the custom, by Roman law, to give priority to the nobility to judge and settle any legal disputation where the family was concerned. Consequently it was in order for Plautius to judge his wife. Next we note that Pomponia is judged in the presence of her own relations, all immediate members of the Royal Silurian Christian household undoubtedly acting in her defence.

It is quite certain that not much defence was needed. Plautius knew his wife Gladys was Christian before he married her, as were all the immediate members of her family, as well as her royal relatives. Theirs was a love marriage, free of all political significance on either side. The fact that they were married in Britain makes it certain that the bond of holy matrimony was sealed by the Priesthood of her Christian faith. Evidently Plautius had a sympathetic leaning to the new faith, for we are later informed that he also became a Christian. Viewed in the light of these circumstances it was a foregone conclusion that Plautius would judge his wife guiltless, which he did.

The Rev. C. C. Dobson, M.A., a keen student of Celtic-Roman history, in his learned works goes into much detail covering this whole situation, pointing out that Tacitus refers to Pomponia as 'a woman of illustrious birth'- an aristocrat. Her marriage to the Roman nobleman bears this out. Plautius certainly recognized her social station to have been equal to his Roman dignity. That she was unusually talented, as well as highly cultured, is borne out by the honour of her Roman-conferred title, 'Graecina'. The Rev. Dobson writes, 'For forty years she was a leader of the best Roman society.' A brilliant woman of wide cultural learning, she was a past scholar in classical literature and wrote a number of books of prose and poetry in Greek and Latin as well as in her native language, Cymric. Their home was a meeting-place for the talented and they were to be as intimately acquainted with the Apostles, Peter and Paul, as Gladys had been with Joseph, Lazarus, Mary Magdalene and the rest of the missionaries at Avalon.

The Roman records state that when the Roman General Aulus Plautius was recalled to Rome, AD 47, 'He took his foreign wife with him.' This statement clearly indicates that his wife was not Roman and, since Plautius was unmarried when he arrived in Britain and was never absent during the years of his command, his wife had to be British.

Gladys and Plautius remained in Britain almost eighteen months after their marriage. The armistice had proved fruitless. The British leaders considered the peace terms unsatisfactory. Caractacus and Arviragus did not linger in Rome; but they returned to Britain and with Arviragus went his Roman wife, Venus Julia. All were faced with an unpleasant situation: Plautius in conducting the war against his in-laws, Caractacus against his sister and brother-in-law, and Arviragus opposing his father-in-law, the Emperor Claudius.

What Claudius and the Roman Senate had underestimated was the unbending temper of the Britons. He was quickly to learn that it was an impossibility for the British to make any compromise where their religion was concerned. His faith was his most precious treasure for which, as he has long proved, he would willingly die but never relinquish. His religion had taught him that his earthly life was but a stepping-stone to the eventual goal of immortality. Following the Atonement, in the Ascension of Christ, he had obtained satisfactory proof of the fulfilment of the promise that death transcended the grave.

It made him both faithful and fearless. Yet he did not willingly seek death. He fully understood that his earthly sojourn was a necessary preparation for the after life. He recognized that Christ had set him free and was solidly convinced that Christianity could only be practised in absolute freedom. Interference with this freedom is what made him the indomitable warrior as the Romans described him. Normally the Briton was a man of peace and a respecter of other peoples' rights. History proves that the ancient Britons were never engaged in territorial conquest or war by invasion except in their own defence, or for punitive reasons.

Ostorius Scapula had replaced Plautius and the war continued for another seven years. Finally, after many bloody battles, the British, under the Pendragon Caractacus, met disaster at Clun, Shropshire, AD 52, by a strange trick of circumstance.

Caractacus was not outmanoeuvred in this last battle by the one General, Scapula. He opposed four of the greatest commanders in Roman history in this action and more. Up to this point things had been going badly against the Romans on the field of battle, as shown by the fact that the Emperor Claudius himself, with heavy reinforcements, came to Britain to support his generals in the field which climaxed the action at Clun.

Opposing Caractacus in the Claudian campaign, in allied command with Aulus Plautius, was the great Vespasian, future Emperor of Rome, his brother and his son Titus who a few years later was to put Jerusalem to the torch, destroy its inhabitants and scatter the survivors of Judah over the face of the earth. Added to this illustrious military assemblage was Geta, the conqueror of Mauritania. As matters became desperate, an urgent appeal for help was sent to the Emperor Claudius. He hastened to Britain, taking with him the 2nd and 14th Legions, with their auxiliaries, and a squadron of elephants. He landed at Richborough, joining his other generals on the eve of the battle of Clun, personally directing the battle which saved the day for Rome.

It took the combined military genius of four great Roman generals, together with the Emperor and an army that vastly outnumbered the British, to bring about this victory. This in itself is the greatest tribute that could be given to the military excellence of Caractacus, the valorous British warrior.

It was a disastrous defeat.

Not only was Caractacus captured but his entire family was taken as hostage to Rome. It was the most complete subjection of any royal house on record by an enemy.

The British Triads commemorate the event as follows:

'There were three royal families that were conducted to prison, from the great, great grandfather to the great grandchildren without permitting one to escape. First the family of Llyr Lllediaith, who was carried to prison at Rome by the Caesaridae. Not one or another of these escaped. They were the most complete incarcerations known as to families.'

Arviragus and his family were not numbered among the captives. Evidently he was more successful than his cousin Caractacus in making his escape at Clun, for we read of him reorganizing the British army and carrying on the war against Rome for many more years.

Among the captives was the wife of Caractacus and his daughter Gladys, as well as his brother who had remained on the battle scene to receive the terms of the victor. Caractacus had been urged to flee so that he might later continue the conflict. However, fate was against him.

Caractacus sought sanctuary from Aricia, the Cartismandua of Tacitus, queen of the Brigantes and a grand-niece of the treacherous traitor, Mandubratius, who acquired infamy during the Julian war. By order of the traitorous queen, Caractacus was taken prisoner while asleep, loaded with irons and delivered to Ostorius Scapula, to be numbered with the many other royal captives and shipped to Rome.

Tacitus, in his *Annals* (bk. XII, ch. 36), writes that the news of the capture of the famed British warrior sped like wildfire throughout Rome. The event was received by the people with greater jubilation than had climaxed any other Roman conquest, including the victories of Publius Scipio, when he brought Syphas to Rome in chains and Lucius Paulus, who led the proud Perses into captivity.

He further states that three million people crowded the streets of Rome to view the captive British King and the Senate convened to celebrate.

Another Roman historian wrote:

'Rome trembled when she saw the Briton, though fast in chains.[48]

---

[48] Morgan, *St. Paul in Britain*, p. 99.

What had this great 'barbarian' chief achieved to cause such a sensation among the high and the low of the conquering Empire? Why was he so feared that the people trembled and shrank from him as he passed by helpless in irons? Fear and respect must have been well deserved to make the Romans cringe in their shoes. Being so dreaded, why did they not dispose of this 'barbarous Christian leader' according to their usual brutal custom?

One is inclined to ponder on the mysterious workings of Providence, as we learn from the contemporary Roman reporters that Caractacus was the first captive kingly enemy not cast into the terrible Tarpeian dungeons. Why? The Roman conquerors were never noted for their clemency. They delighted in humiliating their adversaries, satiating their bestial nature in the most fiendish forms of torture. The greater the renown of their unfortunate victim the less chance he had of escaping the horrors and incarceration of the Tarpeian. This evil experience was specially reserved for the captive kings, princes and great war generals, who were terribly maltreated, starved, and finally strangled to death. Their dead bodies suffered further indignity. With hooks pierced through the broken body, it was kicked and spat on as the mocking soldiery dragged it through the streets of the city, finally to be cast into the nearby river like offal. Yet here was a captive king, leader of the hated Christians, who had conducted a devastating war against Rome over a period of years exceeding that of any other opponent, during which time he had inflicted many disastrous defeats upon the mightiest Roman army ever to march on the field of battle; a warrior who had repeatedly outmanoeuvred the ablest combination of Roman military strategy alone, still feared and looked upon with awe mixed with admiration.

Neither he, nor any member of the British royal family was subject in the least to any physical indignities.[49]

In those nine years of conflict Eutropius reports in his *Roman Records* that thirty-two pitched battles were fought with victory swaying from one side to the other. The *British Annals* report that thirty-nine pitched battles were fought. Is there any wonder, as Tacitus remarks, that people from all parts of Europe poured into Rome to gaze upon this valiant warrior who had so seriously decimated the crack Roman Legions in combat? The record further states that Caractacus, heavily

---

[49] Tacitus, *Annals*, 12:37.

chained, walked proudly with his relatives and family behind the chariot of the Emperor, through the crowded streets of Rome. With this scene before us we can cease to wonder at the series of startling events that transpired from the beginning of the famous trial onward.[50]

On the day of the trial, Tacitus tells us that his daughter Gladys refused to be separated from her father, though it was against the Roman law for a woman to enter the Senate. Voluntarily she walked by the side of Caractacus, up the marble steps into the Senate, as brave and as composed as her father.

The report continues, the Pendragon stood before the Emperor on his Dais and the Tribunal erect, with arms folded on his powerful chest, a noble figure, fearless, calmly defiant, unconquered in spirit. The Senate was crowded to capacity and here again we note another breach of Roman law in the presence of another woman. History tells us that the great Queen Agrippira sat on her throne, on the far corner of the Dais, a fascinated witness to the most famous trial in Roman history.

This man who should have been the most hated as the leader of the Christian army drew admiration from all sides as he stood poised before his sworn enemy, the Emperor Claudius.

Such was the fame of the gallant Christian Briton – Caractacus. As the trial proceeded he spoke in a clear voice, trenchant with the passion of righteous vigour, as he vindicated the rights of a free man. He replied to his prosecutors with words that have lived down through the ages. Probably it is the only episode in this great Christian warrior's life that is remembered by posterity. Free men the world over may read his epic address with blood-warming pride as the pen of Tacitus worded it.

In the words of Tacitus, Caractacus addressed the Senate:

'Had my government in Britain been directed solely with a view to the preservation of my hereditary domains, or the aggrandizement of my own family, I might long since have entered this city an ally, not a prisoner: nor would you have disdained for a friend a king descended from illustrious ancestors, and the dictator of many nations. My present condition, stript of its former majesty, is as adverse to myself as it is a cause of triumph to you. What then? I was lord of men, horses, arms, wealth; what wonder if at your dictation I refused to resign them? Does it follow, that because the

---

[50] Tacitus, *Annals*, 12:36.

Romans aspire to universal domination, every nation is to accept the vassalage they would impose? I am now in your power – betrayed, not conquered. Had I, like others, yielded without resistance, where would have been the name of Caradoc? Where your glory? Oblivion would have buried both in the same tomb. Bid me live. I shall survive for ever in history one example at least of Roman clemency.'[51]

Never before or after was such a challenging speech heard by a Roman Tribunal in the Roman Senate. It is the one solitary case in history. Spoken by a Briton, vibrant with the courageous conviction of a free man.

This noble address was once the proud oration of every British schoolboy; now, like the Songs of Tara, heard no more.

How cheaply today Christians hold this cherished heritage.

For many years students of Roman history puzzled their brains, seeking for a reason or motive that caused the Emperor Claudius to render his remarkable verdict. Why, they ask, did not Claudius demand the customary Roman revenge? The pages of history are full of their brutal 'triumphs': dragging their unfortunate victims behind chariots; trampling them to death under the feet of elephants as they were forced to lie prostrate along the avenue of triumph; thrown to the starving lions in the arena; torn apart on the rack, strangled, burnt or confined to the horrible pit of the Mamertine where they went stark raving mad.

Did the strange intermarriages between princely Britons and Roman aristocrats, which was also to penetrate into his own family, induce Claudius to make his extraordinary decision?

Historians definitely declare to the contrary. Emphatically they affirm that the Roman law was so embedded in the conscience of the Romans, that they would not think, let alone dare to avert traditional ruling.

Nevertheless there and then by order of the Claudian Tribunal, Caractacus, with all the members of the royal Silurian family, were immediately set free. As the decision was rendered, we are told that the whole Senate applauded loudly. And the famed Queen Agrippira rose from her dais, approaching the Pendragon, and his daughter Gladys, shaking hands with each according to British fashion, then embracing

---

[51] Tacitus *Annals*, 12:37.

them, according to the Roman. This display of emotion was another strange deviation from custom.[52]

The only restriction imposed in the pardon of Caractacus was that he must remain at Rome, on parole for seven years, and neither he, nor any member of his family, were ever to bear arms against Rome. To this Caractacus agreed and never once thereafter did he break his pledge. When he returned to Britain seven years later, even though war was then raging between Briton and Roman, led by the unrelenting Arviragus, Caractacus and his family remained aloof, honour bound. While he remained in Rome he enjoyed all the privileges of a freeman. With his family he resided at the Palatium Britannicum – 'the Palace of the British' – which was soon to become world famous in Christian deeds and history. A son[53] had been permitted to return to Britain and rule over the kingdom of the Welsh Silurians in the stead of his father. During the seven years of parole Caractacus was allowed to receive regularly the income from his British estates so that he and his family might continue to live in state, as befitted a royal household.

Why Claudius bestowed such generous clemency upon the royal Britons, knowing full well he could never force them to recant their faith, is something which cannot be reasoned in material form. A greater influence was at work in which all these characters were but pawns on the Divine chessboard, moved in their actions by the inscrutable will of the Almighty, as the astounding events that follow prove so clearly, with St. Paul and this branch of the Silurian royal family holding the spotlight at Rome.

In concluding the chapter on the valiant Caractacus, it should prove of interest to consider the validity of the remark he made in his address before the Roman Tribune, in which he states he was 'betrayed – not conquered'.

Do the facts support his contention?

Undoubtedly they do.

It was the unpredictable conditions that brought about the defeat of the British. Overwhelmed by numbers, as they were, it was circumstance and not arms that wrought the catastrophe.

As stated before, Claudius had brought over to Britain a squadron of elephants, with other reinforcements, to bolster the distressed Legions of Aulus Plautius. This was the first time these strange creatures had been

---

[52] Tacitus *Annals,* 12 :37.
[53] St. Cyllinus, *Records of Jestyn ap Gwrgant.*

seen in Britain. They were introduced into the fight with the hope that their massive charging weight would offset the havoc wrought upon the Roman army by the British war chariots, armed with scythes on their wheels.

Neither the size nor the charges of these monsters dismayed the British. It was the offensive odour of the elephants that distracted and panicked the horses that drove the British chariots of war. Going completely out of control the horses and chariots wrought more havoc within the British lines during the battle than did the arms of the Romans.[54]

Added to this dilemma was the treachery of the Coraniaid, a clan long known for their traitorous dealings. The Romans had succeeded in buying them over. Unknown to Caractacus this insurgent army was hidden to his rear. The enemy had shaped up into the form of a letter L on the field of battle, with the Roman cavalry attacking the British flank. Striving to concentrate on this attack while the frenzied horses ran amok in the centre, the Pendragon was taken by surprise when the hidden Coraniaids attacked into the rear. Defeat was inevitable. Seeing all was lost, Caractacus was urged by his brother and others to flee the field before it was too late. He made good his escape but the betrayal of the Pendragon by his cousin Aricia prevented him from connecting with Arviragus, to carry on the conflict. Thus, by the unhappy accident that attend the fortunes of war, Caractacus stated in truth that he was betrayed and not conquered.

Later Arviragus avenged the treachery of the Coraniaid, warring through their domain and taking a terrible vengeance.

It is of peculiar interest to note that during the nine-year Claudian campaign the Silurians did not receive any reinforcements from the north, nor from Gaul, to whose defence the British had gone on many occasions over the past years. Neither did help come from Hibernia (Ireland) or Caledonia (Scotland). The fact is that help was almost impossible. The Romans used Gaul as a jumping-off place to invade Britain, thus Gaulish aid was prevented. The Roman navy would block the Hibernians, and Caledonia was too sparsely inhabited. At that time the migration of the Scots from Hibernia into the Caledonian highlands had not yet taken place. The powerful northern Brigantes were under the influence of their traitorous Queen who sold out Caractacus to the

---

[54] Cassius Dio Cocceianus, Roman Historian (*c.* AD 150 – 235)

Romans. Aricia was later deposed and the powerful Yorkshire Britons from then on played an important part in firmly rooting the new Christ faith in Britain. In fact many years after, when the faith appeared to weaken, it was the Yorkshire Britons who strengthened the foundation of Christianity that ensured its enduring perpetuation in Britain.

These can be the only reasonable conclusions for the Silurians bearing the brunt of the Roman prosecution. If the whole Celtic nation could have marched as one it is certain that the Romans would have been quickly and decisively defeated and expelled from the Island. With an odd exception, which is ever the rule, there was no unfriendliness among the Celtic peoples. They were staunchly Druidic to begin with, and all showed their eagerness to absorb the instruction of the Christ faith. Throughout the Claudian campaign the Irish and Pictish records tell of an ever-flowing stream of neophytes and delegates from the various kingdoms, journeying to Avalon to receive at first hand instruction from the Arimathean Culdees.

It was a greater authority than that of man which decided the Claudian issue. If it had been otherwise St. Paul would most certainly have been seriously handicapped in carrying out the responsibility placed upon him by our Lord to preach to the Gentiles.

The historic tribute to Caractacus is, that without the aid of his Christian allies he had proven his sterling ability against the Montgomerys and Eisenhowers of his day. By valour of arms and military strategy he had outmatched them. In the quality of his address before the Roman Tribune we see a man of high integrity and intelligence. His oration is worthy of a Winston Churchill. Yet this is the Briton whom short-sighted historians refer to as 'barbarian'. It could be of interest to the despoilers of historic truth to learn that Caractacus addressed the Roman Tribunal in their own language – Latin. This vernacular, not being that of the British, had necessarily to be culturally acquired. We are authoritatively informed that the Celtic priesthood employed their own common language in compiling their sacred works, using Greek exclusively for civil transcriptions. Latin was not adopted in British ecclesiastical liturgies until centuries later, yet Latin was as familiar to their tongue as was Greek and Hebrew. The long association Britain had with Rome in commerce, culture and social affairs had made each conversant with the other on common grounds.

Following the Julian campaign of 55 BC we learn that British citizens were the only people permitted to walk the streets of Rome as freemen. Actually this privilege was older than the Julian report; nevertheless, by this act and statement it is clearly shown that the only people in the world who were truly freemen and freewomen were the British. Freedom was an all-consuming passion with them as Titus, the son of the Emperor Vespasian, was to learn on other fields of battle than that at Clun. Titus fought thirty battles to subdue the short coastal areas of Anglesey and the Isle of Wight without gratifying results.

No Briton ever entered the Temples of Jupiter but, in the ensuing years, thousands of Roman soldiery who served in Britain turned to Jesus, kneeling before the Christian altars with the Christian British.

The banner of the Cross under which Caractacus led the British troops for nine years was to be unfurled at Rome and accepted by the Romans as their national insignia. It was the family of Caractacus who first unfurled that standard at Rome and the family of Arviragus who made it steadfast.

In the end the Silureans conquered Rome for Christ.

CHAPTER 12

THE ROYAL BRITISH FOUNDERS OF THE FIRST
CHRISTIAN CHURCH AT ROME, AD 58

FOLLOWING the famous trial and release of Caractacus, with the rest of the royal Silurian family, we find them settled in the family residence at Rome, on the part of the Mons Sacer, called Scaurus.

Here the British king begins his seven-year parole in absolute freedom.

Caractacus alone is subject to the parole. It was not required of any of the other royal captives. They were free to leave Rome had they so desired. Over a period of time most of them returned to Britain. The first to leave, almost immediately following their pardon, were the two sons of Caractacus: his eldest and his youngest sons, Cyllinus and Cynon. Cyllinus returned to Britain, particularly to take over the reins of government, acting as regent during the absence of his father. Cynon entered the Silurian theological university. The home of the remainder was established in the palatial Roman residence known as the Palatium Britannicum – 'the Palace of the British', or, 'the British Palace'.

At that time it was unlikely that any one of them realized the dramatic part they were to play, under the instruction of St. Paul, in laying down the foundation of Christianity at Rome. They were well aware that the situation was fraught with danger. On it with characteristic British stubbornness they turned their back. They cast the die and unflinchingly dedicated their lives to the Christian service. For this they were to pay with their lives and with their fortunes.

It is an unhappy fact that, as the centuries sped by with their turmoils, these monumental events in our Christian history, with their stark, heart-breaking tragedies, in the main became forgotten. It seemed as though a dark curtain shrouded their glory in sombre shadows. Nevertheless, it is certain that St. Paul's fruitful work could never have been achieved among the Gentiles but for the sacrifices of these noble Britons. The old Greek and Roman Martyrologies, preserved to the present, are most illuminating. Therein are recorded the happenings and dates, in many cases but briefly detailed, but more than enough to give us the story of the pitiful endings of those first great soldiers of Christ. Many of the disciples are completely lost to the record. Nowhere are their names and achievements found. The silence of the grave enfolds them. Many of the tortured bodies never even found a grave.

The Vatican states that there are many thousands of ancient documents in the archives of the Vatican library that have never been read: therefore, it is with pleasure we read of the splendid effort of the Vatican, during the last two years, to microfilm every document, to study and better preserve them. Recently it was announced that copies of these microfilms would be distributed among the various Christian theological centres for co-operative study. In the U.S.A. the Knights of Columbus raised a large fund to purchase a special centre to house these precious records. They are responsible for supplying the Vatican in the first place with the funds that enabled them to produce the first microfilms. It is to be hoped that copies will be as generously distributed among the various Protestant Theological Institutes of learning. Like the mass of ancient manuscripts recently found in the caves of the Dead Sea, it will take years and require the combined intelligence of all to complete this titanic task.

The famous British Museum library in London, the largest in the world, and other great libraries, in Edinburgh, Belfast and Dublin, Marseilles, Rouen, Paris, and many others, apart from the vast accumulation of ancient Church records in England have been most generous in providing co-operation for research. Therein is contained a mass of informative material not possessed by the Vatican. An example is the famous *Myvyrian Manuscript*, a gigantic work exceeding one thousand volumes. It reaches into the dim centuries antedating the record of this story. It is written in the ancient Cymric language of the British and is housed in the British Museum, often referred to as the Bible Museum for the wealth of first-hand Biblical reference it contains. The Magdalen College, at Oxford University, is named for the famous *Magdalen Manuscript* it contains, written by the Archbishop of Mayence,[55] AD 776-856. It brings to life the beautiful story of Mary Magdalene's wonderful work in the service of our Lord in Britain and particularly in Gaul, as told by one of the earliest bishops of the Christian faith.

Just as archaeology has proven the historic facts of the Old Testament, which formerly were regarded as fantasy, so has it with the study of the old tomes lifted the majestic story of the ancient Britons and the work of the Apostles in Britain, out of the realm of legend, myth and

---

[55] Rabanus Maurus.

superstition into the light of reality. The most important part of the founding of the Gentile Christian Church in Britain and Rome is available to us, and the facts regarding the First Church at Rome begin with the Royal Cymric family, domiciled in that city, under the instruction of St. Paul.

Twenty years after the Crucifixion the trial and pardon of the British royal captives took place, in the year AD 52.

Peter first went to Rome twelve years after the death of Jesus, in the year AD 44, eight years after Joseph and his Bethany companions arrived in Britain and two years after the Claudian campaign of persecution began against Christian Britain. Paul did not arrive at Rome until AD 56. This is the date given by St. Jerome, and considered the most authentic. This does not mean that there were not Christians in Rome before the two Apostles arrived, or even before the British Silurians came as captives. There were a number of them present and they are scripturally referred to as 'the Church'. This must not be taken too literally. It did not refer to a material institution; it was a spiritual body in Christ. The number of Christians then at Rome was unorganized, treading in fear. They met secretly in small groups at the homes of various converts to worship, though most of them went underground. The Tiberian and Claudian ban that inflicted death on all who professed the Christian faith was still in effect.

The Bible refers to two Christian churches at Rome: the Jewish Church of the circumcision and the Gentile Church of non-circumcision, presided over by Pastor Hermas; the first being composed of Jewish converts retaining the old practice of circumcision. This group met in secret at the house of Aquila and Priscilla, referred to in *Romans* 16:5. The separation of the two converted groups was in the main the cause of the heated discussion on circumcision between St. Paul and the other Apostles. The Apostle to the Gentiles won the argument, making it plainly known that neither made any difference where salvation was concerned. The Jewish Church did not last. Gradually it became absorbed into the Gentile Christian Church, as proved by the fact that we later find many Jews functioning within the Gentile Church, a number of whom are mentioned as going to Britain with various missions.

At this time bands of converts met in grottoes, but mostly in the catacombs among the dead. The Roman law, perhaps with satirical cynicism, had sought fit to recognize these underground cemeteries with the decree of sanctuary. However, when Christian persecution was at its worst, the Roman soldiery would waylay the worshippers on entering or leaving the catacombs. To avoid capture the Christians made secret entrances and outlets.

Such were the conditions that prevailed in Rome at the time of our story, but unconsciously the tide had begun to turn against the Romans, with the marriage of Arviragus, the Christian King, to Venus Julia, daughter of the Emperor Claudius, AD 45. Venus, known as Venissa, in the British records, had been converted by Joseph after her arrival in Britain with her husband. Since his recall from Britain, Aulus Plautius had resided at Rome with his wife, Pomponia Graecina, the sister of Caractacus, and they are referred to as a Christian family. Plautius, with his position as a nobleman of great wealth and Pomponia, with her brilliance and golden beauty and as a leader of Roman society, certainly would exert considerable influence. Now, the most important and by far the most extraordinary event was to take place that was eventually to swing the tide in favour of the Christian cause at Rome. Strange as it may seem, this incredible situation was created by the Emperor himself, the very man who had sworn by his Edict to exterminate Christianity. Probably it is the most astounding incident in Christian history, showing how God can use even His bitterest enemies to work out His divine purpose.

Following the pardon of Caractacus, a close relationship developed between the two former enemies and their households evolving into a startling climax. Claudius greatly admired the character and extraordinary beauty of Gladys, the daughter of Caractacus. It grew into a deep paternal affection with the result that Emperor Claudius adopted Gladys as his own daughter, a girl who was an exceptionally devout Christian!

Caractacus had two daughters, Eurgain, the eldest, and Gladys, the youngest child. Eurgain had been officially converted by Joseph, the Apostle of Britain, at the same time as her brother Linus. Eurgain was not only the first British woman to be converted to the faith, she is also recorded as being the first female Christian saint in Britain, the reward for her outstanding missionary work to which she devoted her life.[56] Gladys, the younger, was born AD 36, therefore she would be an infant when Joseph and his saintly entourage arrived in Britain, following the Judean exodus of the same year. Joseph baptized Gladys and later confirmed her into the faith with the laying on of hands. Both girls were

---

[56] *The Genealogy Of Iestyn The Son Of Gwrgan.* (Kessinger Publishing: 2004)

profoundly spiritual, devoted to the Christian faith with all the zeal of a Mary Magdalene. Both had been taken to Rome as hostages, with their father and all the other aforementioned members of the royal Silurian families, and had been party to all the unusual circumstances. One wonders with what feelings did Eurgain witness the extraordinary adoption of her younger sister by the Emperor Claudius. The next unusual event was in Gladys' taking the name of her adopted parent.

Henceforth Gladys was known as Claudia.

The Emperor was well aware of the strong Christian convictions of Gladys, and what strikes one forcibly is the fact that the record states that the terms of her adoption did not require her to recant from her faith.

Gladys was not to remain long under the royal roof. The year after her adoption was to see a beautiful romance destined to culminate later in heart-breaking tragedy. In her teens, Claudia was betrothed and married. In the year AD 53, she became the wife of Rufus Pudens Pudentius, an epochal event history could well mark as momentous.

Pudens, as he is most commonly referred to, was a Roman Senator and former personal aide-de-camp to Aulus Plautius. Pudens went to Britain with the Commander-in-Chief at the commencement of the Claudian campaign AD 42.[57]

What could be a stranger circumstance than that of the British Pendragon Caractacus permitting his favourite daughter to become adopted by the remorseless enemy who had brought about his defeat at Clun and see his sister and daughter married to the leaders he had opposed in battle for nine long years, Plautius and Pudens.

Truly the Hand of God works in a mysterious way to perform His Will.

Claudia was seventeen years of age when she married Rufus Pudens. The nuptials did not take place at the Imperial Palace of her adopted father, as one might expect, but at the palace of her natural father, the Palatium Britannicum, a Christian household. It was a Christian marriage performed by the Christian Pastor, Hermas, which proves that Pudens was already a Christian convert. It is interesting to note that they continued to live at the Palatium Britannicum; interesting because Pudens was an extremely wealthy man, owning vast estates in

---

[57] Morgan, *St. Paul in Britain*, pp. 103-107.

Umbria, but he chose to live at the Palace of the British, where their four illustrious children were born.

On the marriage of his daughter to Pudens, Caractacus bestowed the Palace as a bridal gift upon them, with all its spacious grounds.

An idea can be gained of the vast scope and opulence of the British Palace by referring to the domestic routine required to operate the household. The Roman Martyrology, referring to the Pudens, states that Rufus brought his servant staff from Umbria to manage the palatial home. It declares, 'There were two hundred males and the same number of females, all born on the hereditary estates of Pudens at Umbri.'

Adjoining the Palace of the British were two magnificent baths, the largest in Rome. They were named after the children of Claudia and Rufus Pudens, known as the Thermae Timotheus and the Thermae Novatianae. Later the Palace and all the spacious grounds of this great estate were deeded to the First Christian Church at Rome by Timotheus, the eldest son of the Pudens. He was destined to be the second last surviving member of this family and the second last to be martyred. It is recorded that these were the only properties owned by the Christian Church at Rome up to the time of the Emperor Constantine.

Pastor Hermas refers to this munificent home as 'amplissimus Pudentes domus' the 'hospitium', or home of hospitality for Christians from all parts of the world. It was more than this. For many years it was to be Sanctuary, in the true sense of the word, wherein no Roman soldier dare set foot to arrest any member or guest of the Pudens' household.

Such was the home in which the bridal pair began their marital life in the year AD 53.

Many students have puzzled over these extraordinary marriages. Some considered them political alliances. This can be ruled out on two scores. If they were political, war would not have continued but, as history shows, the conflict of arms between Briton and Roman continued, with rare interludes, for over three hundred years. On the other hand, the Roman writers state that the 'British could not be coerced by force of arms or persuasion'. They, more than any other, affirm the unbending nature of the Briton where his hereditary rights were concerned, particularly his religion. Practically all armistices ended in Treaty Alliances, wherein the British kings retained their sovereignty, privileges and freedoms. If conflict had ended in true conquest these privileges would never have been recognized. The Romans imposed their full authority on all the nations they conquered. There must be a valid reason why it was never fully imposed on the British. History shows an unbroken line of kingly successions which alone proves that they were never conquered. Even in the case of Caractacus we see that he retained his sovereignty, his hereditary estates and privileges and this in spite of the fact that Arviragus conducted the war against the Romans without abatement.

Centuries later, when the church acquired political power, it strongly supported kingly succession in the blood strain. It was the very opposite in the Roman Catholic Hierarchy. The Pope made and broke kingdoms subject to the Roman Catholic faith. He alone approved or disapproved of royal marital alliances. The parties involved obeyed or were threatened with excommunication. In this manner the Papal See controlled and expanded the Holy Roman Empire throughout Europe until the time of Martin Luther and the Reformation. The British never were subject to this interference. To do so was to incite immediate rebellion. British royal marriages and succession to the throne have ever been governed by the iron precepts of the British Christian faith. Even today the same law is still adamant, as shown in the circumstances that brought about the abdication of Edward VIII, and more recently in the public declaration of Princess Margaret in her rejection of any marriage that opposed or broke the law of the hereditary rights as declared and set forth in the Christian faith that rules the succession to the British throne.

In the events of our story we have positive proof that the British-Roman marriage alliances were truly an affair of the heart, as shown in each instance, the pagan becoming Christian.

Strange as these marriages appear under the extraordinary circumstances, Martial, particularly, extols them as romances, and his pen is lavish in describing the nuptials of Claudia and Pudens. Martial writes: 'The foreign Claudia marries my Rufus Pudens, she calls him Rufus her Holy husband.'[58]

Undoubtedly the attachment between Claudia and Pudens began in Britain, though one wonders how such a friendly social status could develop when Briton and Roman were engaged at war. No doubt Rufus Pudens Pudentius met Gladys for the first time during the truce period of AD 45, when his chief, Aulus Plautius, married the sister of Caractacus, the aunt of Gladys. Both girls, before assuming their Roman surname, were named Gladys – Princess. At this time the niece would only have been nine years old. It is stated that her extraordinary beauty, which was

---

[58] Vol. 4, p. 18

to make her world renowned, even to exceeding the fame of her illustrious aunt, was then evident. Pudens, then a young man, became attracted to Gladys despite the differences in their ages. Evidently the attraction lingered and prospered over the ensuing years. We know that Pudens did not accompany Plautius to Rome on his recall by the Emperor, AD 47. Today there exists positive proof in the Chichester Museum that Rufus remained in Britain, to the close of the Caradoc-Claudian campaign, AD 52.

While in Britain, Pudens was stationed by Aulus Plautius in command at Regnum, the name for the Roman encampment at Chichester. In the year AD 1723 workers, while excavating some old foundations there, discovered a large stone tablet, which since has been known as the 'Chichester Stone'. Fortunately the inscription it bore had been deeply carved and when restored by the firm of Horseley and Gale the Latin memorial could clearly be read. Translated the inscription is as follows:

'The College of Engineers, and ministers of religion attached to it, by permission of Tiberius Claudius Cogidubnus, the king, legate of Augustus in Britain, have dedicated at their own expense in honour of the divine family, this temple to Neptune and Minerva. The site was given by Pudens, son of Pudentinus.'

This inscription contains a wealth of corroborating support of the presence of the husband of Claudia in Britain at a later date than AD 47, apart from other matters of historic interest. This pagan temple was erected about AD 50, two years before the close of the Claudian war and the return of Pudens to Rome, AD 52. This indicates that Pudens remained in Britain five years after his commander-in-chief had returned to Rome. It also shows that at the time Pudens made the gift of this site he was still a worshipper of the Roman pagan gods; therefore his conversion to Christianity did not take place until a later date. We can be certain that Pudens' recantation from the Roman pagan gods and declaration for Christ took place before his marriage to Claudia. It could not have been otherwise. Their marriage took place within the Palace of the Royal British. The officiating minister was a Christian convert, a kinsmen of Pudens, who also made his home at the Palatium

Britannicum. He was known to St. Paul and St. Peter as Pastor Hermas.[59]

The other note of interest introduced in this inscription is the name and title 'Cogidubnus, the king'. He was not a Roman, though he prefixes his name with Roman titles – Tiberius Claudius. The rulers of the Roman Empire never employed the title 'King'. It was always Emperor – Caesar or Augustus. He was a British king but nowhere in the British Triads is his name mentioned. He was an arch traitor, one of the very few who defected to the Romans. It was he who treacherously betrayed Caractacus in the Claudian campaign. For this despicable act he was honoured by the Roman titles he appends to his own name. His family and estates were guaranteed Roman protection. To the British his name was anathema. He was branded by the most disgraceful name that could be applied to a Briton – 'bradwr', meaning 'traitor'. According to Celtic law death was the penalty for this act and his name forbidden to be spoken. His identity was completely erased from the historic record and the Bards assigned him to oblivion.

While some Britons may have been indifferent Christians, then as now, their patriotism was ever beyond question. Then as now, it burned fiercely within them. No disgrace was so great as disloyalty. They never forgave, stripping the culprit of all honour and mention in their history. This intense patriotism, coupled with severe punishment for military disgrace, continued to be observed within the British Army up to World War I. Military disgrace was a public spectacle. To be 'drummed out' was the one thing every British soldier dreaded. Following conviction by court martial he was arraigned before his paraded regiment, then, one by one, the buttons were torn off his uniform by a common soldier in rank; his insignia ripped in shreds until he stood completely despoiled before all. Then his rifle or sword was broken. This done, he was ordered to depart. All the while the muffled drums throbbed out the tattoo of his disgrace. Officers and soldiers so disgraced were also sent to 'Coventry', an expression meaning that no one who knew him would ever speak to him. Their shame went so deep that they usually left Britain, migrating to some foreign country or to the Colonies, where they changed their name in a futile effort to hide their stigma. But it is said that the ignominy was so deeply etched in their heart that none succeeded in living it down. Many have been known to have committed suicide after

---

[59] *Romans* 16;14.

being 'drummed out'. Such a traitor was Cogidubnus. Tacitus knew him and his pen shared the disdain of the British.[60]

As previously stated, among the British hostages to Rome was Llyr Llediaith, the grandfather of Caractacus. He died shortly after his arrival at Rome. As a result of his death his son, 'the Blessed Bran', the Arch Druid Silurian monarch who had abdicated in favour of his son Caractacus, voluntarily offered himself as hostage to replace his father. Thus we see the necessary characters gradually assembling in Rome in preparation for the role they were all to play in the world's greatest drama under direction of St. Paul.

We now see residing at the Palatium Britannicum the High Priest Bran, King Caractacus and the Queen, his wife; his daughter, the Princess Eurgain and her husband, Salog, Lord of Salisbury; her brother, the immortal Prince Linus, now a Christian priest; the Emperor's adopted daughter, Claudia, and her husband the Senator Pudens; his mother, Priscilla;[61] Pastor Hermas, kinsman of Pudens. Cyllinus and Cynon, the eldest and youngest sons of Caractacus had already returned to Britain. There were other members of the Pudens' Christian household dedicated to the faith but those mentioned are the important figures to remember. The talented sister of Caractacus, the ex-Princess Pomponia Graecina, and her influential husband Aulus Plautius, resided nearby. All were spiritually confirmed Christians except Caractacus and Bran, who were soon to experience the laying on of hands by St. Paul, climaxing their confirmation in the faith in the same manner as is performed by the Priesthood today in the Church of the Anglican Communion.

The following five years, apparently, were years of tranquillity at the Palatium Britannicum.

From the works of the Roman writers of that period we read that the home of Pudens rapidly became the most fashionable and cultural centre in Rome. Martial, the Roman epigrammatist, of Spanish birth, was a constant visitor who valued the scholarship of the Pudens so highly that he freely submitted his works to them for their constructive criticism. In his works, which have been handed down to us, he delights in extolling Claudia's flaxen, blue-eyed beauty, and her literary talent. He says, 'Since Claudia, wife of Pudens, comes from the blue set Britons, how is

---

[60] Tacitus, *Agricola*, 14.
[61] Morgan, *St. Paul in Britain*.

it that she has so won the hearts of the Latin people?' He explains that for wit and humour she had no equal, and her beauty and scholarship exceeded that of her august aunt, Pomponia. Claudia was a fluent linguist and, like her aunt, wrote many volumes of odes and poetry in Greek, Latin and her native Cymric. For over a thousand years her works were treasured in the great Glastonbury library but perished in the great fire, AD 1184. Copies of her hymns, elegies, etc., were contained at Verulam as late as the 13th century. Her British ancestry was never forgotten. Affectionately she was named by the Roman populace, Claudia Britannica Pudentius. Of her, Martial wrote: 'Our Claudia, named Rufina, sprung we know from blue-eyed Britons; yet behold, she vies in grace with all that Greece or Rome can show. As bred and born beneath their glowing skies.'

Rufina was the feminine vernacular for her husband's first name, Rufus. It was a common custom to refer to a married woman personally by replacing her own first name with his. Names then were used rather indiscriminately, which tends to confuse us who retain throughout our lifetime our given name and family name. Consequently it can be bewildering to read of the British Princess by so many names. Gladys-Claudia-Britannica, Rufina-Pudens, and Pudentius.

The dark-haired Romans admired the golden-haired, blue-eyed, pink-complexioned women of Britain. Again Martial sings with praise: 'For mountains, bridges, rivers, churches and fair women, Britain is past compare.'

Martial wrote a long poem describing the nuptials of Claudia and Pudens. He wrote another on the birth of Claudia's daughter, Pudentiana.

In the four years following her marriage Claudia, at the age of twenty-one, was the mother of three children. A fourth child was later born. Timotheus the eldest, and Novatus the youngest, were boys. Pudentiana and Praxedes, born in between, were girls. Names which should never be forgotten. They should be written in red and spiked with nails of gold on the walls in every Christian home. All were martyred.[62]

These four children, added to the family list of names mentioned, residing at the Palace of the British, represent the chief assembly of personalities who officially and openly first declared for the Christian faith at Rome. Fearlessly and with zeal they defied the edicts that were

---

[62] *Roman Martyrologies*.

to follow. They befriended and defended all followers of 'The Way', who sought their sanctuary. Their numbers were legion, apostles, disciples, priests and neophytes.

In *Matthew* 10:11, Jesus said, 'Into whatsoever city or town ye shall enter, enquire who in it is worthy; and there abide till ye go hence.'

Where was there a safer or more worthy home than the Palace of the British? The name it acquired, 'Home of the Apostles', shows it to have been the most popular meeting-place of the Apostles among others.

Claudia's first-born, Timotheus, was named after one of her favourite Apostles who frequented her home, St. Timothy, Bishop of Ephesus. He was closely associated with St. John and St. Paul. To Timotheus, St. Paul refers as 'The beloved son in Christ'. All her children were baptized in Christ and brought up in the presence of apostles, disciples and converts. Cardinal Baronius wrote that Justin Martyr made his home with them.

Even though St. Paul had his residence provided for him at Rome by the Christian following, the Scriptures state that he only resided two years in it during his ten years' association with the city. The common inference is that St. Paul first arrived at Rome in the year AD 58 but, as before stated, St. Jerome placed his arrival at AD 56. He writes, 'St. Paul went to Rome in the second year of Nero.' Nero succeeded Claudius as Emperor.

St. Jerome held a unique place in the post-Christian era of the Catholic Church. By request of the Church he wrote the first most important dissertations of the Christian record. His documentation of the early years of the faith stands unquestioned. A man of intense convictions, he was profoundly devout. Honest and sincere in his writings he was assiduous as to detail. Because of his tremendous knowledge of Christian history and his scholarly excellence, he was especially elected by the Church Fathers to produce the historic literary record; therefore the date he sets for St. Paul's arrival at Rome can be accepted. Moreover, the date is supported by such eminent authorities as Bede, Ivo, Platina, Scaliger, Capellus, Cave, Stillingfleet, Alford, Godwin, Rapin, Bingham, Stanhope, Warner and Trapp, to name a few. This being the date preferred, it allows eight years of contact with Rome in which St. Paul did not reside in his personal home. This fact supports the statements of the contemporary writers who state that St. Paul had his abode with the Pudens. There is a special and particular reason as to why he would prefer to reside with the Pudens at the British Palace, apart from its Christian environment.

Startling as it may be to the reader, facts will prove that living with the Pudens family was the mother of St. Paul and that Claudia Britannica was the sister-in-law of the Apostle to the Gentiles.

St. Paul, writing in his Epistles to those at Rome prior to his coming, says, 'Salute Rufus, chosen in the Lord, and his mother and mine.'

Some have sought to suggest that the woman was St. Paul's spiritual mother. This is entirely ruled out by the facts. A spiritual mother, or father, was one who had converted another. As we all know, Christ had converted Paul on the road to Damascus, and Paul had not been to Rome since before the Judean persecution of Christ's followers, AD 33. Thus twenty-five years had elapsed before his arrival at Rome as an Apostle of Christ. By deduction, Pudens must have been in his late twenties when he married the seventeen year-old British Princess, and at the time of St. Paul's salutation he must have been near his mid-thirties, which shows a long separation between 'his mother and mine.'

Pudens was born on the family estate at Umbri, a Roman state. His father was a Roman Senator, of a long illustrious ancestry. Paul, in describing his Roman citizenship, states that he was a Jew (Benjamite) by race; therefore his parents must have been Jewish Benjamites.[63] From this it is obvious that his mother was probably married a second time, and to a Roman of distinguished birth. Rufus Pudens was born of this marriage. His mother was not a Roman consort as Pudens inherited his father's estates as the legitimate son. If he had been an illegitimate son, born of a consort, the licentious pens of that time, ever ready to declare such an incident, would have said so. On the contrary, Pudens senior and his family are written of in high esteem. Therefore all facts point to a legal marriage, with Rufus as legal offspring. If it had been otherwise, Paul would not have addressed his mother and Rufus with the affection he did.

At the time Pudens donated the ground in Britain for the erection of the temple to Neptune and Minerva at Chichester, he was pagan, following his inherited family religion subject to the Roman gods. This does not prove that his Jewish mother was a pagan worshipper. Born in the Judean faith she may have remained neutral or indifferent. However, it is certain, between the year AD 50 and the nuptial year AD 53, that

---

[63] *Romans* 11:1

both mother and son must have been converted, for we find Priscilla, his mother, a member of the British household, directly following the marriage of Rufus Pudens to Claudia. On the other hand, Paul would not have sought association with his mother and Rufus if he knew they had remained pagan. His salutation proves that Paul knew beforehand that both were then confirmed Christians. He salutes Pudens, 'chosen in the Lord'. This is further supported by the Roman writers of that time who attest that 'all' of the Pudens household at the Palatium Britannicum. were Christian.

From all this we realize that St. Paul and Rufus Pudens Pudentius were half-brothers, each having the same mother. In turn this made the British Princess Gladys the Emperor Claudius's adopted daughter, now known as Claudia Britannica Rufina Pudens Pudentius, sister-in-law to the Apostle of the Gentiles!

Recognizing the facts we can well understand why the ancient writers affirmed that St. Paul, by preference, spent most of his time with the Pudens at the Palatium Britannicum while at Rome. This substantiates other important facts cited in the Roman Martyrologies that, 'The children of Claudia were brought up at the knee of St. Paul.'

Many students of the biblical history of St. Paul are commonly confused by the scriptural report which states that St. Paul spent but two years at his provided home out of the ten years he was associated with Rome. They are conscious of the eight-year gap and ask, 'Where was he?'

If they had sufficiently considered British and Roman history of that time they would have known and also known that when St. Paul was not residing with the Pudens at Rome, he was absent in Britain, Spain, Gaul and elsewhere.

It is interesting to note that St. Paul had other relatives at Rome whom he addressed in his salutations, notably Andronicus, Junea and Herodian. They also became partakers of the Pudens' Christian hospitality. They had been converted long before St. Paul arrived at Rome. They are mentioned in Scripture as being members of the first Christian church in the Imperial City. We can well imagine what a wonderful occasion the arrival of St. Paul must have been at the Palatium Britannicum, AD 56, and the happy reunion between the mother and the two brothers, with Claudia, her children whom he loved so dearly, and other relatives and converts.

From the swiftness of events that followed it is seen that St. Paul lost no time in putting into action his bold plan to erect at Rome, on an indestructible foundation, the first Christian Church among Gentiles above ground. This was the first need and was made possible by a bold act of the British royal family, Claudia and Pudens, in donating their home, the Palace of the British, to be Church at Rome. The sacrificial act is made more courageous in the fact that Nero, the mad Emperor, then sat on the throne of the Caesars.

This was the birth of the first Church of Christ above ground at Rome.

Prior to the coming of St. Paul, the Palatium Britannicum for several years, dating from the marriage of Claudia and Pudens, had been the centre for the Christian gathering to worship. Hermas conducted the services. He was the first minister to the Christian flock in secret session. Now the challenge was openly declared. It was glory or the grave.

St. Paul planned his two greatest adventures in the home of the Pudens; the first, establishing the Church of Rome, which was, as we note, accomplished in part. The second was a notable contribution in Britain in which Bran, Caractacus and Eurgain, his daughter, were to have the leading roles. When St. Paul came to Rome there remained three years of parole for Caractacus to complete. We are told St. Paul confirmed Bran and Caractacus shortly after he arrived at the home of the Pudens, but this is another story to be told in another chapter. Our attention now is still on the action at Rome. A Bishop had to be consecrated to lead the church to its destiny.

Who would this great and grave honour be conferred upon?

Linus, the son of Caractacus, who had remained at Rome, had long before been baptized and confirmed by St. Joseph of Arimathea in Britain. He was a priestly instructor. It was Linus whom St. Paul chose and personally consecrated to be the First Bishop of the Christian Church at Rome. A Prince of the royal blood of Britain, he is the same Linus whom St. Paul addressed in his Epistles. This fact has never been disputed, though seldom brought forth in the light of this reading. St. Peter affirms the fact. He says:

'The First Christian Church above ground in Rome, was the Palace of the British. The First Christian Bishop, was a Briton, Linus, son of a Royal King, personally appointed by St. Paul, AD 58.'

The church still stands and can be seen in what was once the palatial grounds of the Palatium Britannicum, a memorial to the Christianizing endeavours of St. Paul and the expatriate royal British family at Rome with Rufus Pudens. The church is recorded in Roman history under four different names: 1. Palatium Britannicum; 2. Titulus; 3. Hospitium Apostolorum; 4. Lastly, as St. Pudentiana, in honour and memory of the martyred daughter of Claudia Pudens, by which name it is known to this day.

Further corroboration is given to Linus, as the brother of the lovely Claudia and of his appointment to be the First Bishop of the Christian Church of Rome, and is provided in the following extract from *The Apostolic Constitutions:*

> 'Concerning these Bishops who have been ordained in our lifetime, we make known to you that they are these; Of Antioch, Eudoius, ordained by me, Peter. Of the Church of Rome, Linus, brother of Claudia, was first ordained by Paul, and after Linus's death, Clemens, the second ordained by me, Peter.[64]

In this statement Peter himself declared that Linus is the brother of Claudia and first Bishop of the Church at Rome. He further states that Paul performed the ordination and not he. In another statement herein given Peter affirms that Linus was a Briton, son of a royal king. In these statements the common belief that Peter founded the church at Rome, and that the first church there was Roman Catholic in origin, is confounded by the words of St. Peter himself. The Roman Catholic Church was not founded until about three hundred and fifty years later. Clearly Peter states that the first church was established by Linus, through the ordination of St. Paul. He gives the correct year, AD 58.

Clemens Romanus, the second Bishop of Rome, appointed by Peter, affirms the relationship between Linus and Claudia, writing: 'Sanctissimus Linus, Frater Claudiae' (St. Linus, brother of Claudia).[65]

Clemens Romanus knew them all intimately, not only as an intimate guest of the Pudens. He knew of Claudia in Britain, for he was St. Clement of the twelve companions of Joseph.[66] Within twelve years after the martyrdom of Linus he was consecrated the second Bishop of

---

[64] *Book* 7, ch. 46
[65] *Epistola ad Corinthios.*
[66] Clement in an English context, Clemens in the Latin.

the Church by Peter.[67] St. Paul had already suffered his martyrdom. In his works, still extant, Clement tells us that St. Paul was in constant residence at the Palatium Britannicum and personally instructed Linus for his consecrated office. He further writes that the First Church of Rome was founded by the British royal family and that St. Paul personally preached in Britain.[68]

Irenaeus, AD 180, who was also personally acquainted with the first Church, wrote: 'The Apostles having founded and built up the church at Rome, committed the ministry of its supervision to Linus.' This is the Linus mentioned by Paul in his Epistles to Timothy.[69]

This saint was born in Asia and became a disciple of Polycarp, Bishop of Smyrna. Afterwards he became a presbyter of Lyons, in Gaul. From Lyons he was sent as a delegate to the Asiatic churches.

He succeeded Photinus in the Bishopric and was martyred under order of Severus.

Linus, the First Bishop of the First Christian Church at Rome, was also its first martyr. Of this royal Christian family Claudia was the only one to die a natural death. She saw her brother Linus murdered and, years later, her faithful husband, Rufus Pudens Pudentius. He was martyred AD 96. Claudia died the following year, AD 97, in Samnium. This beautiful, glorious woman was spared the agony of seeing her four noble children butchered for Christ. The beloved Pudentiana, immortalized in *The Roman Martyrologies*, and by Martial, was executed on the anniversary of the death of her father, AD 107, during the third Roman Christian persecution. After her martyrdom, the name of the Palatium Britannicum was changed and consecrated by name to her memory. Her brother Novatus was martyred during the fifth Roman persecution, AD 137, while his elder brother Timotheus was absent in Britain, baptizing his nephew, grandson of Arviragus, King Lucius, at Winchester. Shortly after his return from Britain to Rome Timotheus, in his 90th year, suffered martyrdom along with his fellow worker Marcus. Later that same year, in which *The Martyrologies* state, 'Rome was drunk with the blood of the martyrs of Jesus', Praxedes, the youngest daughter of Claudia and Pudens and the last surviving member of the family, was also executed. Thus, by the year AD 140, all of this glorious

---

[67] *Apostolici Constitutiones*, 1:46. (The interval of twelve years was filled by Cletus. He was not appointed by the Apostles; therefore Clement is described in the Apostolic Constitutions as the second.)
[68] 'The extremity of the west', *Epistola*, ch. 5.
[69] *Sancti Irenaei Episcopi Lugdunensis* 3:1.

family were interred by the side of St. Paul, in the Via Ostiensis, their earthly mission in Christ finished.

Priscilla, the mother of St. Paul and Rufus Pudens, reposed in the underground cemetery nearby, named for her memory the Catacomb of St. Priscilla.

In the year AD 66 we are told that Claudia, with her husband and children, rescued the murdered body of St. Paul, interring it in the private burial grounds on the Pudens estate, where they were all to rest together. It was truly a dangerous operation. Christian persecution was again at fever-pitch. One may wonder why the names of others were not mentioned in claiming the body. In a way it was a repetition similar to the circumstances in which Joseph claimed the body of Jesus. Pudens was a Senator and Claudia was still respected as the adopted daughter of the late Emperor Claudius. Many things had happened to show they still had influence with the Imperial Senate. They used it to claim the mutilated remains of St. Paul. Others of the Christian clan, not having influence and being under the Caesarian ban, dared not make the effort. At that time the eldest children of Claudia would only be twelve and thirteen years old respectively. The children being party to the act shows the great devotion they held for the Apostle, who was in all probability their uncle.

The last salutation St. Paul sent out from prison before his execution was to St. Timothy, requesting him to deliver his last fond farewell to the ones he loved dearest on earth, to his sister-in-law, Claudia, and her husband; his half-brother, Pudens; to their children and to his nieces and nephews, whom he had taught with affection at his knee; the beloved Linus, whom he had consecrated and appointed First Bishop; to Eubulus, cousin of Claudia, 'and them which are of the household of Aristobulus'. In only ten years faithfully he carried out the mission to 'go to the Gentiles' as commissioned by his Saviour Jesus Christ. In those years he had established the First Christian Church at Rome and undertaken another mission in Britain, to collaborate with the Josephian Mission at Avalon. In each case his instruments in the divine work were the members of the British Royal Silurian family. How short a time for such a stupendous, noble work. Now it was all over and left for posterity to carry on.

So suffered all those who helped in founding the First Gentile Church at Rome, their glory sealed in Christ, and the spot wherein they laboured and were martyred steeped in their courageous British blood.

No disclaimer can challenge these historic events. In our own time the *Encyclopaedia Britannica* names Linus as the First Bishop of Rome. The Vatican has ever endorsed the facts herein and has kept alive the glorious story. Probably the most authentic record of this great drama is that which can still be seen and read on the wall of the ancient former Palace of the British, the sanctified church of St. Pudentiana. The memorial was carved on its walls following the execution of Praxedes in the second century, the last surviving member of the original Christian band and the youngest daughter of Claudia and Pudens.

Inscribed in these few words is told the noble, tragic story:

'In this sacred and most ancient of churches, known as that of Pastor (Hermas), dedicated by Sanctus Pius Papa (St. Paul), formerly the house of Sanctus Pudens, the Senator, and the home of the holy apostles, repose the remains of three thousand blessed martyrs which Pudentiana and Praxades, virgins of Christ, with their own hands interred.'

How many tourists visiting the Imperial City of Rome take time out to go along the Mons Sacer Way to view this tragic memorial to their faith and humbly breathe a prayer of thanksgiving for the thousands who lie beneath, martyred for our sake?

Eyes fascinated by the splendour of the Vatican Palace and other sumptuous buildings, not one Christian stops to view this hallowed place which played such a majestic part in making the faith they profess theirs to enjoy. All the riches combined in the Vatican cannot equal one iota of the wealth of devotion and sacrifice made for us within these time-weathered walls. Within its sacred precincts trod two of the greatest of Christ's Apostles, Peter and Paul; this the first Christian church at Rome to be established and the second church built above the ground to be created by the British and the Apostles of Christ. They represent the greatest gifts of the British to mankind and to posterity. Unlike the Josephian church erected at Glastonbury (Avalon), the church at Rome is drenched with the blood of martyrs. The valour of the British arms prevented the Roman or any other foreign invader from violation of the Glastonbury sanctuary. This protection was denied, by understandable circumstances, to the church at Rome. They could only die. Theirs is the greatest treasure in blood and sacrifice the British race gave to the people of the world – their cross for Christ that preserved the Word that set men free and saved their soul. How little do modern Christians realize that it was the Royal House of Britain, united with the noble Pudens, that actually made it possible for St. Paul to accomplish his mission, fulfilling the destiny Jesus ordained for him in establishing the faith permanently among the Gentiles? How few know of those gentle women, Claudia, Pudentiana and Praxedes, who gave their all for Christ, their beauty, their talents, their fortunes and their lives. What courage! No wonder the Romans proclaimed in awe: 'What women these British Christians have – what women!' Those gentle hands alone had laid at rest the staggering total of three thousand butchered martyrs within the precincts of their church, the old Palace of the British at Rome. How many more they secreted and buried within the underground catacombs is not known. As one ponders on this dreadful tragedy the soul is shocked.

Now only crumbling, uncared-for walls remain to remind us of its triumph and tragedy yet the modern Christian by-passes it without a look, without a twinge of gratitude or admiration, or a prayer, to be thrilled by the glamour of the Vatican and its cathedrals, basking in wealth and luxury, which had no part in the original planting of the faith, or in establishing and preserving our democratic freedoms.

The inscription on the walls of St. Pudentiana sets the truth squarely before our eyes, with its incomparable drama. To this are added the words of Cardinal Baronius, who writes the following comment in his *Annales Ecclesias*:[70]

'It is delivered to us by the firm tradition of our forefathers that the house Pudens was the first that entertained St. Peter at Rome, and that there the Christians assembling formed the Church, and that of all our churches the oldest is that which is called after the name Pudens.'

The eminent Jesuit Father, the Rev. Robert Parsons, in *The Three Conversions of England*, adds his testimony:[71]

'Claudia was the first hostess or harbourer both of St. Peter and St. Paul at the time of their coming to Rome.'

---

[70] ad 19 Maii
[71] Vol. 1, p. 16.

Who with an atom of intelligence dare deny the authenticity of this dramatic record in Christian history, against the mass of corroborative evidence, simply because their glory has been overshadowed by the ages, lost in antiquity to thoughtless minds? One can search in vain the modern church Calendars of Martyrs for the illustrious names. Once their names led that Calendar of Martyrs with red-letter dates. Of recent years their names have been omitted, giving precedence to others a thousand times less worthy of the honour. Yet we can still turn to the pages of the *Martyrologies of Rome*, *The Greek Menologies* and the *Martyrologies of Ado, Usuard and Esquilinus,* and therein read their glorious stories, noting the Natal Days of each, therein described.

They are as follows:

May 17. Natal Day of the Blessed Pudens, father of Praxedes and Pudentiana. He was clothed with Baptism by the Apostles, and watched and kept his robe pure and without wrinkle to the frown of a blameless life.

May 17. Natal Day of St. Pudentiana, the virgin, of the most illustrious descent, daughter of Pudens, and Disciple of the Holy Apostle St. Paul.

June 20. Natal Day of St. Novatus, son of the Blessed Pudens, brother of St. Timotheus the Elder and the Virgins of Christ, Pudentiana and Praxedes. All these were instructed in the faith by the Apostles.

August 22. Natal Day of St. Timotheus, son of St. Pudens, in the Via Ostiensis.

September 21. Natal Day of St. Praxedes, Virgin of Christ in Rome.

November 26. Natal Day of St. Linus, first Bishop of Rome.

Such is the hallowed record of the illustrious royal British martyrs at Rome:

First to house and openly protect the Apostles.
First openly to teach the Christian faith in Rome.

First to found the Christian Church at Rome.
First to suffer martyrdom for the Christian faith at Rome.

Therein lies the glory and the tragedy, the drama and the triumph of those born to the purple, who died in the purple for Christ; royal princes and princesses, born of a fearless race, converted in Britain by St. Joseph of Arimathea, the Apostle to the British, selected and ordained by St. Paul, the Apostle to the Gentiles, in the name of our Lord and Saviour Jesus Christ, to carry out His mission to the world and to be an unflickering light. Nobly the royal Silurians of Britain sealed their pledge to Christ with their lives; to the last unfalteringly proclaiming the deathless motto of their ancient Druidic ancestors – 'The Truth Against the World.'

It can truly be said that the first church at Rome was the British church, in the true meaning of the word British – 'Covenant People'.

Their Covenant in Christ was untarnished.

CHAPTER 13

DID THE VIRGIN MARY LIVE AND DIE IN BRITAIN?

I N the meantime what about Mary, the mother of Jesus? Once again we are faced with drama as exciting as it is intriguing. Off hand, one feels tempted to ask the doubtful question, Is it true that the Virgin Mary finished her earthly travail in Britain? It seems almost incredible to give an affirmative answer. Circumstance, rather than evidence, would appear to be to the contrary. Yet when one stops to think one quickly realizes how little is generally known about her and how silent the scriptural record is concerning her existence following the Crucifixion of Jesus. One can easily be forgiven for thinking it is too wonderful to be true. Yet the information presented herein appears to provide sufficient evidence to discount any doubt. However, we are entitled to our own personal reservations. In this case it could easily be one of those amazing examples in which truth is stranger than fiction.

Documentary testimony, by no means British, informs us with conviction that Mary, the mother of Jesus, was an occupant of the castaway boat that arrived at Marseilles with the others before mentioned. Other reports take up the story in Gaul, attesting to the fact that Mary was a member of the Josephian Mission that arrived in Britain AD 36. Testimony will be advanced giving a special valid reason for her being with Joseph, her uncle. Other writers take up the theme in Britain, referring to her presence at Avalon with Joseph, Mary Magdalene, the Bethany sisters and others, as unconcernedly as though it were a common matter of fact that should be well understood by all; her life, death and final resting-place is described with a nonchalance that is breathtaking.

But, we ask, did not Jesus entrust His mother, with His dying breath, to the care of His beloved disciple, John?

Yes, He did.

The scriptural record tells us that as Jesus hung on the Cross He tenderly committed His mother into John's safekeeping. John, accepting the charge led Mary away from the tragic scene before her Son expired.

Scripture states: 'From that hour that disciple took her to his own.'[72]

---

[72] *John* 19:27, 'eis ta idia' (idia is possessive pronoun. The word 'home' is not in the text).

As we ponder the text we can read in it a qualifying difference over what is commonly understood by general assumption. The point of importance in the text is the statement that John 'took her to his own'. Most critics have defined the text to imply that John took her as his own, thereby meaning he took Mary to his own home to remain there under his care.

This qualification does not stand up even under a casual study. At that time John, like all followers of 'The Way', was a hunted man. For many years to come, long after the death of Mary, he had no home. The intention, as stated in the text, seems quite plain. John took Mary 'to his own'. His own were the intimate disciples of Jesus, of whom Joseph was the protecting shield, and the Bethany sisters, whose home had been a common meeting-place for Jesus and His disciples.

There is a world of difference between entrusting the care of a person 'to his own', and one requiring the care to be ever personal. The latter is restricted only to the individual. 'To his own' implies a broader meaning, which recorded events corroborate. If it did not it would indeed be strange that such an auspicious trust was not frequently mentioned by John in his writings during his extremely long lifetime. He died at the age of 101.

The facts are that at no time does John ever refer to Mary, nor even in his report of that first greater Easter morning. This omission of his trust is strange and lack of reference to her by John could only mean one thing: the beloved Mary was not with him.

Jesus definitely entrusted His mother to the care of John but the request did not mean she was to be always in John's personal care as much as it meant that John would see her safely provided for. In this case it seems quite reasonable to expect John to turn to Joseph of Arimathea for the necessary protection. We know how greatly his family responsibilities had increased from the time of the infamous trial. Since his lot was henceforth indubitably cast in with that of the apostles and disciples of Christ, there is every reason to believe that Joseph would continue his guardianship of the Nazarene family with a keen awareness. That all the faithful depended on the protection of Joseph while they remained at Jerusalem is well established. Therefore we can reasonably concur that John would entrust his charge to a safekeeping more secure than his own. In those turbulent days, with persecution rampant, none of the faithful could guarantee their future with any degree of assurance. At that time it is quite doubtful if John knew that his selected field of teaching at Ephesus would be less dangerous than the places in which other disciples were to labour.

It must be remembered that despite the hatred borne towards him by the Sanhedrin and possibly dissatisfaction in the local Roman Senate, Joseph remained in a position too powerful for either to contend with. Up to the time of his banishment from Judea, AD 36, he continued to retain his official status as a legislative member of the Sanhedrin, a Provincial Roman Senator, and Nobilis Decurio. So important was this office considered within the Roman Empire that Cicero, remarked ironically, it was easier to become a Senator of Rome than a Decurio in Pompeii.

Consequently the intrepid Joseph could be the only choice.

There are several early documents which bear this out. One reads: 'St. John, while evangelizing Ephesus, made Joseph Paranymphos.'[73] (Paranymphos means to be 'the Guardian'.)

We read in pp. 42 and 71, the statement that St. John and St. Joseph were alone called 'Paranymphos' to the Blessed Virgin. The *Cottonian MS. Titus A* also relates the same facts. British testimony is supplied by Capgrave.

From this we can safely judge that, in the first place, Joseph was the protector of all the faithful band, and later he was officially appointed by St. John to be the guardian of Mary, in which case the mother of Jesus could be ever in his custody and go wherever he went until the end, which the records affirm.

In the last account given of Mary in the New Testament, after the Ascension, we find her 'dwelling among the disciples' in Jerusalem. This would indicate that Mary lived among the families of the faithful, moving from one to the other as safety required. Undoubtedly the watchful eyes of her uncle would know when a change should be made to safeguard her person. As we shall see in the stirring events that followed, Joseph, her Paranymphos, was faithful to the end when he personally laid her to rest, as he had formerly done with the tortured body of Jesus.

Capgrave, in *Novo Legende Anglia*, particularly informs us that John gave Mary into the trust of Joseph, under the peculiar title of being her 'brides man'; that he was present at her death, as were other apostles

---

[73] *Magna tabula Glastoniensis.*

and disciples who came at her bidding to be by her side as Mary breathed her last.

Many are the places claimed for her resting-place, particularly the one in more modern times by the Roman Catholic Church, at a spot near Jerusalem named the Chapel of the Dormition. For many years the priests have pointed out to visitors a ledge, stating that was where Mary's Koimesis, falling asleep, took place. However, none of the places in the East have withstood the probe of investigation. None of the disciples mention her tomb. St. Jerome, recording the sacred places of the East during the fourth century, by special commission of the Church at Rome, makes no reference to the resting-place of Mary, Joseph, or many others, for no other reason than that he knew they were not interred in Judea, or in Rome.

We can be sure that Mary, of her own desire, would never have wished to be left all alone in the land that held for her nothing but danger and memories of stark tragedy. The only happiness left to her on earth was in being associated with those who had been near and dear to her beloved Son. It is impossible to believe that Joseph, her uncle and guardian, would have left her alone in Judea at the mercy of the hateful Sanhedrin. Equally so, it is impossible to believe that the Sanhedrin, when it expelled all the faithful from Judea in the exodus of AD 36, would have allowed Mary to remain. Thus it is only reasonable to believe that the bond of association that held Joseph with Mary and her family since the childhood of Jesus, would be a natural continuance. It gives strength to the documentary evidence which definitely states that Mary remained with Joseph and lived out her life among her dearest friends. Only among them would one expect to find her.

On the other hand, if Mary had wished for her remains to be taken back to Judea for burial, St. Jerome would have known and recorded the fact. He would never have overlooked the important memorial of one held in such affectionate memory, who years later was to become so glorified by the Roman Catholic Church, as to almost overshadow the glory of her Son, Jesus. The Virgin Mary was deified by the Roman Catholic Church in AD 600. She was never deified by the British Church. Christ alone, from the beginning and to date, is the only deity of the Church.

Further contradiction is given to the claim that Mary remained and died in Jerusalem, in the Glastonbury tradition of 'Our Lady's Dowry', bequeathed to her by Jesus Himself, the 'Dowry' being the little wattle temple Jesus built with His own hands at Avalon, wherein He communed with the Father, and which He dedicated to the affectionate memory of His mother. It was to this hallowed spot that Joseph led Mary with his missionary band, when they first disembarked in Britain. When Joseph built the first church at Avalon he continued the dedication, as did St. David when he erected the first stone church, AD 540, over the hallowed wattle temple of Christ, which he had encased in lead for preservation. These points are important to know because the dedications of churches to the Virgin Mary began during the twelfth century, the memorial to Mary at Avalon being the only exception. It could only have been so for a very special reason, particularly since the British never officially deified Mary. It had to be for a specific record.

Actually there is far more substantial evidence to support the Marian residence and demise in Britain than there is to prove Jesus once dwelt on the Sacred Isle, and this in spite of the strength of opinion. Nevertheless the antagonists of the Marian story base their denials on the premise that Jesus was never in Britain; in consequence they claim He could not have erected the wattle temple for her 'dowry'. How the critics can claim intelligence in reasoning to this conclusion is not understandable. The fact is that neither the absence or the presence of Jesus in Britain has a bearing on the subject. Mary's going to Britain with Joseph was a matter of valid circumstances. The atheistical mind jeers in its final challenge, 'Why should Jesus go to Britain? Why should He go to a barbarian country?' The bigotry of the critic is always the same. They never provide an answer to substantiate their challenge. Never once have they attempted to fill in the eighteen-year gap in the life of Jesus, from the age of twelve when He confounded the Pharisees in the Temple, to the age of thirty when He began His ministry. The destructive critic ever assumes that what he does not know about could not have happened. Their minds are cluttered with intellectual weeds.

Let us dwell for a moment on those silent years of Jesus, and see if we can rationalize the circumstances of His life to fit into this unique relationship in Britain, 'twixt mother and Son.

Jesus is frequently referred to as the Carpenter of Nazareth. Being a carpenter, as the Bible says He was, He must have served an apprenticeship, which likely began at an early age. Apprenticeships in Europe and Britain, well within the last one hundred years, often began at the age of fourteen. How long He worked plying His trade is unknown, but we can safely assume that, being aware of His destiny, He must have abandoned His trade early in order to prepare Himself for His great Mission. This being the case He would naturally be attracted to the foremost centres of religious wisdom of His day. One may rightfully inquire why He did not study under the Rabbis of the Sanhedrin. Jesus provides the answer in the contemptuous manner in which He accused them of 'knowing not the Law'.

The facts are readily conceived.

The Pharisees were a sect founded by Pharez, who created the School of Predestination. The Sadducees were founded by Sadoc, a disciple of Antigonus Scohaeus, known as the School of Infidels. These are the fanatics who ruled the Sanhedrin of Jesus's day – those whom Jesus called 'whited sepulchres', full of dead men's bones. He could find no wisdom among them. Where He could find wisdom there He would be certain to go.

The *Rig-Vedas*, the ancient religious books of India, were written *circa* 1500 BC and the Druidic religion antedated that of India, *circa* 1800 BC. The wise men of India record the visit of Jesus among them, stating that He dwelt at Nepal. They also make several references to Britain as a great centre of religious learning; therefore, on several scores, Jesus would know of the eminence of Druidic religious wisdom. He would know from His great uncle Joseph, who frequently visited Britain on his tin-mining excursions. It was popular knowledge among the Greeks and Romans who heavily populated Judea. He would know from His association with the wise men of India and, if tradition is true, He would know from personal contact with Britain, made when His great uncle Joseph took Him on his seafaring trips to that country. Eastern and western tradition claim Jesus completed His studies in Britain. This could be possible. At that time the Druidic universities were the largest in the world, both in size and in attendance, with a listing of sixty large universities and an average attendance of over sixty thousand students.[74] This is affirmed by Greek and Roman testimony which states that the noble and wealthy of Rome and other nations sent their children to study law, science and religion in Britain.

One can well pause to grasp the fact that ancient Britain then had acquired a stature with institutions of learning and attendance rivalling that of the U.S.A. today, in its principal universities. Consequently one

---

[74] Gildas, (*Cottonian MS*).; also Morgan, *History of Britain*, pp. 62-65.

is not left in doubt as to why Jesus might have elected to have studied in Britain.

That Jesus had been absent from Judea for more than an ordinary length of time is proven by the tax incident related in *Matthew* 17:24. The tax collector accosts Jesus and Peter on their arrival at Capernaum, and asks Peter if his Master has paid His tax, indicating Jesus to be a stranger subject to tax. Actually Jesus did not need to pay tax. Capernaum was His domicile, to which the family of Jesus had moved from Nazareth early in His life. Jesus put up no argument, advising Peter to pay the 'stranger' tax, thereby implying He had been absent for so long that He could be regarded as a stranger. By this act Jesus admits an absence of years from His homeland.

Tradition and written testimony assert that Jesus did abide in Britain, and whilst there created a Temple of loving testimony to His mother. This was 'Our Lady's Dowry', to which Joseph, the 'Paranymphos' – 'Bridesman', led her and where she lived her life out in its sanctity. A wealth of ancient writers, ecclesiastical and secular, affirms it. For over a thousand years it was commonly spoken of as 'the church built not by human art'. St. Augustine, during his presence in Britain, was quite familiar with the facts and the existence at that time of this hallowed memorial. Of it he writes with delight and at great length to Pope Gregory, in a letter still extant. He writes with devout acceptance, a part of which reads as follows, from *Epistolae ad Gregorium Papam*:

'In the Western confines of Britain there is a certain royal island of large extent, surrounded by water, abounding in all the beauties of nature and necessaries of life. In it the first Neophites of Catholic Law, God beforehand acquainting them, found a church constructed by no human art, but divinely constructed, or by the hands of Christ Himself, for the salvation of His people. The Almighty has made it manifest by many miracles and mysterious visitations that He continues to watch over it as sacred to Himself, and to Mary, the Mother of God.'

In this brief extract St. Augustine assembles and declares all the salient facts. He identifies it as the 'royal island,' Silurian, where the first disciples of Christ, declaring the Catholic law (Universal Law, not Roman), found a sacred Temple built by the hands of Jesus, and that it was held sacred to Himself and the memory of Mary. This alone is trenchant testimony and written nearly six hundred years after Joseph, Mary and the Bethany group arrived in Britain.

The hallowed sanctity of 'Our Lady's Dowry' is descriptively corroborated by the Saxon historian, William of Malmesbury, who wrote his outstanding works in the twelfth century. He wrote two histories covering the religious subject-matter related herein. His last work, *De Antiquitate Glastoniae*, is most authentic. He was specially commissioned by the Abbot of Glastonbury to write the complete history of the famous church from its beginning at Avalon and was invited to live at the Abbey where he had full access to the world-famous Glastonbury Library. Therein were contained all the original documents from Druidic times, consequently he wrote his history with the benefit of first-hand material, long before the great fire completely destroyed the Abbey and its wonderful library, then considered one of the largest in the world. Consequently, his historic literary work completed at the Abbey, under his commission, is probably the most precious document of the British Christian Church in existence. There are other outstanding works on this subject one can refer to with profit, such as *De origine Ecclesiae Britannicae* by Elvan of Avalon, an illustrious British scholar who had been educated in the School of Joseph of Arimathea at Avalon, AD 180. He is referred to by the eminent Roman Catholic ecclesiastic Pitsaeus, and Cardinal Baronius. *Relat. Hist. de rebus Anglicis Act*, by Pitsaeus; Capgrave's *De Sancto Joseph at Arimathia*; *The Magna Tabula of Glastonbury*, at Haworth Castle; Hearne's *John of Glastonbury*; Bede's *Ecclesiastical History*; Gildas and Geoffrey of Monmouth, among many others, particularly *Glastonbury, The Mother of Saints*, by the Rev. L. Smithett Lewis; Hewins' *Royal Saints of Britain*; Rees' Welsh Saints, of our own times.

The most interesting reading in William of Malmesbury's great work as it concerns this story is where he recites the authentic, well-known story of St. David, AD 540, when he came to Glastonbury to rededicate the new church and his mind was changed by a dream. During the first night St. David slept at Glastonbury, the vision of Jesus appeared to him in a dream telling David that rededication was unnecessary, saying, 'He Himself had long before dedicated the church in honour of His mother and the sacrament ought not to be profaned by human repetition.' St. David obeyed and the original consecration to Mary stood.

In order to perpetuate the historic beginnings of the church and that no mistake should be made at any future time as to its exact site, St. David, AD 546, erected a new stone addition to the old church, over the grave of Mary, and enclosed the original wattle church encased in lead. He caused a pillar to be erected on the site with a brass tablet bearing record to the fact. At the time of the Dissolution, under the edict of Henry VIII, it was still standing. The edict robbed this ancient church, as well as many others, of its ancient privileges, and later, during the Puritan desecrations, the historic Abbey fell into disrepair and decay. Fortunately the brass tablet was recovered in an excellent state of preservation and, according to Archbishop Ussher, 1639, it was treasured in the possession of Sir D. Thomas Hugo at Wells. Later it came into the possession of Sir Henry Spelman, who describes it in his book *Concilia*. The tablet reads:

'The first ground of God, the first ground of the saints in Britain, the rise and foundation of all religion in Britain, and the burial place of the Saints.'

Dean Armitage Robinson excavated the base of the original pillar in 1921. Thus the memorial erected by St. David is today preserved for all to see and to read.

The Rev. Lionel Smithett Lewis, Vicar of Glastonbury, was indefatigable in his research to prove the validity of Jesus and His mother Mary residing in Britain, and painstaking in disclosing the history of Glastonbury from its saintly beginnings at Avalon. In the spring of 1953 he wrote to the author stating that in the past few years he had recovered much more authoritative information from rare old documents he had discovered concerning Jesus and Mary that would prove revelatory on the subject, his one wish then being that he would be privileged to publish this, his last and best work, before he died. He stated, once and for all, that he would prove the validity of the old traditions with incontestable evidence. Unfortunately he died suddenly, a week after writing to the author, at the age of eighty-six. However, his widow, and co-helper and Curate, the Rev. Stacey, have carried out his last request.[75]

[75] This is now published by The Lutterworth Press under the title *St. Joseph of Arimathea at Glastonbury*, and is available from the Covenant Publishing Company Ltd.

This redoubtable researcher for the truth points out the unique place of honour occupied by the Virgin Mary in the Roman Catholic Church from earliest times to date, and states:

'No one better than they (the Roman Catholic Church) know the facts of her (Mary's) life, and no one better than they espouse them. And over the ages the holy ground at Glastonbury has been constantly referred to by them as "Our Lady's Dowry". As such it has always been recognized by the Roman Catholic Sisterhood, who never ceased to pray daily for this hallowed spot at Glastonbury – Our Lady's Dowry.'

This was the spotless legacy Jesus left to His mother Mary, the inheritance bequeathed and built by His own hands and sanctified by his prayers. It was here that Joseph finally laid her to rest, AD 48, while the Claudian campaign was still raging in Britain, four years before the historic events began to happen at Rome at the Palatium Britannicum.

From the earliest times, ecclesiastical and secular chronicles substantiate the story, long before the Roman Catholic Church was founded. It has been carried on through the ages and, apparently, more particularly by the Roman Catholic Church, to present times, as the Rev. Lewis relates above, not only in England but also in France. E. Hutton, in his *Highways and Byways in Wiltshire*, states that it is so referred to in Italy at Assisi. An old English lady, Mrs. Cottrell, of Penwerris, Cornwall, educated at a French convent in Alexandria conducted by nuns who were members of the old French nobility, was taught that St. Joseph of Arimathea took the Blessed Virgin with him to Britain and that she died there. Why would this story persist through the ages if it were not true? The fact that modern Roman Catholics continue to espouse it is rather amazing under present circumstances. Why should they declare the historic facts and daily pray for her resting-place at Glastonbury as 'Our Lady's Dowry' and at the same time show pilgrims and sightseers the stone ledge in the Chapel of the Dormition? Then, nearly nineteen hundred years after, they decided her death to have been a physical translation so celebrated by the Roman Catholics throughout the world in declaring 1954 as the Marian year? To Christians, other than Roman Catholics, this intense glorification of the Virgin Mary seems strange. It is so great in the South American countries that this continent is commonly named 'The Land of Mary'.

The Christian faith of the Celto-Anglo-Saxon Protestants remains firmly entrenched in its original fountainhead – Jesus Christ. The Virgin Mary is regarded as but an instrument in the Divine purpose. There is no passage in the Bible that shows that Jesus regarded His mother as Divine. On the occasion when His disciples told Him that His mother and brethren were present, He asks, 'Who is My mother?', and gives the explanation. Naturally He regarded her dearly, as proven by the dedication and heritage He bequeathed to her at Avalon and, consequently, any evidence brought forth to substantiate her life and death in Britain is of prime interest to all Christians.

When printing was invented, the first book to come off the press was the Bible, and then Wynkyn De Worde printed the life story of St. Joseph. At the same time Pynson printed two accounts of the Arimathean story, copying from old documents, one of which carried these interesting lines:

'Now here how Joseph came into Englande;
But at that tyme it was called Brytayne.
Then XV yere with our lady, as I understande.
Joseph wayted styll to serve hyr he was fayne.'

The intriguing feature of this verse is contained within the last two lines. The chronicler states that Joseph came to Britain, then clearly informs us that Mary was with him and that he cared for her for fifteen years. This length of time closely approximates the number of years Joseph was Mary's Paranymphos, or Bridesman, from AD 32 to 48. The old ecclesiastical records of Glastonbury, confirmed by many other ancient writers, state that the Virgin Mary departed this life in the year AD 48. Coinciding with this, the Abbey records officially declare that St. Mary's Chapel, erected by St. David, was built over her remains.

Melchinus, a native of Avalonia, known also as MaeIgwyn, Celtic bard, historian and philosopher, who lived *circa* AD 450, writes:

'Ye ealde chyrche was built over the grave of the Blessed Mary.'

William of Malmesbury wrote in his *Acts of the Kings of the English* (Bk. 1 ch. 2):

'The church of which we are speaking (Glastonbury) from its antiquity called by the Angles, by way of distinction, "Ealde Chiche", that is the "Old Church" of wattle work at first, savoured somewhat of heavenly sanctity even from its very foundation, and exhaled it over the whole country, claiming superior reverence, though the structure was mean … Men of that province had no oath more frequent, or more sacred than to swear by the Old Church, fearing the swiftest vengeance on their perjury in this respect. In the meantime it is clear that the depository of so many saints may be deservedly called an heavenly sanctuary upon earth …who there more especially chose to await the day of resurrection under the protection of the Mother of God.'

In these words the writer shows the deep veneration in which St. Mary's Church of Glastonbury was held by all, in the fact that they swore the most fervent oath by the Old Church just as we today, in court, swear our oath on the Holy Bible. The plain meaning in the last passage is that the Blessed Mary was buried there.

From the time of her death and for centuries after we are constantly confronted with the desire of holy men and women, disciples, pilgrims, kings and princes from all parts of the world who sought interment in the ancient cemetery at Glastonbury to, as phrased, 'await the day of resurrection under the protection of the Mother of God'.

The list of recorded names, still extant, buried at Glastonbury, is the most illustrious and unique, superior to any other cemetery in the world. This in itself is the greatest testimony to the sacred remains enclosed in that hallowed ground. This ground has always, from time immemorial, been called 'the most holiest ground on earth'; 'the most hallowed spot in Christendom'; 'the burial place of the Saints'.

The mass of testimony supporting this historic incident appears to overwhelm any argument to the contrary. One finds it difficult to believe all this is but a prayerful tribute to a legend without substance. Where there is smoke there is always fire.

There are other historic facts to be considered to support this amazing record that can be seen to this day, irrefutable evidence.

One of the most unique monuments that remain from olden times is the ancient stone that silently stares down on the beholder from the standing outside wall of the Lady Chapel. It bears but two names, 'Jesus – Maria'. This time and weather-worn tablet has puzzled scholars for centuries. Devoid of any other inscription it has ever been recognized as a significant marking, with a definite meaning.

It is commonly asked, 'Why was it put there?' 'What does it mean?'

It has all the hallmarks of a very ancient piece of masonry preserved from the original stone church and replaced in the second new stone church after the disastrous fire of AD 1184.

The late Rev. L. Smithett Lewis, Vicar of Glastonbury, declared that the meaning those two noble names is no riddle.[76] It represents the signature of Jesus, naming the Dowry He had provided for His mother Mary. Truly an amazing document in stone, revealing for all time and to all peoples the ancient title to this hallowed spot at Avalon.

Centuries before Avalon was renamed Glastonbury, by the Saxons, two names were frequently found documented in the writings of the old scribes, definitely referring to something of great importance. Usually no explanation was given, indicating that titles and place were as commonly known to the people of those years as today. Confederation is known to Canadians and the Statue of Liberty to Americans. To the Priesthood and historians of those enthralling years, the two names employed designating the particular place were 'Secretum Domini' and 'Domus Dei'. The first title means 'The Secret of Our Lord' and the second, 'The House, or Home of God'. The explanation given is that the little wattle Temple was the House, or Home of God, because therein He dwelt, and the Secret of the Lord was the Dowry and dedication of the same to His mother. In substance, the ancient stone registers the record and site of 'Our Lady's Dowry'.

This is not myth, legend or unsupported tradition. The title is officially recorded in the ancient names in the famous *Domesday Book*, AD 1086, which reads as follows:

'The Domus Dei, in the great monastery of Glastonbury, called The Secret of Our Lord. This Glastonbury Church possesses in its own ville XII hides of land which have never paid tax.'[77]

Not only is this particular evidence officially recorded in the historic *Domesday Book*, it also corroborates the original deed of the twelve hides of land – 1,920 acres – and its tax-free grant as given to St. Joseph

---

[76] Lewis, L. S. *St. Joseph of Arimathea at Glastonbury*, p. 59.
[77] *Domesday Survey Folio*, p. 249B.

of Arimathea and his companions by the British Prince Arviragus of the royal Silurians when the Bethany group first landed in Britain.

It should be borne in mind that the date given above, AD 1086, is not the date in which the *Domesday Book* was first written. It represents the date in which the Norman King William had all the historic events recorded within the ancient book rechecked and brought up to date to his reign as King of England. The original date and name of this great book is *The Anglo-Saxon Chronicle*,[78] preserved in the British Museum. It was created by King Alfred the Great, AD 871, who commissioned monastic scholars to translate into the Saxon tongue the ancient British history from documentary evidence. The British historians Capgrave and Kemble both wrote that Alfred was given great credit in history for creating laws, institutions and reform. What he did was to restore and enforce the ancient British practices of law, order and religion in existence many centuries before his time. This is borne out by an old record in which it states that Alfred ordered the ancient laws of Dunwal to be codified into the Saxon tongue. Dunwal, or Dunwallon, was the greatest of early British kings and certainly the greatest law maker in British history.[79] He is recorded as Dunwal, the Law Maker. He lived and reigned 500 BC.

However, one cannot help but be impressed by the act of William the Conqueror, Duke of Normandy, hostile to the Saxons by his claim to priority to the British crown, in recognizing the validity of the record of this ancient church and causing the facts to remain perpetuated in the famous historic *Domesday Book*. Not only this, but he openly declared his respect for the sacred Abbey by endowing the church with another Charter, and his royal protection.

Over fifty years before this act of William, another foreign invader, the Danish King Canute, had journeyed to Glastonbury Abbey, 'with a great entourage', and knelt beside the tomb of the former British king, Edmund Ironside, whom he so greatly admired. The historic record is lavish in detail, telling us that the pilgrimage of the Danish king was conducted in splendour, and with 'peacock feathers'. He bestowed on the church munificent gifts and gave to it his enlarged Charter, AD 1032.

---

[78] Parts of the *Anglo-Saxon Chronicle* overlap the period of the *Domesday Book*, the four manuscripts ending with the following dates: A – 1001, B – 977, C – 1066, and D – 1079. The later *Laud MS.* ends in 1154. *Domesday Book* could be a continuation of the Anglo-Saxon Chronicle.

[79] E.O. Gordon, *Prehistoric London*, pp. 101-104; Morgan, *History of Britain*, pp. 42-46.

It is an astonishing fact to remember that, despite the bitter determination of the Roman Empire to persecute and uproot and destroy everything that was Druidic and Christian in Britain, despite the pillaging and ravishing of monasteries, churches and libraries by Roman, Saxon, Dane and Norman, not once was the sanctity of the Abbey defiled. Excepting the Romans, the leaders of the Saxons, Danes and Normans held the old church in awed respect. Under pain of punishment they forbade any of the soldiery to defile its sacred precincts or molest its occupants. Sad as it is to relate, what defilement this hallowed British institution was to suffer was done by its own countrymen and a royal descendant of the famed Christian warrior, Arviragus, none other than King Henry VIII. This despotic monarch not only stole all its precious possessions but robbed it of all its ancient privileges and brutally murdered the last Abbot.

Abbot Whiting was hung, his body quartered and his head stuck on the spike of the church gate and his other parts stuck elsewhere, a dire threat to all who dared challenge the king's despotic will. The Puritans performed the final desecration.

Strange as it may seem, when we consider the unbridled despoiling during the Dissolution, AD 1539-40, and the fanaticism of Cromwell's Puritans, AD 1653-58, the ancient tablet escaped mutilation.

No church in the world has been favoured so many times by Royal Charters as Glastonbury Abbey. Each regal seal declared its sacred historic beginning, attesting to the world-wide reverence held for this sacred memorial to Christ, each a magnificent testimonial to the great truth.

We know that this ancient tablet bearing those two immortal names was hewn by the builders of the first stone church, replacing the one built by Joseph and his saintly companions.

Five years before Mary died she saw the shadow of the persecuting hand of Rome which cast its baleful eye over the Sacred Isle of Britain in the Claudian invasion of AD 43. This time the Bethany family viewed the rising tide of Roman oppression from behind the fearless barricade of British Christian faith and valour. She saw the British army led by its British Pendragons, Guiderius, Caractacus and Arviragus, meet the Roman challenge with the greatest Christian crusading spirit in history, one that has never since been repeated. She heard the clarion call of the British Arch Priests exhort the people to rise in the defence of righteousness. Like the Levites of old, the British Arch Priests, according to ancient Druidic custom, marched in the front ranks of the soldiery, without arms. On their white-shirted breasts they wore the ancient sign of Aaron, the three golden rods, the insignia of the Trinity. Meeting the foe with their deathless slogan, 'The Truth against the world', they were, as even Julius Caesar had said of them a century before, 'careless of death'.[80]

In all probability Mary saw the Christian Mission rise at Avalon, like a fruitful tree, with converts pouring in in an ever-rising wave, and saw them, as well as members of the original Bethany band that came with Joseph to Britain, flow out into other lands to preach the Word, and in many cases die the death of martyrs. At Avalon she would frequently meet the beloved in Christ as they convened with Joseph and his companions to plan their crusading campaigns to Christianize the Gentile world. What a glorious privilege was hers!

It is interesting to know that this sacred burial spot that was to inter a multitude of holy men, kings and martyrs, has been called the British Vale of Jehoshaphat.[81] To the biblical people the Valley of Jehoshaphat was the valley of final judgment. What is more interesting is that Avalon was earlier known as Avilion. This Celtic word has the same word meaning as Jehoshaphat – 'The Isle of Departed Spirits.'

With all the mass of tradition and documentary evidence from Gaul, Brittany, Normandy, Spain, Italy, Constantinople, Rome and Britain, and the great number of name places associating Mary and Jesus with Britain, one feels in his heart it is not possible for it all to be only a beautiful legend without foundation.

How tenderly and lovingly the inspired British poet William Blake 1757-1827, asks the appealing question in his magnificent poem, 'Jerusalem', so popularly sung in Christian communities.

JERUSALEM
And did those feet in ancient time
Walk upon England's mountains green
And was the Holy Lamb of God
On England's pleasant pastures seen?
And did the Countenance Divine

---

[80] Tacitus, *Agricola* xi: 'The Britons, however, not yet enfeebled by a long peace, are possessed of superior courage.'
[81] Lewis, L. S. *St. Joseph of Arimathea at Glastonbury*, p. 70.

Shine forth upon our clouded hills?
And was Jerusalem builded here
Among those dark Satanic mills?

Bring me my bow of burning gold!
Bring me my arrows of desire!
Bring me my spear! O clouds unfold!
Bring me my chariot of fire!
I will not cease from mental fight,
Nor shall my sword sleep in my hand,
Till we have built Jerusalem
In England's green and pleasant land.

William Blake was born in London in 1757, but was familiar with the stories associated with Glastonbury and steeped in its ancient history. He expressed his heartfelt prayers for this, 'the Holiest Ground on Earth', in his beautiful poem, which immediately became adopted as a hymn, familiar to us all.

This hymn was a great favourite of King George V. On special occasions of national significance he would ask for it to be played and sung. He was familiar with the historic story. The Royal Library contains many ancient treasures, including the extraordinary genealogical chart showing the British Royal line to be in direct descent from the royal kings of ancient Israel.

CHAPTER 14

SIMON ZELOTES - MARTYRED IN BRITAIN DURING THE BOADICEAN WAR

FOLLOWING the defeat of Caractacus at Clun, AD 52, and his exile at Rome, Arviragus speedily reorganized the Silurian forces, striking back at the Romans with a fury that exceeded any former combat. Ostorius Scapula was still in command of the Roman armies in Britain, but his forces had become greatly demoralized by the succession of defeats and the terrible savagery of the British onslaughts. In the year AD 53 Scapula suffered a staggering defeat at Caervelin, near Caerleon. Discouraged and broken in health from the years of harrowing warfare, he petitioned Nero to be relieved of his command and return to Rome. This was the year Nero had succeeded Claudius as Emperor of the Romans. Nero accepted Scapula's resignation and he was immediately replaced by Aulus Didius,[82] also known as Didius Gallus. Didius founded the city of Cardiff, which is still known by the Welsh as Caer Dydd – 'The Castle of Didius'.

It is interesting to learn that one of the first acts of Didius on arriving in Britain was to depose Aricia, Queen of the Brigantes, whom he thoroughly distrusted. Her treacherous betrayal of her cousin, Caractacus, had caused her to be held in disdainful contempt by both the Romans and the British. As it was, her own clan had expelled her for adultery.[83]

Didius was impotent in dealing with Arviragus on the field of battle. He suffered repulse and defeat in rapid succession. After a brief command he was replaced by Veranius, AD 57. The latter had no better success, in fact worse. Arviragus drove the Roman forces behind the Plautian wall of fortresses and bottled up Veranius at Verulam. Matters in the field had become so bad for Roman arms that, in desperation, Nero ordered huge reinforcements to be rushed to Britain, under the superlative relieving command of Suetonius Paulinus,[84] then regarded as the ablest tactician in the Roman army. He took with him the Second Augusta Legions, and the famous Ninth, Fourteenth and Twentieth

---

[82] Tacitus, *Annals,* 12:40.
[83] Tacitus, *History*, 3:45.
[84] Tacitus, *Annals*, 14:38, 39.

Legions who carried the victorious legend 'Vicesima, Valens, Victrix'. They were unequal to the occasion. Disaster continued as the British drove the enemy before them, asking no quarter and giving none.

Tacitus bitterly expresses the feeling at Rome which required their most capable generals and finest legions to combat the 'barbarous' British. He writes:

'In Britain, after the captivity of Caradoc, the Romans were repeatedly defeated and put to rout by the single state of the Silures alone.'[85]

The clemency shown the royal British captives at Rome by the Emperor Claudius did not mollify the Silurians in the least. Men, women and priests without discrimination took the field to avenge and arrest the continued tyrannical persecution of Roman savagery. Ruefully Tacitus observes: 'The race of the Silures are not to be changed by clemency or severity.'[86]

Mercilessly they fought pitched battles, stormed forts and Roman encampments, putting Roman settlements to the torch. The record reads: 'The plains and streets ran with Roman blood.'

The more the Romans were defeated the more excessive were their vicious depredations. The culminating climax came under orders from Suetonius Paulinus, to carry out a scorched-earth programme, to destroy everything in their path and particularly to exterminate the seats of Christian learning and all therein. This eventuated in the horrible Menai massacre.[87] Entering the community under pretext of peace, with concealed arms, the Roman soldiery suddenly set upon the inhabitants. Thousands of unsuspecting priests and priestesses and a multitude of people were treacherously butchered in cold blood, men, women and children. The aged and the infants were alike hewn down without mercy.

According to Tacitus, this horrible campaign raged at its worst from AD 59 to 62.

In the year AD 60 the avaricious Roman Prefect, Catus Decianus, had broken the Claudian Treaty with the Iceni, on a false pretext fomented by Seneca, the Stoic philosopher, who at that time held great influence with Nero. Seneca, while renowned as a philosopher of sorts,

---

[85] Tacitus, *Annals*, 12:38-39.
[86] Tacitus, *Annals*, 2:24.
[87] Tacitus, *Annals*, 14:29-31.

was better known as the wealthiest man in Rome, who had obtained his vast fortune by trickery and promoting usurious loans. He had advanced the huge sum of ten million dollars to Prasutagus on the security of the public buildings of the Iceni. Prasutagus, the king, was also an extremely wealthy man. Tacitus says his wealth was rated at Rome as being fantastic. However, the financial transaction was a private matter between Seneca, Prasutagus and his family. Having no political involvement it was outside the authority of Decianus. Nevertheless, Seneca conspired with Decianus to act on the recent death of Prasutagus, completely disregarding the valid claims of the estate. The Roman Prefect needed no second invitation to satiate his greed from the pillage and plunder that would follow. This act of treachery was made more simple for Decianus by reason of an existing Peace Treaty made between Rome, the Iceni and the Coraniaid. This political agreement permitted the Romans to enjoy freedom of travel and residence in the domain of these two British clans. This privilege provided opportunity for Decianus to take the populace by surprise. He struck suddenly with violence, inciting his soldiers to unwarranted brutalities which appalled and drew severe censure from the Senate and Roman writers.

They sacked the British Palaces and public buildings of all treasure, stripping the Iceni nobles of their estates and personal wealth formerly guaranteed to them by the Claudian Pact. To add to the infamy of the act, licentiousness ran rampant.[88] The two daughters of Queen Boadicea, widow of Prasutagus, were publicly raped and Boadicea was whipped. The Menai massacre, already referred to, followed closely on the heels of this bestiality. These combined monstrosities infuriated the British beyond restraint.[89] Their anger swept the length and breadth of the Island with the frenzy of a vendetta. The Roman writers graphically reported that the Roman generals and soldiery alike were stunned with the avalanche of British reaction. In fright the Romans confined their forces within their own encampments.

Despite the fact that the Iceni and the Coraniaid were branded as traitors for deserting Caractacus during the Claudian campaign, these atrocities brought the British clans together in a solid phalanx. The British Queen Boadicea, inflamed by the personal indignities perpetrated upon her daughters and her people, rose in militant defiance to avenge the insults. Her warriors swarmed around her eager for the fray. She was

---

[88] Tacitus, *Annals*, 14:31.
[89] Tacitus, *Annal,s* 14:31-35.

to lead them into battle with a devastating offensive that has caused her name to flame throughout British history as the finest embodiment of Britannia.

To this day Britannia is displayed on the face of British coins in the form of a woman.

Boadicea, the British name meaning Victoria, was a cousin of Claudia Pudens, thus closely related to both Caractacus and Arviragus.

To Arviragus Boadicea sent Venusius, the Pendragon of the Iceni, in an urgent appeal, offering to place the combined forces of the Iceni and Coraniaid under his command. Whether he accepted or not is unstated, probably because the historic record is overshadowed by the brilliant stature of the valorous Queen. We do know that her own Pendragon, Venusius, led the two warrior tribes, but only as second-in-command. Boadicea was the Commander-in-Chief and led her warriors personally into battle. Boadicea was a born warrior chieftainess, undoubtedly the greatest warrior Queen in all history. She had acquired her name, Victoria, by her valour in former military campaigns. Boadicea had always despised the Romans, now she hated them with a chilling bitterness that hungered for vengeance. Historians tell us that in appearance she was a most dramatic, striking figure. The Roman writer, Cassius Dio Cocceianus, states:

'Boadicea ascended the general's tribunal; her stature exceeded the ordinary height of women; her appearance itself carried terror; her aspect was calm and collected, but her voice became deep and pitiless. Her hair falling in long golden tresses as low as her hips, was collected round her forehead by a golden coronet; she wore a tartan dress fitting closely to the bosom, but below the waist expanding in loose folds as a gown; over it was a chlamys, or military cloak. In her hand she bore a spear.'[90]

Such is the portrait of the majestic Boadicea, as she stood surrounded by the 120,000 warriors who had responded to her blazing call for vengeance. To them she delivered an address as challenging and to be as immortal as the one given by her famous relative, Caractacus, before the Roman Senate. Cassius Dio records this address as follows:

---

[90] *Xiphilinus Excerpta*, p. 176.

'I appeal to thee a woman. I rule not, like Nitocris, over beasts of burden, as are the effeminate nations of the East, nor like Semiramis, over tradesmen and traffickers, nor like the man-woman Nero, over slaves and eunuchs – such is the precious knowledge these foreigners introduce among us – but I rule over Britons, little versed in craft and diplomacy, but born and trained in the game of war, men who, in the cause of liberty stake down their lives, the lives of their wives and children, their lands and property. Queen of such a race, I implore thine aid for freedom, for victory over enemies infamous for the wantonness of the wrongs they inflict, for their perversion of justice, for their contempt of religion, for their insatiable greed; a people that revel in unmanly pleasures, whose affections are more to be dreaded and abhorred than their enmity. Never let a foreigner bear rule over me or these my countrymen; never let slavery reign in this island. Be thou forever O goddess of manhood and victory, sovereign and Queen in Britain.'

Having exhorted her followers, the famous Boadicean war began in AD 60. Always in the fore, fiercely inspiring her warriors, Boadicea, with her two daughters riding beside her, led her armies from one devastating victory to another, the scythes on the wheels of her war chariot slashing deep into the enemy lines. Colchester was the first to fall. The Temple, fortified by Roman veterans, held out two days; then disaster overtook them. The Ninth Legion, under Petilius Cerealis, was slaughtered at Coggeshall. Cerealis and a few horsemen were the only ones to escape. The Roman headquarters at Verulam was burnt to the ground and its defenders cut to pieces. It seems as though nothing could stop the furious onslaughts of the British Queen. The Roman populace fled in terror on news of her armed approach. Tacitus states that one Roman Legion that dared to stand ground was cut down to the last man.[91] Her forces had by then swelled to the enormous number of 230,000, clearly indicating that more than the two clans were supporting her punitive cause. It can be fairly assumed that the Silurians, under Arviragus, were participating in this concerted action, since the field of battle had extended into their territory. We do know that the powerful Trinobantes, the warlike clan with whom Julius Caesar signed the Peace Pact of September 26th, 54 BC, had cast in their lot with Boadicea.

---

[91] Tacitus, *Annals*, 14:32.

Tacitus declared that the Silurian state alone had inflicted one defeat after another upon the Romans. Now with at least four of the most powerful warrior clans in Britain massed together under the one standard of baneful vengeance to the number of more than a quarter of a million, there is no need for wonder why the Romans were swept ruthlessly before them. Never before had the British been so deeply wounded and angered by the violation of their native privileges, their religious institutions and personal dignity. The desecration charged them with superhuman determination to avenge. Tacitus reports that over 80,000 Roman soldiers perished in these sanguinary battles, and Catus Decianus, terrified by the violence of the conflict and the horrible carnage he witnessed, took flight, escaping into Gaul.

The greatest single carnage followed the attack on London. At that time it was a populous city, the trade centre in Britain for international commerce. It was filled with Roman merchants and was protected by a powerful Roman garrison.

The assault and destruction of the city is one of the most appalling war records one can read. It was little short of a massacre and shows how intense was the merciless British fury, steeped in a hatred so unnatural to the general British character. Some may consider the quarterless slaughter performed by the British in the Boadicean campaign as unwarranted and diametrically opposed to Christian principles. One should remember, however, that since the Claudian Edict for Christian extermination, beginning AD 42, up to and including the Boadicean war of AD 60, the people and the land of Britain had suffered a persecution at the hands of the Romans for eighteen years which no other nation had experienced. Their towns, religious institutions, libraries and seats of cultural learning had been burnt to the ground with a barbaric insolence unequalled. The defenceless had been massacred. Licentiousness, pillage and plunder of wealth, crops and cattle had been conducted unabated in the vicious Roman pledge to crush the Christian faith and spirit in Britain. People can stand only so much, then anger gets the better of them, often leading to what we may term an excess of violence. The British were only paying the Romans back in their own barbaric coin and unquestionably they saved Christianity for posterity with the sacrifice of their lives and property.

Some historians claim that Suetonius Paulinus, Commander-in-Chief of the Roman forces, terrified at the determined onslaught on London, fled the scene with a few of his troops. This is hardly conceivable. The chroniclers report that the battle for supremacy waged savagely for several days, indicating that the British encountered organized military resistance. Paulinus probably made good his escape when he saw the battle was lost, leaving the destruction of the city, its inhabitants and such Legionaries that remained to the sword of the pitiless British.

Tacitus states that 40,000 of the Roman defenders of London and its inhabitants were put to the sword and the city to the torch.

Next, Boadicea levelled the important city of Verulam, now St. Albans, driving the enemy before her. Such of the inhabitants of Regnum and Rutupium as could, fled before her armies arrived. It is said that the destruction of lives on both sides was so great that the burning towns and cities were quenched in blood. The British Amazon swept westward in an effort to intercept Paulinus. Dion reports many battles fought with the heavy balance of disaster borne upon the Romans. The climax to the victorious Boadicean war ended in a most unpredictable manner in the Midlands, AD 62, very probably near Mancetter in Warwickshire. The contesting armies had met in a savage conflict that was fought from dawn to darkness, with the battle swaying in favour of one side then the other. As dusk set in a section of the British army, led by Boadicea, was separated from the main body. Believing herself trapped and fearing capture (even though the record states the British forces had reorganized, preparatory to a final major assault), rather than fall into the hands of the despoilers and the rapine she knew would follow, the valorous Queen Boadicea, in a last gesture of defiance, committed suicide on the field of battle. As the tragic news swept through the ranks of both sides, it is recorded that Briton and Roman alike were stunned with the calamity of this extraordinary climax. Fighting immediately ceased with each side withdrawing into their own encampment with unbidden consent. The death of this great British queen settled like a pall over all. The woman who had terrified the Romans in life awed them in death. A great sadness descended upon her people. And the Romans, quick to seize an opportunity, took advantage of the situation to come to peace terms with the Iceni.

Under the terms of this new Peace Pact the Romans restored all the confiscated wealth of the royalty, the nobles and the people. The stolen estates were returned to the surviving members of the royal household and to the nobility with all their original privileges. The treacherous transaction of Seneca was cancelled and an heavy indemnity was paid to the Iceni.

How truly the Roman historian wrote: 'Every peace with the British was a signature of defeat.'

The royal Boadicea, majestic in appearance, rich in eloquence, dauntless in war, endowed with the military genius which for two years had outmatched the ablest strategists of Rome, drove their Legions before her arms like sheep to the slaughter. The British heroine who preferred death rather than sacrifice her freedom, a warrior queen with no equal in the colourful pages of history, the avenger of womanly indignities, a champion of the Christian faith, was now no more than a glorious memory.

The Romans wrote that her funeral obsequies were the most magnificent ever bestowed on a monarch. So lavish in pomp and assemblage they gazed in wonder on its splendour, awed and silenced in both shame and fear. Her unhappy death, though spectacular, was an incomparable sacrifice for the preservation of the ancient British freedoms for which she stood.

Boadicea's monumental record is immortalized and enshrined in the magnificent statue erected on Westminster Bridge to her memory. It is one of the finest statues to be seen anywhere in the world. Everyone who views it is impressed with its illustrious majesty. It is created exactly as the ancient Roman writer, Cassius Dio Cocceianus, described her. She stands erect, spear in one hand, and with the other hand holding in check the two rearing chargers, coronet on her brow, with her long hair flowing to the breeze. Her two daughters are kneeling beside her on the floor of her war chariot. Her noble features proudly portray the cast of her fearless character. On the wheels of her chariot are shown the terrible scythes, which were a deadly, slashing war weapon peculiar to the British armaments, dreaded by the Romans.

The sculptor who executed the statuary was truly inspired with the commission. It depicts Christian Britannia on the shores of England, defying the evil powers of the world.

The scene of battle and its tragedy over the centuries are commemorated by place names known to this day as 'Cop Paulinus', 'Hill of Arrows', 'Hill of Carnage', 'Hollow of No Quarter', 'Hollow of Woe', 'Hollow of Execution', 'Field of the Tribunal', 'Knoll of the Melee'. On the scene still exists a monolith called 'The Stone of Lamentation', described as the spot where the great Queen took her life.

On the road to Caerwys was 'The Stone of the Grave of Boadicea', since moved to Downing.

The conflict against the Romans did not cease with her death. The Roman peace made with the Iceni had no effect on other British clans. It is written that her tragic death did not abate the punitive spirit and campaigning determination of the Britons in the north and the west. Under the invincible leadership of Arviragus, Venusius, and the gallant new Pendragon, Galgacus,[92] hostilities vigorously continued against the Romans.

To all this calamity Joseph and his missionary co-workers were sorrowful spectators. But through it all they glimpsed triumph, strong in their faith that the Cause of Christ was safe for all time in the embattled Island realm. Greater sacrifice and heroism was yet to be suffered for Christian welfare but the Flag of Christ was never to dip to any pagan power.

In Pynson's metrical *Life of St. Joseph*, the following lines occur referring to the death of Mary, the Mother of Jesus:

'So after Hyr Assumpcyn, the boke telleth playne;
With Saynt Phylyp he went into France.
Phylyp bad them go to Great Brytayn fortunate.'

These lines inform us that after the death of Mary, Joseph returned to Gaul with Philip, his dearest friend. The last line rather implies that Philip was fortunate in prevailing on Joseph to return to Britain. This would suggest that Joseph, bowed in sorrow, was loath to part from the man who was so close to him that he could understand his grief. Knowing that work was the best antidote for sorrow, Philip urged his friend to return to his mission in Britain where he was so greatly needed. Not only was Philip fortunate in persuading Joseph; Britain was fortunate to receive him back.

It will be noticed that the word 'them' is employed in the last line. Who were 'them'? The word is plural. The answer is provided in the *Magna tabula Glastoniensis*, cited by Bishop Ussher. Every time Joseph went to Gaul he returned with more missionary helpers. On this occasion we are told that among them was his son Josephes, whom Philip had baptized. How long Josephes stayed in Britain with his father is not

---

[92] Tacitus, *Agricola*, 30-32.

stated, but from various records it is quite evident that the son of Joseph journeyed as an emissary between Gaul and Britain. Facts show that Josephes returned to Gaul after arriving in Britain with his father at Philip's request. Joseph remained in Britain as the head of the missionary band at Avalon. In the year AD 60 special mention is made of Joseph going to Gaul and returning to Britain with another band of recruits, among whom is particularly mentioned Simon Zelotes, one of the original twelve disciples of Christ. This is the second time it is specially mentioned that Philip consecrated Joseph and his band of co-workers prior to embarking for Britain. Probably the inclusion of Simon Zelotes indicated an important missionary effort, hence the consecration. This was the second journey to Britain for Simon Zelotes and his last. According to Cardinal Baronius and Hippolytus, Simon's first arrival in Britain was in the year AD 44, during the Claudian war. Evidently his stay was short, as he returned to the continent.

Nicephorus, Patriarch of Constantinople, and Byzantine historian, AD 758-829, writes:

'Simon born in Cana of Galilee who for his fervent affection for his Master and great zeal that he showed by all means to the Gospel, was surnamed Zelotes, having received the Holy Ghost from above, travelled through Egypt, and Africa, then through Mauretania and all Lybia, preaching the Gospel. And the same doctrine he taught to the Occidental Sea, and the Isles called Britanniae.'[93]

In the Bible Simon is often referred to as Simon the Canaanite, because he came from Cana. The Hebrew word for 'zealous' has a similar sound to that of the name of his home town, being 'canna'. The Greek translation of the word is 'Zelotes', the name by which he is best known. His enthusiastic preaching of the Word earned him his zealous surname.

Simon arrived in Britain during the first year of the Boadicean war, AD 60, when the whole Island was convulsed in a deep, burning anger against the Romans, which was never equalled before or after in the long years of conflict between the two nations. Tacitus states that from AD 59 to 62 the brutalities of war were at their worst. Atrocities occurred on both sides but the Romans carried their vicious perpetrations to such an extent that even Rome was shocked. Bearing this in mind we can readily

---

[93] See also Dorotheus, *Synopsis de Apostol.*

understand that any Christian evangelizing outside the British shield would be fraught with imminent danger. At all times the disciples of Christ were oblivious to danger, but when the pressure became too severe invariably they fled the land until matters quietened down. In the year AD 44 a Claudian Edict expelled the Christian leaders from Rome. Many of them sought sanctuary in Britain. Among those who fled to Britain from Rome was Peter.[94] This was the year Simon first went to Britain. He did not come from Rome but from Gaulwhere he had been assisting Philip. Moreover, Simon was directly associated with the Arimathean Mission of Avalon on both his missionary efforts in Britain. As we shall later see it made quite a difference to the British in their acceptance of him whether the missionary came from Rome or Jerusalem.

Simon was unusually bold and fearless, as his surname implies. In spite of the volcanic turmoil seething through Britain during the Boadicean war, Simon openly defied the barbaric Edict of Paulinus, and the most brutal Catus Decianus, to destroy anything and anyone Christian. He decided to conduct his evangelizing campaign in the eastern part of the Island. This section of Britain was the most sparsely inhabited by the native Britons and consequently more heavily populated by the Romans. It was far beyond the strong protective shield of the Silurian arms in the south and the powerful northern Yorkshire Celts. In this dangerous territory Simon was definitely on his own. Undeterred, with infinite courage, he began preaching the Christian Gospel right in the heart of the Roman domain. His fiery sermons brought him speedily to the attention of Catus Decianus, but not before he had sown the seed of Christ in the hearts of Britons and many Romans who, despite the unremitting hatred of Decianus for all that was Christian, held the secret of the truth locked in their hearts.

The evangelizing mission of Simon was short-lived. He was finally arrested under the orders of Catus Decianus. As usual his trial was a mockery. He was condemned to death and was crucified by the Romans at Caistor, Lincolnshire, and there buried, *circa* May 10th, AD 61.

The day of the martyrdom of Simon Zelotes, the devoted disciple of Christ, is officially celebrated by the eastern and western church on May 10th and so recorded in the Greek Menology. Cardinal Baronius, in his *Annales Ecclesiastici*, gives the same date in describing the martyrdom and burial of Simon Zelotes in Britain.

---

[94] Cornelius à Lapide, *Argumentum Epistolae St. Pauli di Romanos*, ch. 16.

Of Simon Zelotes, Dorotheus, Bishop of Tyre, AD 300, writes in his work *Synopsis de Apostol*:

'Simon Zelotes traversed all Mauretania, and the region of the Africans, preaching Christ. He was at last crucified, slain and buried in Britain.'

There are some who think because Simon Zelotes perished in Britain he must have been slain by the British. This could not be at all possible. Only the Romans practised crucifixion. In the first place this form of death was reserved as a gesture of contempt in executing their meanest criminals. During the Christian era it was more viciously employed on the Christians in defiant mockery of all the Cross stood for to all Christians. To the British, and indeed to all Christians, crucifixion was a profanity of the Cross. The historic record leaves no doubt as to who crucified Simon Zelotes.

Some also entertain the belief that Simon Zelotes was the first British Christian martyr. Of the elect, he was the second British martyr. Aristobulus, brother of Barnabas and father-in-law of Peter, was the first to be martyred in Britain. Aristobulus preceded Simon to his reward at what is now St. Albans by a couple of years. The record states he was martyred 'in the second year of Nero'. This would be *circa* AD 59.

Unknown to many, the remains of Simon Zelotes, with many more of the saintly elect, are buried in England, creating the saying uttered the world over, 'Britain, the most hallowed ground on earth.'

The year before the Boadicean war and the two years of its existence, admitted by Rome to be marked with unparalleled horror, are the darkest, most bloodstained years in British history through Roman infamy. Yet they are epic years in British Christian annals, resplendent with noble sacrifice and heroic deeds, outmatching the terror and stark tragedy those years contained. To this notable period the martyrdom of Simon Zelotes added lustre in his last devotional act in serving his Master, with Whom he first walked on the shores of Galilee.

Nearby where this noble martyr perished was the ancestral home of Abraham Lincoln, the great American Christian President. His ancestors migrated from England in the first waves of English colonists to settle in Virginia. The church in which Lincoln worshipped was made an American sanctuary by patriotic, Christian-minded American soldiers of World War II. They made various beautiful contributions to this ancient little church at Boston, Lincolnshire, to the memory of the family, particularly to their illustrious American descendant.

Eighteen hundred years after the martyrdom of Simon Zelotes, in the land of the Lincolns, in America, Abraham Lincoln became a martyr for his humane Christian principles, the same principles which Simon Zelotes taught, for which he was crucified and gave his all in the glorious service of his beloved Jesus.

CHAPTER 15

THE GLORIOUS CAVALCADE

HUMAN nature can be very perverse on occasion, being completely oblivious to experience and sound judgment. It is surprising to hear of people with intelligence so easily victimized by suave tongues and extravagant claims deliberately conceived to misinform and misguide. This human weakness might possibly indicate that people are more prone to accept fiction than truth. Perhaps this is what has given rise to the old slogan that 'truth is stranger than fiction'. To such an extent does this condition exist that truth becomes a matter of serious education in constant conflict to disprove the untruthful who are ever seeking to prove their spurious claims.

Christians are so indoctrinated with the scriptural apostolic records, rightfully, that they would never dream of arguing the point that the Apostles preached Christ in Jerusalem, Egypt, Greece, Rome and Asia, but to mention that they taught in Britain is to tax their credulity. To state that Christianity was brought first to Britain is almost to have them inquire as to the state of one's mental health. The average person is so well inoculated with the belief that Christianity was first established by the Roman Catholic Church at Rome, and that Britain first received the faith through St. Augustine, AD 597, that they take it for granted.

Incredulity is quickly dissipated when one asks, what happened to Christian teaching during the centuries that followed the death of Christ, to the establishment of the Roman Catholic Church in the fourth century? This church was not founded until years after the death of Constantine the Great. Then there is the period that followed to the time when Augustine arrived in Britain.

One has but to turn the pages of the Bible and ask what became of most of the original Apostles, on whose lives Scripture is silent. Where did the unrecorded ones go and where did they die? What of the seventy elect and the following one hundred and twenty elected in Christ and the many that followed, stemming from the teachings of the original Christian multitude?

The biblical travel record of the elect is but briefly given. They all had to be somewhere and achievement certainly followed the sowing of the seed, otherwise where did the Roman Catholic Church obtain the substance to found its own organization? It is only in recent years that the Roman Catholic Church began to scoff at the British record and its claim to priority, but they are 'hoist upon their own petard'. For nineteen hundred years the Roman Catholic Church was the stoutest champion of British priority. It is futile at this later date for them to dispute priority and apostolic succession. The mass of documentary evidence supplied by their greatest ecclesiastics and historians, and even the Popes, substantiates the facts, refuting all modern challenge. For fifteen hundred years the Popes and the ecclesiastical councils sustained British priority whenever it was challenged. For more than six hundred years after the founding of Avalon by Joseph, until the time of the famous Oaks' conference, and the equally famed Whitby Council, when the first official cleavage took place between the two churches, the British and the Roman church existed as sister churches, with Britain accepted as the elder sister, for approximately three hundred years. Though the British church steadfastly refused to recognize the recently instituted authority of the Pope, AD 610, flatly denying the worship of Mary or the use of the term 'Mother of God', proclaimed by the Roman church AD 431, at the Council of Ephesus, or the doctrine of Purgatory, established by Gregory the Great about the year AD 593, they shared the same communion. The Mass had not as then been developed. It was not introduced into the Roman church as an obligatory attendance until the eleventh century. The British church still retained its primitive interpretation of the Christ faith, vehemently declaring in the two councils mentioned that only Christ was the Head of the church and the only means of intercession between man and God, and with no recourse to Purgatory. Though the worship of images and material concepts were being introduced into the church through Roman influence, it still retained a great deal of the original primitive simplicity of worship.

The first six hundred years following the Passion of Christ can truly be called the Golden Age of Christianity, in spite of the fact that these centuries were saturated in drama, romance, tragedy and sacrifice.

The brief glimpse we have taken of the perilous wars and of the violence of the persecutions that swept the sea-girt Isle, leaves us in no doubt as to the invincible courage and unbendable determination of the Christian elect in carrying out the work of our Lord, regardless of consequences. In World War II we were daily thrilled with the heroic exploits of the patriots of the oppressed nations who comprised the Underground. Comparing this record with that of the Apostolic Crusaders of the Cross of that glorious era, the Christian heart must be thrilled through and through as we realize that theirs was no underground operation. Surrounded by evil foes and forces they walked openly into the midst of their enemies, declaring the Word with resonant voices to friend and foe alike, and only too often paying the supreme price, but fearlessly. The record tells us of an endless flow of men and women pouring into Avalon to be converted and baptized, then remaining for instruction to go forth preaching the Word in hostile territory and replacing the glorious ones who had fallen.

Some idea of how great was the multitude of converts who remained for instruction can be gleaned from the record which states that from Gaul alone Philip sent a total of a hundred and sixty disciples to assist Joseph and his companions.[95] That there were others that came from other sources we know, apart from the mission that formed the second church in Britain, sent by St. Paul into Wales. Their fiery zeal was kept aflame by the frequent arrival of others of the Lord's original Apostles, who stayed awhile before setting forth into other lands. Not all of the Bethany band that arrived at Avalon stayed on with Joseph. Some of the most illustrious of his companions he sent back into different parts of Gaul to assist Philip in founding churches, as others qualified to take over their place on the Isle of Avalon.

The first man to be sent back to Gaul by Joseph was Lazarus, but not before the man whom Jesus had raised from the dead had left his timeless imprint on Britain in the work he wrote outlining his rules for living the Christian life. In Celtic *MSS.* they are known as *The Triads of Lazarus*. No better memorial could he have left to prove his identity with Britain. Nowhere else are his laws recorded and nowhere else but in Britain was the word 'Triad' employed, not even in Gaul. The word is Celtic for Law. The Triads of Lazarus are still preserved in the ancient Celtic records of Britain.

He went direct to Marseilles, where he had first arrived at Gaul in the drifting boat with Joseph, and their other companions.

Roger of Hovedon, writing of Marseilles, remarks:

'Marseilles is an episcopal city under the domination of the King of Aragon. Here are the relics of St. Lazarus, the brother of St. Mary Magdalene and Martha, who held the Bishopric for seven years.'

---

[95] Capgrave, John (1393-1464), *De Sancto Joseph ab Arimathea,* quoting an ancient manuscript and the *Book of the Holy Grail.*

The ancient church records at Lyons confirm the same facts:

'Lazarus returned to Gaul from Britain to Marseilles, taking with him Mary Magdalene and Martha. He was the first appointed Bishop. He died there seven years later.'

It is further stated that Lazarus was Bishop of Cyprus before he made the voyage to Britain. This would indicate he was teaching at Cyprus, before the exodus from Judea, AD 36, and having returned to Judea became a member of the Bethany group who occupied the oarless boat on that fateful voyage. He was the first Bishop of Marseilles and built the first church on the site where the present cathedral stands.[96] In the few years he lived to teach at Marseilles he founded other churches. His zealous preaching and kindly disposition left a deep impress in Gaul, to such an extent that he is better remembered in France than is Philip, regardless of the latter's long sojourn in Gaul. In many quarters he is regarded as the Apostle of Gaul and his relics are greatly treasured to this day. At Marseilles, Lyons, Aix, St. Maximin, La Sainte Baume and other places there still remain numerous monuments, liturgies, relics and traditions to his immortal memory. He was the first of the original Bethany band associated with Joseph to die. As the records state he died a natural death seven years after returning to Marseilles. His stay in Britain is reported to have been short, which would place the date of his death between AD 44 and 45.

An interesting report was published in the London *Morning Post*, May 28th, 1923, marking the date of the annual pilgrimage of the French gypsies to St. Maries de la Mer at the mouth of the Rhone. Their tradition maintains that the barque of Lazarus came ashore there with three holy women who remained. From time immemorial to present times the French gypsies make their annual pilgrimage to this sacred spot to venerate the relics of Marie Salome, Marie Jacobs and in particular their black servant, Sara. Mary Salome was another member of the original Josephian band who had been sent forth to preach the Word, known in the British record as St. Salome. Her two other women companions were probably among the unrecorded converts who went to aid St. Salome on her mission. Evidently, as the name suggests, Marie

---

[96] J. Burr, *Remarkable Biblical Characters*. See Taylor, J. W. *The Coming of the Saints*, p. 239, for the inscription in the Church of St. Victor.

Jacob was also a Judean refugee who had drifted to Gaul and Britain. Mention of the black Sara is quite interesting. At odd intervals her name crops up, and in each case shows she was held in special esteem. We note that while the French gypsies made their annual pilgrimage to the spot to venerate the memory of the three women missionaries, Sara, the black maid, is the one to whom they paid especial consideration.

As will be seen by the record it is stated that Mary Magdalene and Martha went with Lazarus from Britain to Marseilles to begin their missionary work in Gaul.[97] There is an interesting statement made by one of the early Bishops of Mayence who said, referring to the many arriving in Gaul from Britain, that each went forth to specially appointed places in Gaul, where they taught and founded churches. Under the direction of St. Philip each followed out their particular assignment in the service of our Lord. Consequently we can understand why Mary Magdalene and Martha did not remain at Marseilles with Lazarus. Martha, the practically minded head of the Bethany household, which had been the favourite resting-place of Jesus and point of assembly for His disciples at Bethany during His Mission, was directed to Arles. With her went the faithful handmaid, Marcella. Martha did not remain long there. Trophimus was sent to Gaul by Joseph and, under the direction of Philip, replaced Martha at Arles. He was consecrated the first Bishop of Arles and there performed an outstanding service. He was energetic, practical and an intelligent organizer. His Christianizing endeavours embraced a large area which formed the district of Narbonne. He became the first Metropolitan of the Narbonne, with Arles as his Bishopric. For centuries it continued to be a prominent stronghold of the Christian faith in Gaul.

Martha and Marcella moved to Tarascon where they settled, spending the rest of their lives preaching, teaching and administering. They both died a natural death, Martha being the first of the two to pass on to her everlasting reward. The record states, 'Marcella was with Martha at her death.' A few years later Marcella, the faithful handmaiden of the glorious Bethany sisters, and their brother Lazarusentered into her well-deserved rest. She, too, had waited on the Lord in the pleasant Bethany home in Judea. She had seen the miracle performed on Lazarus and watched the Crucifixion. Her devotion to her mistresses had carried her with them to Gaul, thence to Britain, and back

---

[97] The identity of Magdalene with Mary of Bethany is a subject of controversy, but the French Church regards them as one.

again to Gaul where she helped Martha to plant the Cross of Christ and nurture it with their love.

The early records show Maximin, Eutropius, Trophimus and Parmena leaving Britain for Gaul, joining with those already mentioned. Parmena is not listed among the original companions of Joseph at Avalon. The other three are named among the twelve companions. As we have seen, Trophimus joined with Martha at Arles, where she later left for Tarascon. Maximin is described as joining with Mary Magdalene at Aix where both spent out their life. Both died a natural death. Maximin was the first Bishop of Aix, and there are found numerous memorials and relics of Maximin, and particularly of Mary Magdalene. The area is saturated with her memory. Mary's classic beauty and her rich voice, extolled in reverence and pleasure by all who knew her, endeared her so deeply to the hearts of the people among whom she laboured that she was adored as a Saint before she died. Her undying devotion to her Lord throbbed through her teachings of the Word. The most hardened soul melted to her preaching, and she converted, as we are told, 'multitudes to the faith'. The ancient documents resound with her glory.

One, if not the most outstanding document treating of her life, was written by the famed Maurus Rabanus, Archbishop of Mayence,[98] AD 776-856, *Life of Mary Magdalene*. This precious *MS.* is owned by Oxford University, where it is preserved and treasured in the College Library bearing her name, the Magdalen College Library. There are many manuscripts older than the Rabanus *MSS.*, some written about the same time, but none as illuminating. In his Prologue the eminent Archbishop states that his information was written 'according to the accounts that our fathers have left us in their writings'.

In his work he supports all the earlier records of the gathering in Gaul, the Josephian entourage arriving in Britain, confirming the date. He tells of the many of Joseph's companions returning to Gaul to preach and teach. He writes:

'Therefore the chief, St. Maximus, the blessed Parmenas, the arch deacon Trophimus and Eutropius, bishops, and the rest of the leaders of his Christian warfare, together with the God-renowned Mary Magdalene and her sister, the most blessed Martha, departed by way of the sea ... They came near to the city of Marseilles, in the

---

[98] Mainz.

Viennoise province of the Gauls, where the river Rhone is received by the sea. There, having called upon God, the great King of all the world, they parted, each company going to the province where the Holy Spirit had directed them, presently preaching everywhere, "the Lord with them", and confirmed the Word with signs following.'

Eutropius was the first Bishop of Aquitaine.

Here we have eight of the original Josephian band that arrived in Britain back in Gaul, after receiving their final instructions from Joseph, who consecrated them before they left the sacred Isle of Avalon.

Some are inclined to think that Marie Jacob, one of the three venerated women to whom the French gypsies paid reverence at St. Maries de la Mer, was none other than the Mary Cleopas, recorded in the British Bethany band. It is quite possible. We note in the biblical records that names are changed and interchanged. Mary was the wife of the Roman whom Jesus converted. Since there is no record of him, following the exodus, he probably had died, in which case it was not uncommon for a woman to revert to her ancestral family name. Being a Judean and a near relative of the Virgin Mary, her claim could be of the family branch of Jacob, and so be known as Mary Jacob. If this is the case, this would make nine of the original Bethany band sent forth by Joseph to preach and found missions and churches in Gaul.

The Gaulish and Celtic chronicles affirm that most of the ancient French Bishoprics were founded by the companions of Joseph, other Culdees and former neophytes, all stemming from the sacred sanctuary at Avalon. Sidonis, Saturninus and Cleon are reported as teaching in Gaul on various occasions, supporting other missionaries and returning to Britain. Joseph also contributed in like manner and his name is well associated with the founding of the church at Morlaix and Limoges.

It is stated that St. Martial, of the elect twelve, was the only one who never left Avalon to go abroad. He remained throughout his lifetime converting and teaching neophytes, as the right hand of Joseph.[99] In the same report it is interesting to note the statement that with Martial there remained at Avalon his parents, Marcellus and Elizabeth, and also St. Zacchaeus. The mention of the latter three names proves the illustrious assemblage of faithful Judeans finally domiciled in

---

[99] An old French cantique, or song, refers to *Eutrope et Martial, Sidonie avec Joseph*. See Taylor, J. W. *The Coming of the Saints*. (Available from the Covenant Publishing Company Ltd.)

Britain, aiding Joseph at Avalon in his great work while great battles between Britons and Romans were being fought around them. From time to time we find other Judeans, many relatives of the twelve disciples of Jesus, arriving at the sacred stronghold in Britain, bending their efforts in the evangelizing mission.

Parmena, who accompanied Maximin, Eutropius and Trophimus into Gaul from Britain, was a disciple of Joseph. He was appointed the first Bishop of Avignon. Drennalus was also a disciple of Joseph.

He first went to Gaul in company with Joseph to found the church at Morlaix. This done, Joseph appointed Drennalus to Treguier, where he remained after being installed as the first Bishop of Treguier.

The British crusaders in Christ were not limited to GaulThey journeyed into other lands founding missions and erecting churches. Three of Avalon's missionaries were responsible for founding the three great mother churches in Gaul, Helvetia (Switzerland) and Lotharingia.

The illustrious Beatus, who founded the church in Helvetia, received his baptism and education at Avalon. He was the wealthy son of a prominent British noble, his pre-baptismal name being Suetonius. It is of interest to note that Beatus was baptized at Avalon by St. Barnabas, the brother of Aristobulus, sent in advance by St. Paul to Britain to represent the Apostle to the Gentiles. In the scriptural record he is referred to as Joses, the Levite, who changed his name to Barnabas, meaning 'Son of Consolation', the same Barnabas who, together with St. Paul, founded the church at Antioch, AD 43 (*Acts* 11:22). Barnabas combined with St. Paul, Joseph and his brother in expanding the church in Britain, particularly in Wales. His stays were short but effective. It was on one of these excursions into Britain, after his brother Aristobulus[100] was martyred, that he baptized the noble Beatus who, on finishing his novitiate, was consecrated a Bishop. He selected Helvetia as his missionary field. Before he left Britain he disposed of all his wealth and used it to ransom prisoners of war on the continent, making his headquarters at Underseven (Unterseen) on Lake Thun. Beatus introduced Christianity into Switzerland, erecting hospitals and churches, building a band of devoted missionaries who continued his great work throughout the centuries. It was in the humble dwelling he first built on his arrival in Helvetia that he spent his last days. He died in his cell, AD 96. This ancient cell is preserved and can be seen today on the shore of Lake Thun. The Venerable Bede and Cardinal Alford

[100] St. Ado, Archbishop of Vienne, *Adonis Martyrologia*, March 17.

mention his noble missionary work in their writings, and he is commemorated in the *Roman Martyrologies*.

Another extraordinary British zealot who graduated from Avalon was Mansuetus. He went to Glastonbury (Avalon) from Hibernia (Ireland) where he was born, a member of the Celtic aristocracy. His evangelistic career was profoundly notable. He had journeyed to Avalon three years before the Claudian campaign began and according to Arnold Mirmannus, Mansuetus was converted and baptized by Joseph, AD 40. At Avalon he became closely associated with the intrepid St. Clement, also forming a great friendship with St. Peter, when he sought sanctuary in Britain, AD 44. Only death was to break these enduring connections. Later he was sent to Rome with St. Clement on his first mission. On the request of St. Philip he went to Gaul where he founded the great Lotharingian Church, frequently referred to as the Mother Church of Gaul. Cardinal Alford, in *Regia Fides Britannica*, writes that Mansuetus was consecrated the first Bishop of the Lotharingians AD 49, with his See at Toul. He also founded the church at Lorraine. His missionary zeal was indefatigable. He travelled far and wide, meeting a great number of the original Apostles and disciples of Christ, with whom he laboured. Probably for this reason he is referred to as 'the friend of all the disciples, and their pupil', and as 'a disciple of St. Peter'. Mansuetus had mingled with the royal Silurian families while at Avalon, therefore it is but natural to know he was a constant visitor at the Palace of the British at Rome after Claudia had married Pudens. He was a friend of Linus, the first Bishop of Rome and brother of Claudia. After the death of St. Clement, Mansuetus became the third official Bishop of the British Church at Rome. Thus we have three disciples of Avalon, instructed by St. Joseph, to become, in succession, Bishops of Rome. Mansuetus extended his preaching into Illyria, where he was martyred AD 110, thirty years before the last member of the royal family of Claudia Pudens was slain. This record is reported in *Mersaeus De Sanctis Germaniae* and confirmed by L'Abbé Guillaume.[101]

The Natal Day of Mansuetus is given in the *Gallican Martyrologies* as September 3rd.

The eminent St. Clement, in the British Bethany record named St. Clemens, was another outstanding British missionary, stemming from Avalon, and the friend of Mansuetus, already referred to, with whom he

---

[101] L'Abbé Guillaume, *L'Apostolat de S. Manouel*, p. 38.

was associated in the early evangelizing of Illyria. He perished long before Mansuetus received his martyrdom. St. Clement succeeded Linus as the second Bishop of Rome. In this document there is a curious record of succession which states: 'Clemens became Bishop twelve years after Linus.'

Iltigius, in *De Patribus Apostolicis*, quotes St. Peter as saying:

'Concerning the Bishops who have been ordained in our life time, we make known to you that they are these. Of Antioch, Eudoius, ordained by me, Peter. Of the Church of Rome, Linus, son of Claudia[102], was first ordained by Paul, and after Linus's death, Clemens the second, ordained by me, Peter.'[103]

In every case but one the records of succession as given above have all agreed that Clement was the second Bishop. The one exception states that Cletus succeeded Linus and agrees that Clement followed twelve years after Linus was martyred, as the third Bishop of Rome. While the twelve-year gap is commonly sustained, yet all other references place Linus, Clement and Mansuetus as first, second and third, and with no mention of Cletus. My conclusion in the case is that Cletus, functioning in the British church at Rome, along with the children of Claudia Pudens, was not in an official capacity due to the grave Christian disturbance at that time. The three related were officially appointed by apostolic consecration. After Clement was lodged in Rome he became known as Clemens Romanus and is the one referred to by St. Paul in his Epistle.[104] All records state he was ordained by St. Peter.

The life and works of St. Clement are referred to in the Oxford edition of Junius in *Son of Claudia*, and by Iltigius.

Another noble Briton, born to the Silurian purple, was Marcellus. He received his conversion and baptism at Avalon, a number of years after Joseph had passed on to his eternal rest, by the hands of those who followed. He also went to Gauland there founded the church at Tongres, being its first Bishop. He later founded the princely archbishopric at Tréves, over which he ruled. For centuries this diocese dominated the Gallican church. Some records confuse this Marcellus as being the

---

[102] Publisher's note: there is some ambiguity in the sources concerning whether Linus was the brother of or the son of Claudia. (See p.122 for the children of Claudia.)
[103] *Apostolic Constitutions*, 1:46.
[104] *Philippians* 4:3.

teacher of Linus before the latter went to Rome as one of the royal captives with his father Caractacus. This is a mistake, as the date is far too late. Linus was taught at Avalon by Marcellus, the father of Martial of the original Bethany band. Marsseus and Pantalin both state that Marcellus the Briton was martyred AD 166. The *Tungrensian Chronicles* confirm this fact.

The Gallic records state that for centuries the Archbishops of Tréves and Rheims were all Britons supplied by the mother church at Glastonbury-Avalon.

St. Cadval, another famed British missionary, going out from Glastonbury, founded the church of Tarentum, Italy, AD 170. The cathedral at Taranto is dedicated to him and his achievements are reported in the Vatican Catalogue of Saints.[105]

It is impossible to catalogue the list of devoted British disciples and missionaries who went out of Avalon to preach the Gospel in other lands. Their names are legion, many of them laying down their lives in the final sacrifice, to be buried in unknown graves in foreign lands. During the golden Christian era, centuries before the Roman Catholic Church was established, the British missionaries comprised the bulk of the Christian army of crusaders. They, more than any others, established the Christian faith on its firm foundation, and against the deadliest opposition and persecution on record. Their fiery zeal flamed across the known world like an unquenchable fire. As one fell a hundred more were ready to step into the martyr's footsteps proclaiming the faith with a challenging insistence.

Despite the fierce conflicts that raged throughout Britain against Roman tyranny, Avalon was ever a safe sanctuary for apostle or neophyte. To this hallowed haven many of our Lord's original disciples came: Lazarus, Barnabas, Zaccheus, James, Luke, Simon, Paul and Peter, of whom we have positive record, leaving only three not definitely chronicled, Matthew, Mark and John, though it is recorded that at the death of Mary all the living original band were present at her request. Their names were unmentioned in the record but we know Stephen and James, the brother of John, could not be present. Judas Iscariot had been banned on his betrayal of his Master and had committed suicide. Stephen was the first martyr, being stoned to death at Jerusalem, AD 33. James, brother of John, both sons of Zebedee, was

---

[105] *Moronus de Ecclesia Tarentina.*

beheaded AD 44,[106] by order of Herod Agrippa. The executioner of James was possibly Herod, King of the Chalcis, the father of Paul's companion and co-worker, Aristobulus.[107]

Of James the Just, the brother of Jesus, Flavius Dexter, quoting the ecclesiastical Benedictine historian, Cressy, in his Church *History of Brittany*, states: 'In the one and fortieth year of Christ (AD 41) St. James, returning out of Spain, visited Gaule and Britain.'

Other records confirm this date of his first visit to Britain, and some records claim he was present at the death of Mary at Avalon, AD 48. James was the first Bishop of Jerusalem, calling together the first Apostolic Church there. This is the first Council of the Appointed on record. The next Council was called by Constantine the Great, three hundred years later. James was closely associated with Paul, preaching to the Gentiles. While the record and his memorial tablet state he worked mostly among the Greeks, he is given credit for founding the Spanish Church.[108] One can readily note his great interest in working among the Gentiles by reading the *Acts of the Apostles*. In *Acts* 21:18 it tells how Paul meets James, the brother of Jesus, to whom he speaks of the great works God had wrought among the Gentiles by his ministry. The text in *Acts* 15:14 is of curious interest. James tells his brethren that Simeon had said, 'God at the first did visit the Gentiles, to take out of them a people for His name', and so had declared the prophets.

James was stoned to death at Jerusalem by the Jews nearby where Stephen met the same fate, AD 62, four years before Paul suffered martyrdom.[109]

Of St. Luke, Professor Smith in *Dictionary of Christian Biography*, says that St. Luke taught in Gaul, Dalmatia, Italy, Macedonia, principally in Gaul, and that he made frequent trips to Britain, visiting the sainted company at Avalon. The Rev. Morgan, in his marvellous work *The Saints in Britain*, gives a remarkably detailed insight into the travels and work of the apostles and disciples as they came in contact with Britain and laboured there.

Barnabas was to meet his death in Cyprus, where he was stoned to death. He was buried by St. Mark, his young kinsman, outside the city.

---

[106] *Acts* 12:1.
[107] Hewins, Prof. W. A. S. *The Royal Saints of Britain*, (London: Chiswick Press) 1929 p. 29.
[108] Sant Iago, Patron Saint of Spain.
[109] Josephus, *Antiquities*, xx, 9: 1.

The record says that, as he laid Barnabas in his grave, Mark placed on his breast a copy of the *Gospel of St. Matthew*.

Each life is a part of the indestructible chain of 'The Way', welded link by link by the unswerving devotion and fearless sacrifices of the apostles, the disciples and the countless followers of Christ. Forged on the anvil of persecution and purged in the crucible of Christian blood, this golden chain links us with the marvellous past with the assurance that God still reigns in the heavens and Christ is ever the bond between our Father and His earthly children.

It is strange to note the passage in *Martyrs of the Coliseum*, by the Roman Catholic priest, A. J. O'Reilly, wherein he states that St. Ignatius is recognized by the Roman Catholic Church as being the first Christian martyr, AD 107. St. Ignatius was a disciple of St. John, who consecrated him the third Bishop of Antioch. It is he who is supposed to have been the child Jesus took on His knee when He made the reference to becoming as little children, related in *Matthew* 18:3. St. Ignatius was martyred on the order of Trajan, cast to the wild beasts in the Coliseum and devoured.

The claim made by the Rev. O'Reilly is incongruous. Nowhere does the Roman Catholic Church support the statement. What about all the other Christians murdered in the Coliseum? What about the martyrdom of all the Apostles and disciples recorded herein and those not recorded? What of the martyrdom of Pudens and his children? What of Peter and Paul, whom the Roman Catholic Church claim to be the foundation of their church? They, too, were brutally martyred. What of the early martyrs catalogued in *The Vatican Catalogue of Saints, The Roman Martyrologies*, *The Ecclesiastical Annals* of Cardinal Baronius, *Regia Fides* by Cardinal Alford, and the many others? The records herein of those who died for the faith are all supported by the official documentation of the Roman Catholic Church and its top-ranking authorities. It shows how in some cases the Reverend Fathers of the Roman Catholic Church are as ignorant of the historic record as many of the Protestant ministry.

Such ignorance reminds one of the recent polls taken of the students in the American universities, asking them to name the Fathers of the Revolution and other outstanding historic events in American life which one would expect to be commonly known. The answers were an appalling record of ignorance. Only too plainly it teaches us how easily those raised in the indulgent security of a prosperous age forget their national heritage to such an extent as to rate it almost meaningless.

It would seem only when the glory has departed from them do people remember, when it is too late. To remember is to appreciate and stoke the fires of loyalty.

Little known, or little remembered, as the related incidents in this book may be, probably the knowledge that St. Peter laboured in Britain with the Josephian-Jerusalem Mission at Avalon is less known.

There is an interesting and curious record chronicled by Cardinal Baronius, who writes: 'Rufus the Senator received St. Peter into his house on Viminalis Hill[110], in the year AD 44.'

One is apt to confuse the name with that of Rufus the Senator who, nine years later, on his return from Britain to Rome, married Claudia, the adopted daughter of the Emperor Claudius, the natural child of Caractacus. The latter went to Britain with his commander at the beginning of the Claudian campaign, AD 43, and remained there until AD 52. Therefore, he was absent in Britain when St. Peter visited his parental home AD 44. As we have seen, after his marriage to Claudia, he forsook his parental home on Viminalis Hill, and also his estates in Umbria, to live at the Palace of the British. He also became a Senator, but in this record it is obvious that St. Peter visited the father of the younger Rufus. This is curious, as we recall that, while in Britain, Rufus the younger donated the land at Chichester for the pagan temple, evidence that he was not then converted. Under these circumstances one can reasonably ask why Peter went to the parental house on Viminalis Hill?

The answer is obvious. The royal British family, not having then been taken into captivity, were not resident at Rome. Peter would go at least to visit the home of a friend, while Rufus Pudens may have been an indifferent supporter of the Roman pagan religion, as indicated by his second marriage. Priscilla, the wife of Rufus, would be known to Peter as the mother of Paul and sympathetic to his visit. We know later she is recorded as a Christian in the household of her son at the Palatium Britannicum. It is an interesting record, more so since it was in that year Peter first arrived in Rome. It was also the year of the banishment decree when all Jews in Rome were forced to flee to escape the Claudian persecution administered to them as well as to the Christians.

---

[110] Viminal Hill, Rome – lat. *Collis Viminalis*

Peter fled direct to Britain. This is affirmed by Cornelius á Lapide in his work *Argumentum Epistolae St. Pauli ad Romanos*, in which he answers the question as to why St. Paul does not salute St. Peter in his *Epistle to the Romans*. He replies: 'Peter, banished with the rest of the Jews from Rome, by the edict of Claudius was absent in Britain.'

Peter, acting as a free-lance missionary, stemming from Avalon, preached in Britain during the Caradoc-Claudian war. While in Britain he became well acquainted with the members of the two branches of the Royal Silurian House of Arviragus and Caractacus. He knew the children of Caractacus years before they went into Roman captivity. Years after, when the British family became well established in Rome, he was naturally attracted to the home of the Pudens at the Palatium Britannicum. The visits of both Peter and Paul, with the family of the Pudens, is referred to in Scripture. Other ancient records state that the children of Claudia and Rufus Pudens were raised at the knees of Peter and Paul and other disciples, particularly naming St. Paul, for reasons stated in a former chapter.

There is plenty of evidence to show that Peter visited Britain and Gaul several times during his lifetime, his last visit to Britain taking place shortly before his final arrest and crucifixion in Nero's circus at Rome.

In Gaul Peter became the Patron Saint of Chartres, by reason of his preference to preach in the famous Druidic rock temple known as the *Grotte des Druides*. This is considered to be the oldest Druidic site in Gaul, on which is built the oldest cathedral in France.

Of his visits in Britain we have the corroboration of Eusebius Pamphilis AD 306 whom Simon Metaphrastes quotes as saying: 'St. Peter to have been in Britain as well as in Rome.'

Further proof of Peter's sojourn in Britain was brought to the light of day in recent times when an ancient, time-worn monument was excavated at Whithorn.[111] It is a rough hewn stone standing 4 feet high by 15 inches wide. On the face of this tablet is an inscription that reads: LOC. STI. PETRI APV.STOLI, or (of) *the place of Apostle Peter.*

The eminent Dean Stanley, writing in his works of the beloved Apostle, claims that the vision that came to St. Peter and foretold his doom: 'Knowing that shortly I must put off this my tabernacle, even as our Lord Jesus Christ hast shewed me' (2 *Peter* 1:14), appeared to St. Peter on his last visit to Britain, on the very spot where once stood the

---

[111] Candida Casa, Whithorn Priory: Early Celtic Christian settlement.

old British church of Lambedr (St. Peter's), where stands the present Abbey of St. Peter, Westminster. Shortly afterwards Peter returned to Rome, where he was later executed.

The first church dedicated to Peter was founded by King Lucius, the British King, who was the first by royal decree to proclaim Christianity the national faith of Britain at Winchester AD 156.

The church was erected AD 179, to the affectionate memory of St. Peter, in commemoration of his evangelizing labours in Britain. It is still known as 'St. Peter's of Cornhill' and bears the legend on its age-worn walls relating the historic fact and dates by the order of King Lucius, the descendant of Arviragus, preserved to this day for all to see and read.

During his lifetime Peter was the Apostle who suffered most for his Master. One can believe how his heart must have ached with remorse whenever he recalled the tragic scene in the Garden, the shocking betrayal by Judas, and the realization of his Master's prophetic words that before the cock crowed he would have denied Him thrice. In his heart he had never denied his Lord. He loved Jesus too dearly. We can only believe that in the panic of the fear-ridden events the weakness of the flesh momentarily prevailed. We fellow humans, possessing the same seeds of frailty, can understand and better admire and love Peter as he rose above all storm and persecution, spiritually and physically triumphant, vindicating his verbal lapse of loyalty.

The anguish he endured as a spectator at the infamous midnight trial in the Sanhedrin must have been soul-wracking and the disappearance of the body of Christ from the tomb must have stunned him as he looked in on its emptiness. How gloriously he redeemed his character!

As he took leave of the sceptred Isle of Britain to return to Rome to climax the last chapter of his splendid life, emotion must have touched him as he said his final farewells to the beloved Joseph and the remaining old Bethany comrades at Avalon. He feared not what might occur to him in the remaining time. He weighed the glory of his reward in soon being with the One he adored and his life magnified.

In the long period of incarceration that followed his arrest at Rome he was to suffer dreadfully.

Maliciously condemned, Peter was cast into the horrible, fetid prison of the Mamertine. There, for nine months, in absolute darkness, he endured monstrous torture manacled to a post. Never before or since has there been a dungeon of equal horror. Historians write of it as being the most fearsome on the brutal agenda of mankind. Over three thousand years old, it is probably the oldest torture chamber extant, the oldest remaining monument of bestiality of ancient Rome, a bleak testimony to its barbaric inhumanity, steeped in Christian tragedy and the agony of thousands of its murdered victims. It can be seen to this day, with the dungeon and the pillar to which Peter was bound in chains.

This dreaded place is known by two names. In classical history it is referred to as Gemonium or the Tullian Keep. In later secular history it is best known as the Mamertine. At this time it is not out of place to pause in our story to describe this awesome pit, if only to provide us who live so securely today with a slight reminder of what the soldiers of Christ suffered for our sake, so we may be quickened the better to appreciate the substance of our Christian heritage.

The Mamertine is described as a deep cell cut out of solid rock at the foot of the capitol, consisting of two chambers, one over the other. The only entrance is through an aperture in the ceiling. The lower chamber was the death cell. Light never entered and it was never cleaned. The awful stench and filth generated a poison fatal to the inmates of the dungeon, the most awful ever known. Even as early as 50 BC the historian Sallust describes it in the following words:

'In the prison called the Tullian, there is a place about ten feet deep. It is surrounded on the sides by walls and is closed above by a vaulted roof of stone. The appearance of it from the filth, the darkness and the smell is terrific.'

No one can realize what its horrors must have been a hundred years later when Peter was imprisoned in its noisome depths.

In this vile subterranean rock the famed Jugurtha was starved and went stark raving mad. Vercingetorix, the valorous Druidic Gaulish chieftain, was murdered by the order of Julius Caesar.

It is said that the number of Christians that perished within this diabolic cell is beyond computation – such is the glory of Rome.

One can re-read the denouncing words of the noble Queen Boadicea, with profit. She branded them for what they were. These people of the Roman purple, who scorned all their enemies as barbarian, were the greatest and most cruel barbarians of all time.

How Peter managed to survive those nine long dreadful months is beyond human imagination. During his entire incarceration he was manacled in an upright position, chained to the column, unable to lie down to rest. Yet, his magnificent spirit remained undaunted. It flamed with the immortal fervour of his noble soul proclaiming the Glory of God, through His Son, Jesus Christ. History tells us the amazing fact that in spite of all the suffering Peter was subjected to, he converted his gaolers, Processus, Martinianus, and forty-seven others.

It is a strange and curious circumstance that the chair, or throne of Pius IX, at the Vatican Council, was erected directly over the altar of Processus and Martinianus.

Peter, the Rock, as he predicted, met his death at Rome by the hands of the murderous Romans, who crucified him, according to their fiendish manner. He refused to die in the same position as our Lord, declaring he was unworthy. Peter demanded to be crucified in the reverse position, with his head hanging downward. Ironically enough, this wish was gratified by the taunting Romans in Nero's circus AD 67.

Such was the timbre and mettle of the valiant, glorious cavalcade of saints who permeated the hallowed Isle of Britain, with their presence and their devotion to Christ.

Amid the tragedy of wars and persecutions in which the bloodiest battles for Christendom were fought on British soil, repelling the hated Romans, the carnival of blood and death in the Roman arenas reached abnormal proportions. The popular sport of the Roman pagans was the torture, mutilation and destruction of the Christians.

They screamed with moronic delight as the famished lions tore and mangled the kneeling, praying Christians, old and young, women, children and babies in arms. They made wagers on the staying ability of the British warrior in his fight to the death. As one Roman Gladiator was slain another took his place until, overcome with fatigue from continuous combat, the British Christian warrior was finally butchered. Roman writers reporting these carnivals of murder wrote that the courage of the Briton was indomitable. With their dying breath and last mite of strength they would hurl themselves upon their foe in a last superhuman effort to avenge. They stated that it was not an uncommon sight for Briton and Roman to die together, impaled on each other's weapon.

The teachers of the faith, the elderly, the women and children, met their end serenely with quiet prayer on their lips, proudly defiant. It is said that the mothers would push their children forward to die first, so that they following were sure life was extinct and their children spared the agony of being dragged around the arena by the mauling animals.

The courage of the women awed the Romans, causing them to whisper, 'What women these Christian Britons have. What women!'

The sadistic Roman could never understand or analyze the cold, remorseless courage of the Christian British with its silent, savage ferocity. It made their craven hearts quaver. Not understanding immortality, they could not understand a faith that made its believers 'fearlessly indifferent to death', as Julius Caesar wrote.

The valour of the British evoked Roman admiration and at the same time increased their fears which forbade them to offer one mite of mercy. The pitiless nature of the Roman against the Briton was born out of cowardly fear more than anything else.

In Christianity the Roman Caesars began to see the handwriting on the wall, proclaiming their imperial doom, and it was the Britons that sealed it by their faith.

Following the death and interment of Mary, the mother of Jesus, at Avalon, it became a passionate desire of the disciples, holy men, pilgrims, kings and other notables to be interred within 'the hallowed acres of Glastonbury' (Avalon) where, with Mary and the other apostles and disciples, it is recorded that they: 'Especially choose to await the day of resurrection.'

There are many records still in existence reporting the claim that many of the martyred were brought to Britain to be buried in the sanctified haven at Avalon and elsewhere in Britain.

The heroic Constantius, of Lyons, who saved the city of Clermont, in Auvergne, from Euric, the Goth, AD 473-492, tells in his work *Life of St. Germanus,* how he took the relics of all the Apostles and martyrs from Gaul, to place in a special tomb at St. Albans in Britain.

This record is of particular interest, supplying the one link missing in earlier records and confirming, to a point, much later records.

The earlier records are cited by Maelgwyn of Avalon, who writes: 'Joseph of Arimathea, the noble decurion, received his everlasting rest with his eleven associates in the Isle of Avalon.'

Here, as can be seen, is one missing. Twelve companions arrived in Britain and thirteen if we count Marcella, the handmaid of Martha, as reported by Cardinal Baronius. Which one is missing? It is thought to have been Lazarus, who was the first of the illustrious band to die.

The later records say that *all* of them were interred in Britain, which would indicate that the missing one was among the relics of those whom

Constantius returned to Britain from Gaul, where Lazarus had died at Marseilles.

But what of Peter and Paul?

Did they remain buried at Rome, in the grave where the loving hands of Claudia, Pudens and their children had placed them?

We do know that the martyred Pudens family were never disturbed from their final resting-place beneath the floors of the first Christian Church at Rome, which before was the famed Palace of the British.

Of Peter and Paul there is confusion, mystery and deliberate misinformation concerning the place where their bodies found their last resting-place.

The Martyrologies inform us that the Pudens, after retrieving the body of Paul, interred it on their estate on the Via Ostiensa road. We know from the historic records of the Emperor Constantine, first Christian Emperor of Rome, that he, knowing where the mutilated body of Paul lay, caused it to be excavated. He had it placed in a stone coffin, and over the spot built a church, still known as St. Paul's Without-the-Walls, meaning the church and his body are outside the city walls of Rome. The original church perished and a larger one was built on the site. Fire destroyed this in 1823. In the present church built after the fire, but still bearing its ancient name, a Benedictine priest is ever on guard before a grille on the floor of the High Altar. On occasion, for the benefit of special visitors, the priest moves the grille, lowering a light through the floor into a cell beneath, revealing to the eyes a crude slabstone on the floor bearing the name 'Pauli'. But there is no stone casket to be seen.

What happened to it and to the body?

The positive answer is found in a document written by Pope Vitalian to the British King Oswy, AD 656. The letter is still in existence. Probably to the astonishment of many, the letter states that Pope Vitalian permitted the remains of the bodies of St. Paul and St. Peter, with the remains of the martyrs St. Lawrence, St. John, St. Gregory and St. Pancras, to be removed from Rome to England and re-interred in the great church at Canterbury. This historic record is beyond refutation.

From St. Pancras is named St. Pancras Station, one of the large railroad terminals in London. At one time on this site there stood a cross erected to the memory of St. Pancras who preached on that same spot. The full facts concerning this amazing incident are related by the

Venerable Bede, AD 673-735, in his *Ecclesiastical History of the English Nation.*[112] Learned British historian Bede was held in high esteem by both the British and the Roman Catholic Church. While he was a sincere advocate of the novel papal faith, introduced by St. Augustine, AD 596, he was dogged in his support of the British church and to its claim of priority in establishing the Christian faith first in Britain, a fact not disputed by St. Augustine nor by Pope Gregory at Rome. Bede is recorded as the 'Father of English learning', being the first to translate the New Testament into English. All Christians are familiar with the beautiful story of Bede translating the last chapter to his scribe as he lay dying in his barren cell, expiring within a few minutes after concluding the last verse in the Gospel of St. John, reciting the 'Gloria'.

Regardless of the preservation of the letter sent from Pope Vitalian to King Oswy, Bede, being a man of devout character and erudition, would never make a false report on such an important matter as the transfer of those saintly bodies from the care of the Roman Catholic hierarchy at Rome to England if it were not so. His stature in the Augustinian church is noted in the record that the Venerable Bede is a canonized saint in the Roman Catholic Calendar.

The common belief was, and still is among the Roman Catholic laity, that the body of St. Paul rests beneath the high altar in the cathedral at Rome, erected to his honour; but it is well known in the high places in both Christian churches that for many centuries only his empty stone sarcophagus remains in the vault.

Professor Kinnaman, the learned American scholar and archaeologist, in recent times has in his book *Diggers for Facts*, this reference to St. Paul's life work, writing:

'The real earthly remains of the Apostle to the Gentiles sleep in the soil of England beyond the reach of the arm of the Roman law.'

What of the tablet seen in the vault at St. Paul's Without-the-Walls? Is it the lid of the stone coffin, supplied and inscribed by order of Constantine? The stone sarcophagus is in St. Paul's Cathedral at Rome, but his body rests with St. Peter and the many other saints in England, described by historians as 'the most hallowed ground on earth'.

---

[112] *Book* 3, ch. 29.

CHAPTER 16

ST. PAUL'S MISSION IN BRITAIN

S INCE the beginning of time when the peoples of the earth amalgamated into kingdoms, the pages of history are filled with the spectacular conquests of ambitious kings and mighty Caesars who, by military subjection, built mighty empires to their name. Backed by powerful, organized armies, with the wealth and resources of the nation behind them, the conquerors slaughtered and trampled underfoot the peoples of other nations whose only offence was to defend their land and homes.

Even as history extols their despotic fame it writes their pitiful obituary, exemplifying the words Jesus spoke in rebuke to Peter when he had slashed the ear off an offending servant's head with his sword: 'All they that take the sword shall perish with the sword.[113]

History books are the graveyard of military dynasties which rose and fell by the sword to satiate the ambitious greed of so many murderous conquerors. Such is the record of Empire, thousands of years before Christ, and in the two thousand years that have followed.

In comparison, imagination is staggered as we contemplate the achievements of that handful of apostles and disciples who first stood for Christ.

Penniless, suffering poverty, incarcerated, tortured, exiled and without a weapon in their hands, each stood alone in the midst of imperial hostility as they conquered the world for Christ, a conquest that has endured and thrived for two thousand years. Empires have come and gone with the flag of Christ waving over their dust as majestically as the day it was unfurled when the British armies, led by Guiderius and Arviragus, defeated the Romans in the first battle of the Claudian campaign, AD 43.

Thus are the words of Jesus vindicated. Yet, in spite of the glaring truth, a major portion of the world today, more than ever, believes the sword is mightier than the Word. We see it as the Communistic regime seeks to bring the rest of the world under their tyrannical heel of slavery. Despite their faults and frequent backsliding for two thousand years it

---

[113] *Matthew* 26:52

has been the Christian Anglo-Saxon world that has stood against the evils of material despotism and won. Often alone and overwhelmingly outnumbered, they have fought for the freedom of man's spirit wherever it was challenged.

God has said, 'Ye are My people. Ye shall not perish from the face of the earth.' In the same breath God warns us that we shall be scourged with rods for our backsliding, meaning that we shall pay a price for our waywardness. We shall be punished with Pearl Harbours and Dunkirks. Then He says, when we are on the verge of disaster He will 'not make a full end' of us and save us out of our trouble so that we may triumph.

What a bitter price we unnecessarily will pay.

Read carefully the reports written by our great commanders in battle who could report no other explanation for victory, when all seemed lost, but a miracle.

Further tribulations are bound to come. We shall pay a great price. We have asked for it. The punishment can be minimized if we but open our ears and hearts to the Word of God and our Saviour Jesus Christ; if we will but listen to the words of the apostles and disciples of our Lord, as our forefathers did in ancient Britain, and gird ourselves with the strength of divine promise, as they did.

St. Paul laboured among the Gentiles to fulfil the promise which James said Simeon had declared, that God would take a people out of the Gentiles for His name, who would keep His Word, His Laws, and the Sabbath.

Are we those people? Scientists, scholars and ecclesiastics think so. St. Paul certainly believed so. His founding of the first Christian church at Rome implementing the British royal converts was his triumph, to be culminated in his special mission to Britain by other members of this same royal family of Christians. Before he had gone to Rome he had sent his representative to Britain, in Aristobulus, the father-in-law of St. Peter. He was one of the original seventy elected by Christ and was the brother of Barnabas. It was his wife on whom Jesus wrought the miracle as recorded in St. Matthew's Gospel. In his epistles St. Paul sends his greeting 'to the household of Aristobulus'. It is stated that Aristobulus was in Britain before St. Paul wrote his epistle to the Romans.

Aristobulus was ostensibly Paul's forerunner in Britain, sent by the Apostle to the Gentiles to prepare the way for his own particular mission, which was to follow later, and to be separated from the Josephian Mission. In the preparatory stages Aristobulus was associated with Joseph but never attached to the mission at Avalon. He laboured in the part of Britain now known as Wales. In those far-off centuries the whole Island, now divided into England, Scotland and Wales, was covered by the one name - Britain. The brother of Barnabas was exclusively connected with the most southern branch of the royal Silurians, the family of Caractacus, in Wales. Previous to the coming of Aristobulus to Wales, the father and grandfather of Caractacus had already planted the Christian seed in their own particular domain. As we have seen, when Joseph and his companions arrived in Britain, AD 36, Bran, the father of Caractacus, had abdicated his throne in favour of his son in order to assume his office as Arch-Druid of the Silures. His seat was at Trevnan, where Caractacus was born, in the parish of Llan-Ilid, Glamorganshire. Llyr Llediath, father of Bran, the King Lear of Shakespeare, founded the first Christian church in Wales at Llandaff, after his conversion and baptism by Joseph. On the merging of the Druidic with the Christian faith all the members of the Bran-Caradoc dynasty were converted by Joseph.

The Princess Eurgain, eldest daughter of Caractacus, was the first to be baptized, and immediately following the order was her grandfather, the Arch Druid Bran, her great-grandfather Llyr Llediath, then her brother Linus, who later became the first Bishop of Rome and then her husband Salog, Lord of Salisbury, all at the hands of St. Joseph.

Her father Caractacus, and his son Cyllinus, who became regent in his father's stead during the latter's captivity at Rome, and Cynon the youngest son, were baptized in Rome by the hands of St. Paul.

Of Cyllinus, it is interesting to note that during his reign he is given credit for introducing into Britain the christening of infants with Christian names. Prior to this the British followed the old Hebrew method of naming a person by one name only, and adding the word 'ab', meaning 'of', or 'son of'. Tracing the lineage of a person under the old Hebrew principle was a difficult matter.

Support for the credit given to Cyllinus is evidenced in the following extract from the family genealogy as given by his descendant, Jestyn ap Gwrgant, Prince of Glamorgan, in the eleventh century:

'Cyllin ab Caradoc, a wise and just king. In his days many of the Cymry embraced the faith in Christ through the teachings of the saints of Cor-Eurgain, and many godly men from the countries of Greece and Rome were in Cambria. HE FIRST OF THE CYMRY

GAVE INFANTS NAMES; for before, names were not given except to adults, and then from something characteristic in their bodies, minds or manners.'

The quotation in capitals is by the author to draw attention to the historic fact. Incidentally, Cyllin and Caradoc are the true Celtic names of father and son. Caractacus and Cyllinus are the Roman versions.

All the children of Cyllinus were baptized in the faith. In later years he also abdicated his throne, in favour of his younger brother, Cynon. Like his grandfather, Bran, he took up the Cross, becoming a priest in the Christian faith. In the British Celtic Annals he is registered as St. Cyllinus.

Llyr Llediaith, the grandfather of Caractacus, was among the group of royal captives taken to Rome, AD 52. Shortly after the famous trial of the British Pendragon before the Emperor Claudius in the Roman Senate, Llyr died at Rome. His son Bran, being an Arch Priest, was not subject to the surrender but, voluntarily, on hearing of his father's death, offered himself as hostage in place of the deceased Llyr. After the parole of his son, Caractacus, he remained with the Silurian family, dwelling at the Palace of the British in Rome. With the exception of the sons of Caractacus, who had returned to Britain to take over the reins of government, they were all residing in the Empire City when Paul arrived, AD 56. Then followed two years of instruction under St. Paul of the royal group who were to establish his mission in Britain. Aristobulus had journeyed to Rome from Britain to meet Paul and plan the evangelizing commission. From years of former service with Paul, Aristobulus was well acquainted with Paul's intentions. He knew he was to be an important factor in this great work among the selected Gentiles and his previous experience in Britain had given the aged disciple a good insight of the groundwork, most of which he personally had laid, with the aid of Llyr, Bran and Joseph. Nevertheless Paul's mission was designed to be distinctly separate from the Avalon Mission. Perhaps herein lay the weakness, for Paul's mission to Gentile Rome was not to endure.

While the royal house of Caractacus sponsored the mission, it was Eurgain, the eldest daughter of Caractacus, who actually was the chief sponsor, endowing the mission with munificent gifts and lands.[114]

---

[114] St. Prydain's Genealogy, which refers to Eurgain as the first female saint of Britain.

In the year AD 58 the Paulian mission was ready to leave Rome to begin their work in Britain, in the territorial section known as Cambria, the ancient name of the Caradoc domain now known as Wales.

Only Caractacus was subject to the seven-year parole, the rest of the British royal hostages were free to leave at any time they wished.

The record states that Bran, after being consecrated by St. Paul at Rome, left one year before his son Caradoc, whose parole did not expire until the following year, AD 59. With Bran went Aristobulus, who had been consecrated the first Bishop of Britain by St. Paul, his sons Manaw, Brennus, Ilid and Cyndaw as supporting missionaries. The last two named were Judeans. With them was Eurgain and her husband Salog, Lord of Caer Salog, or old Sarum, Salisbury. He is described as being a Roman patrician who had married the daughter of Caractacus prior to the disaster at Clun, AD 52. Again we see a mingling of the Roman aristocracy with the royal British. They arrived at Llan-ilid (meaning 'consecrated enclosure'), Glamorganshire, erecting a church as a memorial.

Eurgain is recorded as the Patroness of the Paulian Mission at Llan-ilid, and for that reason it became more commonly known as the Cor-Eurgain Mission. There she founded the first Cor, or choir, and from that time onward it was considered the finest choir in the world. This magnificent tradition has been continued over the centuries in unbroken sequence by the Welsh, being the basis of the world-famous Eisteddfod held every year by the Druidical Order of Wales, when they congregate in Druidic costume and ceremony to renew the glorious past with the present. There the famous choirs can be heard singing by the descendants of those courageous noble Christians. In the annual choir contests held throughout the world the Welsh Eisteddfod has never lost pride of place.

Once yearly, the famous Welsh choir visits the United States and Canada where, in a series of recitals, their magnificent voices delight and thrill all who hear them. Yet how little is it known by the audiences that this wonderful choir is a distinct link with St. Paul's mission to Britain nearly two thousand years ago.

Aristobulus was installed as the first Bishop at Llan-ilid, with Bran remaining as chief High Priest of Siluria at Llandaff.

In the Cymric language Aristobulus is known as Arwystli-Hen and Arwystli-Senex. Hen is Celtic for aged, just as Senex is the Roman term.[115]

Unfortunately, the aged Aristobulus was to meet with a tragic end within a year of his return to Britain with his royal companion. Unlike the Paulian Mission, which had come direct from Rome, the Josephian Mission had come direct from Jerusalem. It had no contact with Rome. Joseph also had the advantage of being well known to the British by his former interests in the tin mining of Cornwall and Devon. He was so well received by them that he was considered as one of them. On the other hand, the inveterate hatred of the British for Rome, and anything associated with it, persisted with an unrelenting detestation. Anything tinged with the Roman stigma was cause for grave suspicion. The Blessed Bran, writing in his journals, said they were hard put to induce the British to accept anyone or anything that came from Rome. It was only their love for the devout Bran and the lovely Eurgain, and their proud loyalty to Caractacus, that made them willing to meet half-way the Roman religious delegates. Aristobulus was well respected by the Silurians; he had come to them from Jerusalem, through Spain, and was known to be loved by Joseph and the Avalon band.

Aristobulus in his preaching zeal journeyed far beyond the territory of the Silurian shield into the lands of the British Ordovices, whose hatred for the Romans was bitter and black. This blinded them to the facts, and he was unknown to them. Aware of the many ruses the Romans had instigated against the Britons in order to trick them into submission, they allied the presence of the aged elder brother of Barnabas to some form of Roman political treachery, in which religion played an hypocritical part of the scheme. They rose and slew him, given as the year AD 58 or AD 59, according to present reckoning.[116]

Aristobulus was the first British bishop and the only one martyred by them. St. Alban, however, was regarded by Rome as the first British martyr at what was ancient Verulamium, still to be seen thanks to archaeological restoration. A church existed in Alban's time and, after his martyrdom, Offa, king of the Mercians, founded the Monastery of St. Albans, to his memory, in AD 793, Roman bricks from ancient Verulamium being used in its structure. The pre-Roman Belgae

---

[115] Triads: *Myvyrian Archaiologies*, vol. 2.
[116] Alford, *Regia Fides*, p. 41.

foundations, and the early Christian witness, instituted a continuous worship in this spot.

Centuries later the Romish church criticized the British for their great lack of martyrs as compared to their own record. The leaders of the British church informed them that the disciples of the British church lived to preach and teach the Gospel and not die for it unnecessarily. If their life had to be the only sacrifice, that they would gladly give. We know they gave it abundantly, but at the hands of the enemy and not by the hands of their own countrymen except in this one tragic circumstance. It was well known that the priests of the Roman church viewed martyrdom as a notable, worthwhile gesture to such an extent they became frantic. Many deliberately sought martyrdom before they had achieved anything worth while.

There is another popular claimant to the honour of being the first Christian martyr in Britain identified with the church of St. Albans. It is a Christianized Roman soldier, named Alban, during the Diocletian persecution in Britain two hundred and fifty years later, who aided a hunted British priest to escape by wearing his robe, drawing pursuit to himself. On being recognized, the Roman officer ordered a soldier standing nearby to execute the culprit. The soldier refused, admitting that he, too, was a Christian, with the result that both soldiers were immediately beheaded. Tradition claims they were buried together on the spot where they were killed and a church erected on the site was named St. Albans.

Alban was the first Christian Roman soldier martyred in Britain by the Romans, but by no means the first Christian martyr in Britain. All authentic records, including *The Genealogies of the Saints in Britain*, name Aristobulus as the first of our Lord's disciples martyred in Britain, with Simon Zelotes being a second martyr shortly after.[117]

The first church erected on the site of St. Albans was built, as stated earlier, by the remorseful Ordovices to the memory of Aristobulus. Following the death of the Roman soldier Alban and his companion two hundred and fifty years later, the old church was reconstructed, enlarged and renamed St. Albans, by which it is known to this day.

Of the aged, beloved friend of St. Paul and father-in-law of St. Peter, Aristobulus, there exists an abundance of authentic records from which the following are quotations from the original.

---

[117] Dorotheus, *Synopsis de Apostol.*

Cardinal Alford, who ranks second only to the erudite Cardinal Baronius as an authoritative historian of the Vatican, was one of the very few British ecclesiastics to achieve high position in the Roman Catholic Church. He was a native-born Briton whose original name was Griffiths. He changed his name to Alford on joining the Jesuit Order. In fact one can look in vain for the name of a British Pope during the years when the two churches were somewhat in agreement. None would accept the office, definitely refuting any mortal claim to being Christ's appointed Head of the Church. Only He was the Headstone.

Alford writes:

'It is perfectly certain that before St. Paul had come to Rome, Aristobulus was absent in Britain.'

In the *Martyrologies* of the Greek Church we read:

'Aristobulus was one of the seventy disciples and a follower of St. Paul the Apostle, along with whom he preached the Gospel to the whole world, and ministered to them. He was chosen by St. Paul to be the missionary bishop to the land of Britain. He was there martyred after he had built churches and ordained deacons and priests on the island.'

Dorotheus, Bishop of Tyre, writes AD 303:

'Aristobulus who is mentioned by the Apostle in his Epistle to the Romans, was made Bishop in Britain.'

Haleca, Bishop of Augusta, adds:

'The memory of many martyrs is celebrated by the Britons, especially that of St. Aristobulus, one of the seventy disciples.'

In the *Adonis Martyrologia* we read:

'March 15. Natal day of Aristobulus, Bishop of Britain, brother of St. Barnabas the Apostle, by whom he was ordained Bishop. He was sent to Britain where, after preaching the truth of Christ and forming a church, he received martyrdom.'

The reference in the above to the ordination of Aristobulus as Bishop by his younger brother Barnabas, was a much earlier appointment and did not apply to Britain. Following this ordination he first went into Britain, with Barnabas, as an exploratory agent of St. Paul. The consecration conferred on Aristobulus at Rome, as Bishop of Britain, came much later, AD 58.

Some may surmise that St. Paul's appointment of the aged disciple was in conflict with St. Joseph's office and mission. This is not so. Joseph is never referred to as Bishop of Britain. His title is more outstanding as the Apostle of Britain. His mission preceded the Paulian Mission under Aristobulus by twenty-two years. The year following the demise of Aristobulus, St. Philip re-consecrated Joseph as Chief Priest in Britain, AD 60.

The title, Bishop of Britain, was not again conferred on any missionary who followed after Aristobulus. Of his coming to Britain, the *British Archaic*, or *Genealogies of the Saints*, has this to say:

'There came with Bran the Blessed from Rome to Britain, Arwystli Hen (Senex-old), Ilid, Cyndaw, men of Israel; and Maw, or Manaw, son of Arwystli.'

A district on the River Severn, in Montgomeryshire, from time immemorial perpetuates the presence and name of Aristobulus in the original Cymric vernacular – Arwystli.

The *Greek Menology* also gives March 15th as the day of the martyrdom of Aristobulus.

Thus is established in brief form the positive evidence that Aristobulus actually laboured and was slain in Britain, corroborating the contention that St. Paul did establish a working Christian mission in Britain.

The year of the death of the Bishop of Britain was the same year that saw the end of the parole of Caractacus at Rome, AD 59. He said his farewell to his beloved youngest daughter, Gladys, now Claudia Pudens, and to her noble husband, Rufus, and their four children. The parting with his eldest son, Linus, now the first Bishop of Rome, must have been sad, for war was still raging in Britain, with his cousin, the valorous Arviragus, carrying the assault against the greatest commanders in Roman military history. The rest of his family had all returned to Britain. The famed Palace of the British at Rome would no longer house him. He had given it as a dowry to his daughter at her marriage to Rufus Pudens, along with its magnificent estate and baths. There is no record that he ever returned to Rome. That was hardly possible. He had taken oath never to lift arms against the Romans as long as he lived. This oath he kept, but he was still a dominant figure in British authority and it is understandable that any visits he may have wished to make to Rome may have been misconstrued by either side. The mad Nero had succeeded the Emperor Claudius in the Roman hierarchy, and Christian persecution was blazing with renewed malice.

On his return to his native land he built a castle at Aber Gweryd, now St. Donat's Major, in Glamorganshire. Unlike his father, his grandfather, or his children, he did not take any religious vows or office. It appears he aided his sons in governing his people and strongly supported the Christian movement without jeopardizing his oath. He ended his days peaceably, dying a natural death. This noble Briton, who had shaken Imperial foundations, was laid to rest beside his wife, his father Bran, and grandfather Llyr, in the Cor of Ilid in Siluria, where later were to be gathered Cyllinus, Cynon, Eurgain and Salog, all heroes in Christ, all of whom died a natural death in the light and joy of their Lord.

Following the death of Aristobulus, the Princess Eurgain became the chief influence in the Paulian Mission. The famous *Iolo MS.* states that Eurgain founded twelve colleges of Christian Druids for Culdee initiates at Caer Urgan, or Cor Eurgain. These colleges she endowed bountifully, developing them to the highest estate in theological learning. The greatness of Cor-Eurgain endured for centuries after her death, the only great memorial to endure to the testimony of St. Paul's Mission in Britain. From here many of the greatest teachers and most able missionaries flowed out in a constant stream, on into the tenth century. Her love for music and excellent talent created the first Christian choirs. Eurgain was as talented as her younger sister, Claudia, and her famed aunt, Pomponia, writing hymns and anthems that rang throughout the land in chants of praise and glory. Her attention to the education of the young in the many schools she provided is a noble record. The beautiful Princess Eurgain devoted her entire wealth and life in the service of Christ. The records state that she was the most beloved woman in Britain. Eurgain was the first female convert in Britain and the first Christian female saint. Her illustrious life is chronicled in the

Genealogy of the Saints in Britain, a beautiful woman, a noble princess, a shining star in the diadem of Christ.

On the death of Aristobulus, Ilid, 'a man of Israel', who had gone with Bran and Aristobulus to Cambria, took charge until Paul arrived. Prior to his membership in the Paulian Mission little is known of him except he was a Judean convert out of Rome. In the Cymric Triads he is shown as a very capable, energetic leader. His devout, efficient administration endeared him to the Silures. He spent many years of his life in Cambria, espousing the original plan St. Paul had conceived with the aged Bran and Aristobulus. Financed by the royal Silurian family, and by the personal efforts of the Princess Eurgain and her brother, the abdicated Cyllinus, there was built a magnificent church and university and many new schools in Cambria. The *Iolo MS.* says, 'He afterwards went to Glastonbury, where he died and was buried, and Ina, king of that country, raised a large church over his grave.' King Ina's church at Glastonbury Abbey, built AD 700, was excavated in recent years. By neglect it has since been covered. It is interesting to note that he is numbered first on the long list of Cambrian saints, listed in the *Genealogy of the Saints in Britain.*

In some of the ancient records Ilid is claimed to have been a son of the Decurian Joseph of Arimathea, the Apostle of the British.

The loss of his aged friend was a grievous blow to St. Paul. He had sent his salutations to his friends at Rome, including 'the household of Aristobulus'.

It is claimed that Paul landed at what is now a suburb of the great naval port of Portsmouth, known over the ages and to present time as 'Paul's Grove'. From there he evidently made his way into Cambria, where it is claimed he founded the famous Abbey of Bangor. The doctrine and administration of the Abbey was known as Pauli Regula – 'The Rule of Paul'. Over each of its four gates was inscribed his motto: 'If a man will not work, neither let him eat.' All the Abbots that followed considered themselves as the direct successors of Paul.[118] Each was specially elected, was usually of royal descent. It later developed into a monastery and is named by St. Hilary and St. Benedict as the 'Mother of Monasteries'. Its educational curriculum was of the highest order, attracting thousands of scholars. Its membership is stated by Bede to have risen to two thousand one hundred. Its twentieth Abbot was the

---

[118] Morgan, *St. Paul in Britain*, p. 177.

famous Pelagius who fought so strenuously against the novel papal teachings. They described his defence of the ancient British simple faith as the Pelagian Heresy.

It is doubtful if Paul stayed long enough in Britain to see the famous Abbey of Bangor completed. He knew his time was short and he sought to make the best use of it in his fervent evangelizing mission, chief of which was his special attention to his British Mission. While there he left his impress in writing his rule for a godly Christian life, recorded in *Ancient British Triads*, as 'The Triads of Paul the Apostle'. Nowhere else are they recorded and nowhere else is the term 'Triads' employed outside Britain, which favours acceptance of their Pauline origin. They are as follows:

TRIADS OF PAUL THE APOSTLE

'There are three sorts of men: The man of God, who renders good for evil; the man of men, who renders good for good and evil for evil; and the man of the devil, who renders evil for good.

'Three kinds of men are the delights of God: The meek; the lovers of peace; the lovers of mercy.

'There are three marks of the children of God: Gentle deportment; a pure conscience; patient suffering of injuries.

'There are three chief duties demanded by God: justice to every man; love; humility.

'In three places will be found the most of God: Where He is mostly sought; where He is mostly loved; where there is least of self.

'There are three things following faith in God: A conscience at peace; union with heaven; what is necessary for life.

'Three ways a Christian punishes an enemy: By forgiving him; by not divulging his wickedness; by doing him all the good in his power.

'The three chief considerations of a Christian: Lest he should displease God; lest he should be stumbling-block to man; lest his love to all that is good should wax cold.

'The three luxuries of a Christian feast: What God has prepared; what can be obtained with justice to all; what love to all may venture to use.

'Three persons have the claims and privileges of brothers and sisters: The widow; the orphan; the stranger.'

The preservation of the Triads of Paul the Apostle is due to the Cor of Ilid, of which Ilid, the 'man of Israel', was chief architect and chief priest.

In Merton College, Oxford, there is an ancient *MS.* which purports to contain a series of letters between St. Paul and Seneca. In them are several allusions to St. Paul's residence in Siluria. It is known as the *Paulian MS.*

Bishop Burgess writes:

'Of Paul's journey to Britain we have as satisfactory proof as any historical question can demand.'

A casual study of the life and works of St. Paul, after his arrival at Rome, shows blank periods which Scripture does not explain. They total a silence of six years. The general opinion, supported by the secular records, is that those years were spent in Gaul, and principally in Britain. We know he returned to Rome from Cambria, AD 61, and was imprisoned there. Again he returned to Britain and Gaul. Edouard de Bazelaire traces the path of Paul's travel, circa AD 62, along the Aurelian Way from Rome to Arles, in Gaul. With him was Trophimus, one of the original Josephian band, previously referred to, and Crescens, whom he sent to Vienne, where he found the church at Mayence, being the first Bishop there. Scriptural records support this in which Paul refers to the sickness of one of his disciples whom he was obliged to leave in Gaul.

The Rev. R. W. Morgan writes:

'There are six years of St. Paul's life to be accounted for, between his liberation from his first imprisonment and his martyrdom at Aquae Salviae in the Ostian Road, near Rome. Part certainly, the greater part perhaps, of this period was spent in Britain, in Siluria or Cambria, beyond the bounds of the Roman Empire; and hence the silence of the Greek and Latin writers upon it.'[119]

---

[119] Morgan, *St. Paul in Britain*, p. 175.

In Wales, as in Gaul, the memory of Paul's work among them is almost entirely lost. The only enduring memorials to Paul's presence in Britain, of note, are to be found in England.

Llandin – London, is referred to as the 'Areopagus' of Britain, arising out of the instance that St. Paul preached from the summit of Ludgate Hill. The famous St. Paul's Cathedral is erected on the site, and the ancient St. Paul's Cross may well mark the spot where St. Paul stood as he preached the Gospel to the British.

This, and much more, is confirmed in the *Long Lost Chapter of the Acts of the Apostles* (*The Sonnini MS.*).

The presence and preachings of St. Paul in London became so deeply associated with that city that he was made the Patron Saint of London, and his emblem, the sword of martyrdom, is incorporated in the coat of arms of this great metropolis.

A common question often arises in discussions of the ability of the Apostles to preach understandably to the people of different tongues. In what language did St. Paul address the British? Did he speak the Celtic tongue or Latin? It is an interesting but difficult question to answer.

Philologists have pointed out the great similarity of the ancient Celtic language with the ancient Hebrew, in which case it would not have been difficult for Paul to have preached to the British in the Cymric language. We know that the ancient British on a large scale were familiar with Greek, which was as common an international language of those days as English is today. Paul wrote all his epistles in Greek, and for a long time after the apostolic age Greek was the language of the Church of Rome. Among the educated, Latin was well known. Caractacus addressed the Roman Senate at his famous trial in Latin; therefore neither side would experience any difficulty in speaking or hearing.

Moreover it was the common practice of Christians from the beginning to read the Scriptures in the vulgar tongue. It had ever been the Druidic custom to speak in the vernacular. According to 1 *Corinthians* 14:9, the Word of God forbids praying and preaching in an unknown tongue. Paul emphasized this in the canon he laid down for the Corinthian Church. He says:

'If I know not the meaning of the voice, I shall be unto him that speaketh a barbarian, and he that speaketh shall be a barbarian unto me ... I had rather in the church speak five words with my understanding ... than ten thousand words in an unknown tongue.'

It was not till the reign of Charlemagne that Latin became the language of the church services. Latin as the language of prayer and worship was also imposed by Pope Gregory I in the year AD 600.

The British church ever opposed this practice and were the first to demand its abolition, and the first to print and preach the Bible in their own language.

Bishop Ussher, in his *Historia Dogmatica*, writes:

'No two causes contributed so much to the declension of Christianity and the progress of Mohammedanism, as the suppression by the Church of Rome of the vernacular scriptures, and her adoption of image worship.'

Worship of images and relics was first introduced in the Roman Church Council by Pope Hadrian I, AD 788. In the Bible this is called idolatry and is severely condemned (*Exodus* 20:4,5; *Deuteronomy* 27:15; *Psalms* 115).

Probably the place where Paul is most commemorated is Malta, where he was shipwrecked. At Valleta stands the beautiful church of St. Paul Shipwrecked, erected to his memory and rescue from the sea.

It is certain that, if it had not been for the vigorous support of the Paulian Mission in Cambria by the Princess Eurgain and her relatives, his efforts would have completely failed. We cannot help but feel regret that so little was perpetuated, even during the activity of the Cor Eurgain, to his memory and those faithful workers who issued through Rome. It can be well said that the success of his mission during its existence and presence in Cambria was due to the magnificent efforts of the Caradoc Silurian family and had a profound influence in the promotion of Christianity in Wales. Following the death of Paul the Cambrian church renewed its close ties with Avalon. The deep affection Eurgain and her relatives held for Joseph who first converted and baptized many of them always remained. Among the common people their allegiance never deviated from Joseph or the Mother Church at Avalon. They could not or would not accept that which came from Rome. In this alone is found the answer. Yet they could not and did not fail to recognize the deep affection Paul held for the children of

Caractacus and the children of Claudia. It was too evident. His love for Linus was unbounded. We see this preserved in an unusual relic in the Vatican Museum. It is in the form of a glass medallion depicting a contemporary portrait of the heads of Linus and Paul, proclaiming their undying friendship and close association during those drama-packed years.

Paul fulfilled the mission of his Saviour, Jesus Christ, to go 'far hence unto the Gentiles', the merit of which has throbbed and thrived for two thousand years, and will continue to live firm in the hope of the great promise, till He shall come again.

Eloquently St. Clement sums up the magnitude of the achievements of the Apostle to the Gentiles. Being one of the original Bethany band that dwelt at Avalon with Joseph, he knew St. Paul intimately and long before he followed in the office of his beloved friend Linus, as Bishop of Rome. He writes:

'To leave the examples of antiquity, and to come to the most recent, let us take the noble examples of our own times. Let us place before our eyes the good Apostle, Peter, through unjust odium, underwent not one or two, but many sufferings; and having undergone his martyrdom, he went to the place of glory to which he was entitled. Paul, also, having seven times worn chains, and been hunted and stoned, received the prize of such endurance. For he was the herald of the Gospel in the West as well as in the East, and enjoyed the illustrious reputation of the faith in teaching the whole world to be righteous. And after he had been in the extremity of the West, he suffered martyrdom before the sovereigns of mankind; and thus delivered from this world, he went to his holy place, the most brilliant example of steadfastness that we possess.'

'Extremity of the West' was the term used to indicate Britain. Capellus, in History of the Apostles, writes:

'I know scarcely of one author from the time the Fathers downward who does not maintain that St. Paul, after his liberation, preached in every country of the West, in Europe, Britain included.'

Theodoret, fourth century, writes: 'St. Paul brought salvation to the Isles in the ocean.'

Ventanius, sixth century, Patriarch of Jerusalem, speaks very definitely of St. Paul's visit and work in Britain, as does Irenaeus, AD 125-189; Tertullian, AD 122-166; Origen, AD 185-254; Mello, AD 256; Eusebius, AD 315; Athanasius, AD 353; and many other chroniclers of church history.

If further confirmation is needed it is supplied in the records of the Roman, Eastern, Gallic and Spanish churches, all of which attest to the fact that St. Paul evangelized in Gaul and Britain.

St Paul's Cathedral at night time.

CHAPTER 17

GOOD KING LUCIUS NATIONALIZES THE FAITH

B Y the year AD 140 all the original apostles, disciples and all those who had been associated with them had passed on into their eternal rest; the last being the noble children of the glorious Claudia and Rufus Pudens. St. John had outlived all the original three groups elected by Jesus. He lived to the remarkable old age of 101 years.[120] Joseph, the Apostle of the British, had died AD 82, at Avalon.[121] A few of them had lived to see fulfilment of the command to go to all corners of the world and preach the Gospel, and had seen the Christian platform on which each had laboured firmly established. Their lives were the nails that held it fast. It seems almost impossible to believe that this handful of men and women could have achieved such a formidable conquest in so short a time.

Undoubtedly it is the greatest and most enduring world conquest in the history of time. Unarmed these gentle, valorous champions of goodwill conquered the evil forces of the mightiest armies of the ancient world, their only weapon the promise of Christ.

Within sixty-six years after the Incarnation prominent Christian centres were strongly entrenched in many foreign lands. In the foregoing chapters we have seen, like the roots of a bay tree, how the endless flow of Christian workers streamed out of Britain into GaulRome, Germany, Switzerland and other countries, evangelizing and building sturdy Bishoprics in numerous cities of importance. Apart from those listed can be added Jerusalem, Samaria, Caesarea, Lydda, Antioch, Damascus, Antioch of Pisidia, lconium, Lystra, Ephesus, Smyrna, Sardis, Thyatira, Pergamos, Philadelphia, Caesarea in Cappadocia, Laodicea, Colosse, Galatia, Athens, Corinth, Thessalonia, Berae, Philippi, Cyprus, Crete, Alexandria, Rome, Malta and Spain. Britain and Gaul have been discussed.

In comparison, the missionary progress made by the Christian world in the last one hundred years is minute. In spite of the vast sums of money provided and expended, under far more favourable conditions, the impress made by our churches and missionaries in India, China,

---

[120] Irenaeus speaks of him as still living in AD 98, and Jerome dates his death as sixty-eight years after the Crucifixion.

[121] July 2nd, AD 82, according to Cressy.

Japan, Africa and elsewhere is not heartening. Since the middle of the last century ungodliness and atheism has developed alarmingly within the Christian nations. The Gallup polls claim that the majority of the Christian world believes in God and worship, but the empty churches and pitiable financial support given to them hardly substantiates the claim. The difference between the teachers and the people of the Christian golden era and the present luxury Christian era is that our ancestors gave heart-service. Today it appears to be purely lip-service. Virtually the Lord's Day is lost and is nothing more than a Roman holiday.

As the wings of death swept the spirits of the glorious cavalcade to their well-earned reward, other disciples stemmed from the many Christian centres in an ever-growing army to take their place, preaching the Word with fiery tongues. The missionary band that flowed from Britain still provided the greatest number in the field. Avalon was still the citadel of the Christian faith. For the churches labouring in other foreign fields, particularly Rome, the task was filled with grave personal danger. They lacked the invincible protection of the British warriors; they stood alone and were to continue to do so for more than one hundred and fifty years before a British army, led by its royal warrior chieftain, was to smash the Gates of Rome and crush pagan opposition for ever.

In Britain there had long been peace between Roman and British armies. Recognizing the futility of the strife and the decimation of her Legions from war in Britain, Rome found her military defence so weakened that she was hard put to defend her own frontiers. Tacitus states that from AD 43 to 86, sixty major battles had been fought on British soil. From AD 86 to 118, only one Roman name appears in British history, Neratius Marcellus. The great Roman commander, Agricola, who had experienced the mettle of British valour on many a battlefield, was more broadminded than any of his predecessors.[122] He was convinced that the Britons were oblivious to persecution and war. Like Julius Caesar he realized that defeat or privation had the adverse effect of discouragement on this warrior nation, inspired with the fire of the Cross. He effected a more humane policy by inaugurating a treaty that held no chains. Wisely he incorporated the British as allies of the Roman Empire, recognizing all their native freedoms and kingly

---

[122] See Tacitus, *Agricola*, ch. 4 for his character.

prerogatives. In AD 120 the Emperor Hadrian enlarged on the treaty, which merely permitted the Romans to hold certain military bases in Britain. The peace treaties of Agricola and Hadrian created the long peace between Rome and Britain that lasted up to the Diocletian persecution, *circa* AD 300.

In the year AD 137 St. Timotheus, son of Claudia Pudens, had journeyed from Rome to baptize his nephew King Lucius at Winton (Winchester), at the same time consecrating him Defender of the Faith, as legal, royal successor to his ancestor, Arviragus, upon whom Joseph had conferred the original honour. This began a new wave of evangelism in Britain which, it is said, had somewhat waned since the death of Joseph. To a certain extent this can be understood: rarely do we find the successor of a strong, vigorous founding leader equally as dominant; nevertheless, as one reads the long list of teachers that continued to pour from Avalon and Cor Eurgain, filling new Bishoprics at home and abroad, there appeared to be little flickering of the light.

However, there is no doubt that the enthusiastic religious zeal that Lucius now supplied infused a vigour more akin to the energy that inspired the founders of the Josephian Mission at Avalon and the Pauline Mission in Cambria, particularly knowing that he was a direct descendant of the royal Silurian kingdoms of Cornwall and Cambria.

According to his genealogy Lucius was son of Coel, son of St. Cyllinus, son of Caractacus, son of Bran, son of Llyr. By intermarriage he was also directly descended from Arviragus, of the Cornish-Devon Silures. This made Lucius the great-grandson of both Caractacus and Arviragus, truly a majestic heritage.

It is strange how the Roman names of the early British kings cling to the pages of the English history books, in preference to their original Celtic names. Because of this the writer finds himself obliged to concur in order to avoid any confusion in the reader's mind in referring to historic data.

His native name was Lleurug Mawr. Because of his exemplary religious life and his outstanding achievements in church and state, he was termed in Celtic Lleuver Mawr, meaning the 'Great Light'. However, the name by which he is best known is the Latin interpretation Lucius. The Romans latinized his name to Lucius from the Latin 'Lux', which carries the same implication as the Celtic to the Romans, the 'Great Luminary'.

It is interesting to note that Lucius made his royal seat at Caer Winton, romanized to Winchester, as it is still known. The city was founded by the brilliant British king, Dunwal Molmutius, renowned in British history as one of 'the Three Wise British Kings', the Great Numa, or Law-maker. He made Winchester his royal capital, 500 BC, instead of the older capital London. It was also known as the 'White City', due to the white chalk walls with which he surrounded the city. Even after, when London was re-established as the royal capital of Britain, Winchester continued to be known as the 'Royal City'. The city was founded on an ancient Druidic Gorsedd site. Some of the stones are still preserved in the old public buildings. Many great British kings made royal Winchester their capital. William the Conqueror refused to consider his first coronation valid until crowned a second time at Winchester, 'to justify his rightful claim to the British throne, where all true British kings had been crowned'.

The most notable event in the meritorious reign of King Luciuswas performed in the year AD 156 when, at the National Council at Winchester, he established Christianity as the National Faith of Britain.

By this act he solemnly declared to the world that Britain was officially a Christian nation by Act of Parliament. This Act is described in the British Triads as follows:

'King Lucius was the first in the Isle of Britain who bestowed the privilege of country and nation and judgment and validity of oath upon those who should be of the faith of Christ.'

In so few words is described one of the most momentous events in Christian history, officially establishing Lucius as the first Christian king by national act of Council. His great grandsires, Caractacus and Arviragus, were Christian kings in person but they had not proclaimed it by a national order in Council over the realm. The time then was not propitious. Their era was the period of acceptance, conversion, organization and the vanquishment of their mortal enemy, the Romans, in defence of the faith; years of preparation by the diligence of the apostles, their disciples, and those that followed after. The great British Edict was joyously welcomed by Christians in other lands. Sabellius, AD 250 shows this national establishment was acknowledged elsewhere beyond the confines of Britain. He writes:

'Christianity was privately confessed elsewhere, but the first nation that proclaimed it as their religion, and called itself Christian, after the name of Christ, was Britain.'

Genebrand declares:

'The glory of Britain consists not only in this, that she was the first country which in a national capacity publicly professed herself Christian, but that she made this confession when the Roman Empire itself was pagan and a cruel persecutor of Christianity.'

This statement by Genebrand is important, proving the invalidity of the claim by the Roman Catholic Church, centuries later, that this epochal act of legislature was brought about by the Pope Eleutherius of Rome. In striving to justify their claim, Romish writers of the seventh century sought to confuse the dates. The ironical fact is that no allusion was made to this claim by the church at Rome until after the Italian-Augustinian Mission in Britain, AD 597, over four hundred and forty years after the Act had been declared. Why the centuries of silence if it were true?

The flat rejection by the British Bishops on their first meeting with St. Augustine, who sought to coerce the British church into the novel Papal system, so angered him and his Romish retinue that he began to institute a rejection of all British priority to her native claims in being the first to accept and establish the Christ faith. They had said:

'We have nothing to do with Rome. We know nothing of the Bishop of Rome in his new character of the Pope. We are the British Church, the Archbishop of which is accountable to God alone, having no superior on earth.'

Blackstone, the great English jurist, wrote:

'The ancient British Church was a stranger to the Bishop of Rome, and all his pretended authorities.'

Sir Francis Bacon, writing in *Government of England*, says:

'The Britons told Augustine they would not be subject to him, nor let him pervert the ancient laws of their Church. This was their resolution, and they were as good as their word, for they maintained the liberty of their Church five hundred years after this time, and were the last of all the Churches of Europe that gave up their power to the Roman Beast, and in the person of Henry VIII, that came of their blood by Owen Tudor, the first that took that power away again.'

A number of writers in modern times have supported many of the statements made by Augustine and his followers, taking for granted what they read from the Romish writings. They could not bother to check the record.

Actually, the spiteful Augustine and his cohorts outsmarted themselves. Gregory I, who commissioned Augustine to go to Britain, was not officially Pope. The slovenly historians dishonoured him. The title of Pope, or universal Bishop, was first given by Emperor Phocas, AD 610. He created the office to demote and spite Bishop Ciriacus of Constantinople, who had justly excommunicated him for his having caused the assassination of his predecessor, Emperor Mauritius. Phocas first offered the title to Gregory I, who was then Bishop of Rome. Gregory refused the office. It was accepted by his successor, Boniface III. He was the first to assume this false title.

One has but to read *Luke* 22:24-26; *Ephesians* 1:22-23; *Colossians* 1:18; and 1 *Corinthians* 3:11 to see that Jesus did not appoint Peter to the headship of the Apostles and expressly forbade any nation to do so.

In later years it became a habit with many Roman Catholic writers to refer to all the former Bishops of Rome as Pope, even to Linus and Paul. The Apostles of Christ never heard the term and Peter and Paul in making their elections specifically nominate the elected as Bishops only. As Bishops they were all known in Rome until the inauguration of the Papacy, AD 610, and in Britain even during the alliance with Rome the heads of the British church were never anything but Bishops, and they alone inherited apostolic succession in an unbroken line from the original Apostles of Christ.

In their efforts to sway the minds of the people Augustine, and a few who followed later, sought to debase the facts and confuse the dates, in a futile effort to convince those not allied with the Roman Catholic hierarchy that all Christianizing eminence was created by them. Due to the record of the correspondence issued between King Lucius and Eleutherius, Bishop of Rome, the spurious claim was made that Lucius pleaded with the Bishop to send his representatives to Britain to convert him and nationally proclaim Britain Christian.

All British and Roman records attest to the fact that Lucius was confirmed and baptized in the faith by his uncle, St. Timotheus, as stated before. He was baptized in the famous Chalice Well, at the foot of the Tor at Avalon, May 28th, AD 137. In the year AD 167 he commemorated the event by building St. Michael's on the summit of the Tor, which was the largest Druidic Gorsedd in Britain. This memorial was destroyed in the earthquake that shook Glastonbury, AD 1275. The present St. Michael's was erected on the same site. It is a most imposing monument. It can be seen for miles before one enters the ancient town of Glastonbury. Standing on its high eminence it reaches into the sky like a giant finger, proclaiming to all who see it the monumental events of the auspicious life of King Lucius.[123]

In the year AD 170 Lucius founded the majestic church at Winchester, now known as Winchester Cathedral, and familiar to thousands of Canadian soldiers in World War II garrisoned at Winchester as the Battle Abbey of the British Empire. Therein repose its greatest warriors and therein is preserved the elaborate casket of the grandfather of Alfred the Great. Also the Round Table of King Arthur's fame is preserved in the County Hall.

Twenty-seven years after Lucius had nationalized Britain in the Christian faith he sent his two emissaries, Medwy and Elfan, to Rome to obtain permission of Bishop Eleutherius for the return to Britain of some of the British missionaries aiding Eleutherius in his evangelizing work within the Roman Empire, in order that he, Lucius, could better carry out his expansive Christian programme in Britain.

Gildas, Geoffrey of Monmouth, Bede, Urban, John of Teignmouth and Capgrave, referred to 'as the most learned of English Augustinians whom the soil of England ever produced', support the date of return of the emissaries of King Lucius from visiting Bishop Eleutherius at Rome, as that given in the British annals, AD 183, over a century and a half before the Roman Catholic Church was founded. Cardinal Baronius not only denounces the Augustinian claim but in detail recites the whole record from the year AD 36 onward.

---

[123] *Vide* Capgrave, John of Teignmouth, *Book of Teilo*, and William of Malmesbury.

Bishop Eleutherius, in his letter to King Lucius, AD 183, plainly shows that he is aware that Lucius possessed all the necessary knowledge of the Christian teachings beforehand and needed no advice from him, and that he had no part in the nationalizing of Britain in the Faith, or in converting or baptizing the British king, otherwise he would have referred to the matter that had occurred twenty-seven years previous to his letter. By this he shows how unjustified is the claim of the Church of Rome, let alone the Roman Catholic Church, which was not yet dreamed of. John Foxe, the talented author of *Acts and Monuments,* reproduces the controversial letter as Eleutherius wrote it to King Lucius[124]:

'The Roman laws and the Emperors we may ever reprove, but the law of God we may not. Ye have received of late through God's mercy in the realm of Britain the Law and Faith of Christ. Ye have with you within the realm, both the parts of the Scriptures. Out of them, by God's grace, with the council of your realm take ye a law, and by that law (through God's sufferance) rule your kingdom of Britain. For ye be God's Vicar in your kingdom, according to the saying of the psalm, "O God, give Thy judgment to the King."'

Medwy and Elfan returned to Britain with Dyfan and Fagan, both British teachers who had first received their schooling at Avalon.

Elfan, Dyfan and Fagan were appointed Bishops in Britain. Elfan succeeded Theanus, first Bishop of London, who died AD 185. The Welsh authorities state that he presided over a congregation of Christian Culdees at Glastonbury (Avalon), before he was sent to Rome with Medwy. Pitsaeus, the Roman Catholic Canon, in his *Relationes Historicae de Rebus Anglicis*, says that Elfan, known as Elvanus of Avalon, was brought up at Glastonbury and was educated in the school of St. Joseph of Arimathea, and that he wrote an informative work concerning the origin of the British church. On being elected as the second Bishop of London, Elfan was the first prelate to occupy the new church erected by King Lucius in memory of St. Peter, a church which has remained famous throughout the centuries of Christian history as St. Peter's on Cornhill, London.

---

[124] Foxe, John *Acts and Monuments of the Church; containing the History and the Suffering of the Martyrs* (Foxe's *Book of Martyrs*) new revised edition Seymour, Rev. M.H. (London: A Fullerton & Co.) 1850 p.75

Medwy was made a Doctor of Theology by the king.

It seemed that the three newly-appointed Bishops shared Lucius's deep affection for Avalon and sought to restore it to its original conception, as first founded by St. Joseph with his twelve companions.[125] From Winchester they journeyed to the Sacred Isle of Avalon, of which Geoffrey of Monmouth writes as follows:

'There, God leading them, they found an old church built, as 'twas said, by the hands of Christ's Disciples, and prepared by God Himself for the salvation of souls, which Church the Heavenly Builder Himself showed to be consecrated by many miraculous deeds, and many Mysteries of healing. And they afterwards pondered the Heavenly message that the Lord had specially chosen this spot before all the rest of Britain as the place where His Mother's name might be invoked. They also found the whole story in ancient writings, how the Holy Apostles were scattered throughout the world. St. Philip coming into France with a host of Disciples sent twelve of them into Britain to preach, and that there, taught by revelation, they constructed the said chapel which the Son of God afterwards dedicated to the honour of His Mother; and that to these same twelve were given twelve portions of land for their sustenance. Moreover, they found a written record of their doings, and on that account they loved this spot above all others, and they also, in memory of the first twelve, chose twelve of their own, and made them live on the island with the approval of King Lucius. These twelve thereafter abode there in divers spots as anchorites – in the same spots, indeed, which the first twelve inhabited. Yet they used to meet together continuously in the Old Church in order to celebrate Divine worship more devoutly, just as the kings long ago granted the said island with its surroundings to the twelve former Disciples of Christ, so the said Phagan (Fagan) and Deruvian (Dyfan) obtained it from King Lucius for these twelve companions and for others to follow thereafter. And thus, many succeeding these, but always twelve in numbers, abode in the said island during many years up to the coming of St. Patrick, the Apostle of the Irish.'

In this manner, at Avalon, the beautiful past was renewed by Fagan and Dyfan, following in the steps of the Nobilis Decurio and his twelve

---

[125] Lewis, L. S. *Glastonbury, Her Saints*, pp. 10-11.

saintly companions, and the many others of the illustrious company of Christ.

Returning to the famous letter of Eleutherius to Lucius, we note the remarkable statement naming Lucius 'Vicar of God'. This is the first time that title was ever bestowed on a king and that a British king and by the Bishop of Rome. By this act the church at Rome declared Lucius to be the head of the church and not they. However, Lucius did not accept or use this honourable title. He recognized the admonition of the Bishops of the British church and of all Christian Britons inured in the faith, that Christ alone was the Head of the Church and the true representative of the Father. Instead, Lucius was named, 'the most religious King', a title which every British ruler since who has sat on the British Throne has held.[126]

Lucius also established the three famous Archbishoprics at London, York and Caerlon on Usk. In the year AD 179 he built the historic St. Peter on Cornhill. This church is often referred to as the first Christian church erected in London, of which Elfan was installed as the first Bishop. During the ensuing centuries this church was enlarged but was destroyed in the Great Fire of London which almost completely levelled the ancient city. The tablet telling the history of this great church, embedded in the original walls, survived the Great Fire, and has since been preserved over the mantel of the fireplace in the vestry. It bears the following inscription:

'Bee it knowne to all men that the yeare of our Lord God 179, Lucius, the first Christian King of the land, then called Britaine, founded the first church in London, that is to say, the church of St. Peter upon Cornehill. And hee founded there an Archbishops See and made the church the metropolitane and chief church of the kingdome; and so indured the space of 400 years unto the coming of St. Austin the Apostle of England, the which was sent into the land by St. Gregoire, the doctor of the church in the time of King Ethelbert. And then was the Archbishops See and Pall removed from the forsaid church of St. Peter upon Cornehill into Dorobernia that now is called Canterburie and there it remaineth to this day. And Millet a monke which came into this land with St. Austin, hee was made Bishop of London and his See was made in St. Paul's church. And this Lucius king was the first founder of St. Peter's

---

[126] Lewis, L. S. *St. Joseph of Arimathea at Glastonbury*, p.18.

church upon Cornehill. And hee reigned in this land after Brute 1245 yeares. And in the yeare of our Lord God 124, Lucius was crowned king and the yeares of his reign were 77 yeares.'

Among other wonderful churches King Lucius founded was the church at Llandaff and the church at Cardiff, known today as St. Mellors, which is still referred to as Lucius's Church. He also founded the beautiful church of St. Mary de Lode in the city of Gloucester, where he was interred. In later year, AD 679, this church was enlarged and beautified by the Christian king of the British Mercians, Wolphen.

It is commonly stated that the Emperor Constantine was the first to have the coin of the realm stamped with the sign of the Cross. The statement is an error. King Lucius, the ancestor of Constantine, was the first to mint his coins displaying the sign of the Cross on one side and on the other side his name 'Luc'. In the collection in the British Museum exist two coins depicting the reign of King Lucius, bearing the motifs as stated. Of interest is the fact that Arviragus, maternal ancestor of Lucius, was so bitterly opposed to all that was Roman that he made acceptance, or circulation of Roman coins among the British, a capital offence. This refusal to accept Roman coinage by the British lingered well into the reign of Lucius. From Claudius, whom Arviragus first opposed on the field of battle, to the reign of Emperor Hadrian, no coins of intervening Roman Emperors are to be found in Britain. From Hadrian onwards complete series of Roman coins are found. An examination of the coinage exhibit in the British Museum substantiates these facts and the notable omission. The coins of Arviragus are considered to be the most magnificent minted. An eminent numismatic expert made the remark:

'Wherever a coin of the British King Arviragus is shown in any coin collection, it stands out as a gem.'

The coins of Cunobelinus bear the inscription on one side of his name 'Cuno', on the reverse side a galloping charger and the plume of three ostrich feathers.

The interesting part is that the coins of these three famed British kings were all minted at Colchester. Historians pay little attention to this ancient city. Focus is all on the great centres such as London, Winchester, York, Edinburgh, Canterbury and others. Few are as steeped in British tradition, where so many notable events had their beginnings, events that are milestones in the destiny of nations and, in particular, Christianity, as we shall see as we pursue our story.

Colchester is a quiet little city today, but what a mass of startling history it contains for those who have the energy to part the curtains of time and examine the records.

Of all the great disciples of Christ, King Lucius is in all probability the least known. To the average person his name has no meaning. All he did to solidify the Christian foundation is not even considered, let alone remembered. Historians by-pass him as though he never existed, in spite of the wealth of information describing his life and achievements at hand. The talented Foxe, in his *Acts and Monuments*, wrote:

'The said Lucius after he had founded many churches, and given great riches and liberties to the same, deceased with great tranquillity in his own land, and was buried at Gloucester.'

King Lucius died December 3rd, in the year AD 201, after a long reign of seventy-seven years. The learned Alban Butler[127] states that Lucius was buried first at St. Mary de Lode, the lovely church he founded at Gloucester, then later was reinterred in the other church he built, St. Peter's on Cornhill, for which church he had a deep affection. Much later, his remains were again translated to Gloucester where they were placed in the choir of the Franciscan church by the Earls of Berkley and Clifford, which church, the Church of the Grey Friars, was founded by these two famous families.

There is another record concerning the death of King Lucius, chronicled in the *Roman Martyrologies*, which states that Lucius abdicated his throne and with his sister, St. Emerita, travelled as a missionary through Bavaria, Rhoetia and Vindelicia, meeting a martyr's death near Curia in Germany. According to an old transcript recorded circa AD 685, Lucius, king of the British, and his sister Emerita, are buried in the crypt of the old cathedral at Chur (Coire), the capital of the Grisons Canton, Switzerland. Cressy the Benedictine, who wrote following the Reformation, quoting from these old chronicles, recites the above in his book *Church History of Brittany*. Students of the life of the illustrious King Lucius state that the *Roman Martyrologies* have the British king confused with the religious Bavarian King Lucius, who was martyred near Curia in Germany.

---

[127] Butler, Fr. Alban *The Lives of the Fathers, Martyrs and other Principle Saints* (1756).

In *A Guide to the Cathedral*, compiled by the Rev. H. Haines in 1867 at Gloucester, he writes:

'King Lucius was baptized on May 28th, A.D. 137, and died on December 3rd, 201. His feast had been given on both these days, but the latter is now universal.'

There exists a wealth of material extolling the exemplary life of Good King Lucius, among which are the writings of Bede, Nennius, Elfan, Geoffrey of Monmouth, Cressy, William of Malmesbury, Ussher, who states he had consulted twenty-three works on Lucius: Rees, Baronius, Alford, *The Book of Llandaff*, *Welsh Triads*, *The Mabinogion*, *Achau Saint Prydain*, and many other reliable works, all of which pay noble tribute to this famed Christian monarch, who devoted his entire life as a disciple in Christ's service, to the benefit of the Christian world which has forgotten him.

The lasting benefits of the wonderful achievements of King Lucius on the realm endured for well over one hundred years after his death. The people and the land thrived in peace and prosperity.

The Venerable Bede, writing AD 740, sums up the picture in a few brief words, but in his characteristic eloquence:

'The Britons preserved the faith which they had nationally received under King Lucius, uncorrupted and entire, and continued in peace and tranquillity until the time of the Emperor Diocletian.'[128]

The savage Diocletian persecution broke the peace and produced the conquering Constantine, known to history as the Emperor Constantine the Great, a direct descendant of Lucius, Arviragus and Caractacus, a stalwart champion and disciple of the Christian faith.

The seed never perished, enduring from one generation to another. In times of peace its strength coursed beneath calm waters, ever ready to crash to the surface in stormy conflict to defend the priceless heritage as circumstances demanded. In every case it was a prince of the royal blood who stalwartly and often heroically stood forth to meet the challenge of battle oppression. And in each case the Defender of the Faith was a true lineal descendant of those valiant British kings and

---

[128] Bede, *Historia Ecclesiastica Gentis Anglorum* (Bede's *Ecclesiastical History of the English People*) Book 1, Chapter 4.

queens of so many centuries ago, even as is today Queen Elizabeth I of the United Kingdom and the British Commonwealth.

Publisher's Note.
Despite the agreement of authorities that King Lucius was baptised by his uncle, St. Timotheus, in the year AD 137, there seems uncertainty as to the place of baptism: Winchester, Glastonbury, and by implication Gloucester, being listed in this chapter. The Gloucester reference implies baptism there, but could be a reference to that at Glastonbury, thus narrowing the field to two. The place, however, is not the important factor here; the fact of baptism is.

CHAPTER 18

THE EMPEROR OF CHRISTENDOM CONSTANTINE THE GREAT

T HE great peace which had settled over the Island, beginning with the Treaty of Agricola, AD 86, continued for a period of two hundred years. During these two centuries there is no mention of any British-Roman conflict. Historians are silent, leaping the two-hundred-year gap as though nothing had occurred in the tight little island of Britain; then they take up the record in the year AD 287, to recite the usurpage of the Roman Emperor's crown when Carausius, a Menapian by birth, who was then the Admiral of the Roman fleet, landed in North Britain, marching to York, where he had himself proclaimed Emperor.

Since the fall of London, under the arms of Queen Boadicea, the city of York had become a popular resort of the Romans. From this ancient British city, first known as Caer Evroc, several Roman Emperors had functioned, probably deeming it a safer haven to rule from than the city of Rome, rife with jealousy, intrigue and assassination. Several Roman Emperors are buried within the walls of this age-old citadel of the Brigantes.

It was at Caer Evroc – York, where Caractacus was betrayed and delivered to the enemy by his relative, Aricia, Queen of the Brigantes, and where she was denounced and dethroned by her own people. For centuries before Christ it had been the centre of enamelling craftsmen and the La Tène art.

Briefly, profane history tells us that Carausius reigned as Emperor from York for seven years and was then assassinated by Allectus, his minister, AD 294. The assassin reigned for two years and then fell in battle against the forces of Constantius Chlorus, who succeeded Allectus as Emperor. He also ruled his Empire from York for ten years. With him began one of the most momentous chapters in Christian history, beginning in a maelstrom of persecution and slaughter exceeding the brutal Menaii bloodbath of the Christians by Suetonius Paulinus and the Boadicean atrocities under the malignant direction of Catus Decianus, AD 60 to 62.

Actually the stupendous events that began to be enacted with the reign of the Emperor Constantius Chlorus had their start in the lovely city of Colchester, thirty-one years before Constantius assumed the Roman purple.

The old Celtic name for Colchester is Camulodunum, the city where Cunobelinus and his son Arviragus minted their excellent coinage. It was also the royal seat of King Coel.

King Coel reigned at Colchester, once the royal seat of Cunobelinus, his ancestor, endowing the churches with munificent gifts. The remains of King Coel's castle can still be seen at Lexdon, a suburb of Colchester.

In the year AD 265 a daughter was born to King Coel in his castle at Colchester who was to become world renowned as Empress Helen of the Cross. Helen was the Graeco-Roman interpretation of the British name Elaine. As the Empress Helena Augusta she is best known and so recorded in the brightest annals of Roman history. This beautiful, accomplished woman was a noble counterpart of her famous predecessors, the Princess St. Eurgain and the beloved Claudia (Gladys) Pudens. Raised in a Christian household and educated in its religious principles, her natural talents were developed to a high degree by the best scholars and administrators in the land. Steeped in the traditions of the faith, she espoused all that is Christian with intelligence and with courage. Helen possessed one attribute greater than either of her famous royal female predecessors, her capacity for political administration. While her regal husband and son stood out eminently in the art of diplomacy, all facts and records prove that her capacity in this direction played a prominent part in their imperial destiny. The Christianizing of the Roman Empire would undoubtedly have been delayed centuries but for her energy and devotional support.

As usual, profane history merely describes Helena in her role as Empress. No mention is given of her ancestry and brilliant heritage. To all Roman historical records the Empress Helena is made to appear as a Roman native, wife of a Roman, and the mother of an illustrious Roman son, none of which is true. They were British to the core.

Melancthon writes: 'Helen was unquestionably a British Princess' (*Epistola*, p. 189).

Even to many academic intellectuals the statement that the Empress Helena and her eminent son were Britons could appear startling. Yet none would deny that the first record of Constantius Chlorus[129] and

---

[129] 'Chlorus' means 'pale' and could be a reference to descent from a blond family, his Dardanian ancestry being Trojan.

Helena began in Britain. Before Constantius defeated Allectus at York he was the recognized Emperor of Britain, Spain and Gaul. At that time the boundaries of Gaul extended far into the European continent, embracing Belgium, Holland and part of Germany. Tréves (Trier) was long the capital of Belgic Gaul. With this record historians begin the Constantinian story, becoming more profuse following the proclamation of Constantius at York as Emperor of Rome. He was the first monarch to be legally recognized as Emperor over the fourfold domain by the populace of the four countries. Only he, and his extraordinary son, Constantine the Great, were ever to acquire imperial sway over this vast Empire, an amazing fact which historians have strangely overlooked.

Six years before Constantius became world Emperor, at the request of his wife Helena he renewed and enlarged the Archbishopric of York, AD 290. After that York became an outstanding royal and religious city in Britain. In the pre-Christian era, as Caer Evroc, it was one of the Druidic centres, continuing so under the Josephian Mission until King Lucius nominated London, York and Caerlon on Usk as the three great Archbishoprics of Britain. Later, Caerlon on Usk was displaced for the city of Canterbury, which replaced London as the chief ecclesiastical seat. These three Archbishoprics have remained throughout centuries until now the great Anglican religious centres, in the following order: Canterbury, London and York.

Canterbury, with its Archbishop, is still recognized throughout the world as the head of the Protestant Anglican Communion. Its Bishops, wherever they may be, are the only ecclesiastics that have inherited and hold true, unbroken succession from the original Apostles, Paul, Peter, and Joseph the Apostle of the British.

The Empress Helena is given credit for founding the first cathedral at Tréves, after the elevation of her husband to be Emperor of Rome. It became her favourite continental residence and, because of her manifold gifts to the city, she was held in the highest esteem and made the patroness of Tréves. The former British princess became titled 'Helen of the Cross', due to the claim that she found the cross of Christ buried near Jerusalem, AD 326. One of the greatest art treasures still in existence is the one entitled 'Helena', created by the renowned artist Cima da Congliane,[130] AD 1459, showing the beautiful royal daughter of King Coel of Colchester with the cross of Christ.

---

[130] Giovanni Batista da Conegliano.

Due to her association with Tréves, and that of her Emperor husband Constantius and their noble son Constantine, this city had closer contact with the early British monarchs than any other on the continent. The present cathedral is built on the site of the palace her husband, Constantius Chlorus, built. Indeed, the basilica of the palace forms the actual walls of the cathedral. Her son, Constantine the Great, erected at Tréves an imperial palace on the same pattern as that of his grandfather's castle at Colchester, the ruins of which can still be seen.

It is said that anyone who has seen the ruins of King Coel's castle in the suburbs of Colchester, and later viewed the ruins at Tréves, is so intrigued with the similarity they bear that the picture of one is easily mistaken for that of the other.

Of further interest is the claim that the original castle now known as Edinburgh Castle was erected by Constantius for the Queen Empress Helena, and that a great portion of the present walls were part of the walls of the original castle.

With the exception of the church dedicated to Mary, the Mother of Jesus, at Avalon, Glastonbury, the practice of making church dedications to women did not begin until about the twelfth century. However, we know that Cor Eurgain was erected and consecrated to the daughter of Caractacus during the lifetime of the Princess Eurgain and Joseph of Arimathea. It was chiefly a university of learning and choral training, with a chapel in its enclosure. To Helena is given the distinctive honour of being the first woman to have a church erected to her glory, several hundred years before the practice began in the twelfth century, and being proclaimed a Saint.

The church of St. Helen was built at Colchester, her birthplace. From ancient times to the present this city has, for its coat of arms, borne the symbol of Helen of the Cross. It is in the form of a cross with three crowns for its arms. Thus, in silent form, is the noble record perpetuated in the city in which she was born and also her son Constantine, the champion of Christendom.

With devout pride the descendants of British Christians in the British Commonwealth, America and elsewhere may point to the fact that the only sainted female dedications made between the one to Mary at Avalon, and those appearing a thousand years later, were to the royal ancestors of their own race, relatives to each other in the royal blood strain: first, the dedication of the church formed from the British Palace at Rome to Pudentiana, the daughter of Claudia and Rufus Pudens, following his martyrdom; second, Cor Eurgain in Wales, dedicated to the Princess Eurgain, aunt of Pudentiana; and, thirdly, to St. Helen at Colchester, daughter of King Coel, Queen Empress of Rome.

Strangely enough, some have stated that Helen was never Empress of Rome but a concubine of the Emperor, Constantius Chlorus. There are ever twisted minds seeking to debase the most noble. However, written records, and they are legion,[131] confound them beyond remotest question. Certainly no person who was not a reigning king or queen would have coins struck with their name, declaring them as such. In the Vatican Museum and the British Museum can be seen coins struck with her name, proving that she was Empress by the title of Augusta. The coins read, 'Flavia Helena Augusta.'[132]

Sulpicius Severus says: 'Helen reigned as Empress with her son.'

Helena lived seventy-one years. She died AD 336. The later years of her life were spent in working diligently for the faith at Constantinople, the city which her son founded, and for him named. Helena was assiduous in collecting and preserving relics of the early Apostles found in and around Jerusalem. Posterity can be eternally grateful to this gracious woman who contributed so abundantly of her fortune in searching for and restoring ancient manuscripts and documents, as well as personal effects of the Apostles.

Her husband, the Emperor Constantius Chlorus, had died thirty years before her in AD 306 at the city of York, where he is buried.

Prior to the ascent of Constantius to the throne of the Roman Empire, tragic storm-clouds had gathered on the continent, particularly at Rome, where revolution and assassination had been disposing of one Emperor after the other. There was a confusing medley of predatory Romans who raised armies, laying claim to the throne of the Caesars. The infamous Diocletian held the reins at Rome, and on his orders began what is often described as the worst persecution of the Christians in the year AD 290. In his Edict, he ordered churches to be pulled down, the sacred scriptures to be gathered together and burnt, along with other Christian literature on which they could lay their hands. Libraries, schools of learning and private homes were equally destroyed. Again the lions roared in the Coliseum. The prisons were filled and streets ran with the blood of martyrs. No Christian was spared, regardless of age or sex. Even the babes in arms of Christian parents were cruelly destroyed. The

---

[131] Archbishop Ussher lists twenty authorities; cf. Morgan, *St. Paul in Britain*, pp. 164-165.
[132] Lewis, L. S. *St Joseph of Arimathea*, p. 138 (note).

Diocletian persecution is described as the tenth Christian persecution, beginning with the Claudian Edict, AD 42. The Emperor Diocletian struck with sudden appalling savagery at the Christians. He blamed them for the series of disasters over the years that had decimated the Roman arms to such an extent that they were no longer able to defend their own frontiers successfully, let alone conquer as formerly. Rome was on the decline; her glory was fast waning. Diocletian sought to avert national disaster by ordering the extermination of the Christians, their churches and other possessions. This bestial cruelty lasted for eighteen years. The persecution flamed across Europe for several years before it struck the shores of Britain. Again the Romans were frustrated by the incredible zeal of the martyrs who died with prayer on their lips, or ringing exhortations. They saw the common people destroyed, showing the same disdain for death as had their Christian forbears. This infuriated Diocletian to more fiendish practices, in which he later was aided by Maximian, who became co-ruler with him over the continental Roman Empire. Brutal as was Diocletian, it is written by the Romans themselves that Maximian was worse. His ferocity and atrocities are claimed to be beyond description. He caused his finest Legions, exclusively composed of Gauls, to be butchered to the last man because they were Christian. He was blind with maniacal hate.

The Diocletian persecution reached Britain, AD 300, where again the Romans sought to destroy Christianity at its source. The Emperor poured a huge army into Britain, while Maximian carried on his destructive course on the continent. Constantius Chlorus had already been proclaimed Emperor of Rome at York. The British kingdoms were better united. As one they responded to the battle call of Constantius. Previously the British had fought years in deciding each Roman conflict, with victory swaying from one side to the other. Yet, within one year, Constantius terminated the Diocletian persecution in Britain, inflicting staggering defeats on the Roman arms, driving them back to the continent, AD 302. However, before victory crowned the British armies, the Romans had inflicted great destruction, levelling churches, universities and libraries, and sacking towns. The slaughter was terrific, totalling a list of British martyrs that far exceeded the total inflicted by all the former persecutions combined. It is stated that the loss of British lives was beyond computation, not so much on the field of battle as in the slaughter of the harmless, defenceless people and priesthood.

Gildas, the early British historian, informs us that the British church lost the following eminent prelates by martyrdom: Amphibalus, Bishop of Llandaff; Alban of Verulam; Aaron and Julius, citizens and presbyters of Chester; Socrates, Bishop of York; Stephen, Bishop of London; Argulius, his successor; Nicholas, Bishop of Penrhyn (Glasgow); Melior, Bishop of Carlisle; and about ten thousand communicants in different grades of society. The thousands of others who perished in Britain will never be known, any more than is known of the countless multitude of Christians who were slaughtered on the continent for the sake of the faith.

Following the expulsion of the Romans, we are told that the Emperor Constantius and his Queen Empress diligently began to restore the destroyed churches. It was a titanic task, speaking highly for the Christian devotion of this royal family who poured their personal fortune into the restoration. During this process of rehabilitation the Emperor Constantius Chlorus died at York, AD 306 and there he was laid to rest. Immediately, his son Constantine assumed the purple and at York declared himself Emperor of the Roman Empire. For the next six years Constantine remained in Britain, building many new churches and institutions of learning after he had completed restoration of those destroyed. During this time Diocletian, and particularly Maximian, continued their destruction of Christian lives on the continent.

Peace restored in Britain, Constantine, the famed son of famous royal Christian parents, began to prepare to cross the seas to the continent where his dramatic destiny was to unfold. He massed a powerful army in Britain, composed wholly of British warriors. With them he sailed, landing in what today is Germany. The two armies clashed together on the banks of the Tiber where the British, under the generalship of the Emperor Constantine, won an overwhelming victory. Maximian was completely routed and persecution ended. Constantine, with his British warriors, marched victoriously on to Rome, where he met with an uproarious welcome. Amid great rejoicing he ascended the Imperial throne, officially acclaimed by the Senate and the populace of Rome as Emperor.

By hereditary right he was Emperor over Britain, Gaul and Spain, succeeding his father's claim to power in Rome by virtue of conquest at York, which he confirmed by victory over Maximian on the banks of the Tiber.

This was the greatest territorial dominion over which one Roman Emperor reigned, alone and at peace. It was also the last time.

His first act as Emperor of Rome was to declare Rome Christian, ending for ever Christian persecution within the Empire, *circa* AD 312. Henceforth Rome began her history as a Christian nation. In nationalizing the faith, Constantine had done for Rome what King Lucius had done for Britain one hundred and fifty years earlier. In the great Christianizing work that followed, the gracious Helen, his mother, stood by his side and, as Severus said, reigned with her son as Empress.

As we sum up the picture one may well exclaim, 'What a paradox!'

The first Christian church founded at Rome by the British royal family! The same family under Arviragus are the first to be given the sign of the Cross for their emblem. In order, their descendants under Lucius nationalized the faith in Britain and planted the sign of the Cross for the first time on coinage; the grand-daughter of Lucius, Princess Helen of Colchester, preserving the faith in her homeland, her husband smashing the Diocletian persecution and, finally, her illustrious son, backed with a British army, conquering the city of Rome; Constantine, a Briton, nationalizing the faith in Rome. What irony of fate! The Romans who first set out to destroy Britain and Christianity are finally converted to the faith, nationalized in Christ by the same British, with a Briton reigning on the Imperial throne and British warriors defending the faith where, for three hundred years, persecution of the Christians had prevailed.

History has no counterpart to this strange drama. The Divine pattern was now almost complete, and Constantine was to seal it.

Forgotten is this long train of disciples but the majesty of their great deeds lives with us in the Christian democracies sprung from them.

How many today realize that Constantine the Great was a Briton? Few, if any, except for the seekers of truth who have read the scrolls. Many think the fact is too fantastic to be true and discount it without searching. To them the eminent Cardinal Baronius speaks:

'The man must be mad who, in the face of universal antiquity, refuses to believe that Constantine and his mother were Britons, born in Britain.'

Over twenty European authorities affirm this fact. The descent of Constantine is listed in *The Panegyrics of the Emperors*, and the genealogy of his illustrious lineage given by his descendant, Constantine Palaeologus, wherein is provided in detail all the records and proof and circumstances of his wonderful career.

Polydore Vergil, in his *History of England*, exclaims:

'Constantine, born in Britain, of a British mother, proclaimed Emperor in Britain, beyond doubt made his natal soil a participator in his glory.'

Sozomen, in *Ecclesiastical History*, writes:

'The Great Constantine received his Christian education in Britain.'

And Pope Urban says in his *Brief Brittannia*:

'Christ shewed to Constantine the Briton, the victory of the Cross for his sceptre.'

The Emperor Maximus Magnus who, with his victorious British army, overran the continent AD 387, then withdrew into Gaul, where they peopled Brittany, sprang from the Great Constantine. Quoting from Hewins' *The Royal Saints of Britain*, we read:

'The Emperor Maximus Magnus or Maxen Wledi was a Roman-Spaniard related to the Emperor Theodosius, and of the family of Constantine the Great, and of British royal descent on his mother's side.'

All records prove that Constantine was heir and legal representative of the royal Christian dynasty of Britain, a true representative of the royal church which he permanently established by Imperial Edict in the pagan city of Rome. He made land gifts to the church at Rome, whose only previous gifts were those bequeathed to the church by the Caradoc-Pudens royal family: the Palace of the British and its estate, reminiscent in the church known as St. Pudentiana, the first church at Rome above ground. The objects of Constantine the Great's life are clearly exemplified by him in one of his Edicts, wherein he says:

'We call God to witness, the Saviour of all men, that in assuming the government we are influenced solely by these two considerations: the uniting of the empire in one faith, and the restoration of peace to a world rent to pieces by the insanity of religious persecution.'

He bent all his efforts to this end. Two years after he was hailed Emperor at Rome he created and commanded the first Christian church council since the one recorded by St. James in the *Acts of the Apostles*. This important church council took place at Arles, AD 314. The second great council was held at Nicaea, AD 325. Constantine personally presided at this council, of which it is recorded, out of three hundred and eighteen Bishops present, only ten were Latin-speaking. The third great council was held at Constantinople, AD 337. It is known as the Council of Byzantium or Constantinople. Although the Bishop of Rome was present, it is interesting to note it was the Bishop of Constantinople who presided. At every council, the representative of each country took his seat in the order in which each land had received Christianity. At all times, at every convention that ever followed, the British Bishop retained the first seat. Nearly a thousand years later, when Italy and Spain challenged the priority of Britain, it was the Pope who vetoed the complaint by stating that Britain held priority of place by reason of her being the first nation to accept the faith of Christ.

For twenty years Constantine laboured to extend the system of constitutional Christianity, long established in his native land. Like his mother, the Queen Empress Helena, he had inherited the British sympathy for the Eastern church rather than the Roman. For them, British faith stemmed from Jerusalem, not Rome. For this reason he, with his mother, set up his government at Constantinople and there transferred the Imperial Throne of the Caesars. It is stated that during his long reign he only made two short visits to the Italian capital. Constantinople, York and Colchester were his favourite places of residence. As Virgil wrote, 'he made his native sod a participator in his glory'.

There is documentary evidence in existence which reports that he restored lands and the ancient forest rights of the Diocese of London, together with the Gorsedd lands of his grandfather King Coel, son of Lucius, in the royal city of Camulodunum – Colchester, the city being in the Diocese of London. In this manner he followed the practice of his regal predecessors, Arviragus to Lucius. In the British Triad III he is recorded as being the first Emperor to extend royal patronage to all who assembled in the Faith. This fact is again mentioned in connection with the three Archbishoprics of the Isle of Britain.

There are some remarkable similarities between the practice and observance of Christianity which, as we have seen, was a flower planted and flourishing on Druidic soil, and the Israelitish 'church' or 'congregation in the wilderness'.

The Levites, in the old patriarchal system, were charged with the service of the Tabernacle and the Temple. They, being in charge of the Sanctuary, had no inheritance in the land as had all the other Tribes of Israel. They were not paid for their services. It was provided for them out of the tithe. The tribe of Levi is known as the Priestly Tribe, but all Levites were not priests. Apart from performing the ecclesiastical functions of the Temple, they performed the functions of civil servants. As one modern writer puts it:

> 'The Levites include not only those who waited about the altar; but the educational or teaching staff of the nation, as well as judicial officers represented by judges and magistrates. The administration of justice, or at least the whole legislative side of it, the provision for the poor, the system of national education, as well as the custody and transmission of the Scriptures, besides the conduct of sacrificial worship and the songs and services of the Temple were in the hands of the Tribe of Levi.'

In addition, the Levites furnished the majority of the judges, clerks, registrars, censors, keepers of the records, the geometricians, genealogists and superintendents of weights and measures. The tithe represented the divine economic system, through the law of righteousness, including the principle of distributive justice.

The Druidic economic law was exactly the same and naturally continued in the merging of the Druidic with the Christian principles of the faith. For thousands of years this practice was so embedded in the minds of the people it was normally carried on throughout the Golden Era of the church in Britain. The magnificent gifts of the British kings to the church were simply an enlargement of the tithe on their part to the glory of God for the advancement of the Christian faith.

The Queen Empress Helena and her son, Constantine the Great, were probably the greatest contributors of wealth to the Christian cause.

The Harvest Feast, better known today as Thanksgiving, was the time when the people brought to the church in early Druid and Christian times their gifts of the field. The decoration of churches with the products of the field is but a modern gesture of the age-old harvest tithing custom.

Following the Golden Era, *circa* AD 600 the tithe began to lose some of its original substance, chiefly caused by the Danish invasions and desecration of the holy places by the Norsemen. Again we see a British king stand forth to preserve an ancient godly law. In AD 854 King Ethelwulf, a Christian Saxon king, by order of a Royal Charter in Parliament, caused the state and the church to recognize the tithe as a national institution. Quoting from this Royal Charter, which is in the British Museum, we read:

'The tenth part of the land of the Kingdom to God's praise and His own eternal welfare.'

This deed was written at Winchester and the Charter placed on the Cathedral altar in the presence of St. Swithin and the assemblage of the Witan (Saxon Parliament), and consecrated to the service of Christ. Thus was the patriarchal law of Israel, and of the Druids, re-established.

The years of the reign of Constantine the Great and the Empress Helenaare the brightest pages in Roman history. Constantine freed the Christians for ever from further persecution. The horrible pit of the Mamertine was closed. The blood-soaked arena of the Coliseum was dry and the great walls began to crumble into decay from misuse. It was an era of peace quietly maintained by Constantine's British Legions.

The apostolic claim to the heirship of Peter is inconceivable. Peter was never addressed as Bishop of Rome, let alone Pope, by St. Paul, or any of the Apostles or early Bishops of the church. Yet the impressive text which appears in gorgeous blue letters around the golden dome of St. Peter's deliberately seeks to proclaim the heirship to visitors to Rome, who see the text:

'Thou art Peter, and upon this rock I will build my Church, and the gates of hell shall not prevail against it.'

Linus and Clement, the first and second Bishops of Rome, knew Peter intimately, along with the apostolic throng. Quite obviously they were also unaware of the claim of Peter's supposed election. St. Paul addressing the church at Rome in his Epistles, makes no reference to Peter as Bishop, or as having any direct association with the Gentile church. The crowning fact is that if St. Peter had been known as the 'Supreme Head of the Church and Vicar of Christ on Earth', the Council of Jerusalem, AD 46, which met to settle a heated dispute between Peter and Paul, ending in the latter's favour, never would have accepted St. James, brother of Jesus, and Apostolic Bishop of Jerusalem, as its presiding chairman. And certainly Peter could not have been on trial if he were Pope.

Gore, in his *Roman Catholic Claims*, dispenses the claim, along with the present charge that no one belongs to the true church unless under the authority of the Bishop of Rome. The argument is worthless. The Papacy as we know it, and as William the Conqueror, Henry VIII, and Queen Elizabeth I knew it, is not in and of the Primitive Church of Christ. It is devoid of all scriptural recognition. It evolved out of a combination of circumstance and pressure politics, based on a series of documents proven by all historians to be 'the Forged Decretals'.

Constantine, steeped in the heritage of the primitive faith in Britain, would be the last man to suggest, let alone endorse such a sacriligious act. Gregory the Great, who sent Augustine to Britain, rejected the title of Pope, claiming to be no more than 'first among equals', which is the position today existing among all Bishops stemming from apostolic succession in the Anglican Communion.

The sons of Constantine preserved the Christian principles of their great parent. They were the founders of the Byzantine Empire but their august lives do not affect our story except in the case of one descendant. Oddly enough, he is best known as 'the Prince of the Sanctuary'. Professor Rhys says that Ambrosius Aurelianus[133] was the grandson of Constantine the Great. He was the son of Jovin, who married a daughter of the Emperor and became King of the British Cotswolds. He was brother to Uther Pendragon, uncle of the romantically famed King Arthur. It is strange how these ancient religious responsibilities appear in Britain and always within the office of the British royal family. The subject becomes more intriguing when we learn that the standard of this

---

[133] See also Hewins, Prof. W.A.S., *The Royal Saints of Britain*, pp. 52-56.

227

grandson of Constantine bore the sign of the lion. This takes us a long way back into Old Testament history.

When the dying Jacob nationalized the twelve tribes under the name of Israel, the two chief offices representing the power of the government and authority of the Temple were bestowed on two members of the twelve tribes of Israel. To Judah was given the Sanctuary – the Temple; and to Ephraim the Dominion – governmental power. Judah thus became the Keeper of the Sanctuary and his son the Prince of the Sanctuary. His ensign was a lion, still known as of old as the Lion of Judah. The sign of the ten tribes under Ephraim was the bull. They were known historically as the 'Bull Tribe'. Their standard bore the insignia of a white bull. Finally, thousands of years later we find these same insignia all appearing in Britain and demonstrative of the same ancient royal religious authority. First the bull sign of Ephraim, employed by the Druids; then the cross under Arviragus; now we have the lion as the emblem of the Prince of the Sanctuary, and today all these signs are combined on the royal standard of the British monarchs. In all sincerity we may ask the profound question. Is it all a coincidence, or is it the working of divine destiny as proclaimed by the prophets?

Only time will tell the fulness of the hidden scroll.

Little is left to us today reminiscent of the life and great Christian achievements of Constantine the Great and his devout mother, the Empress Helena. For nearly fourteen hundred years the Sword of Constantine was a treasured relic among the British Coronation regalia. As the king was crowned and the ring of the Church was placed on his finger, the Sword of Constantine was handed to him as a symbol of his heritage as the defender of the Christian faith. During the Cromwellian desecration of the churches the fanatical Puritans seized, among many other treasures, the coronation crowns, jewels and other regalia. Many precious jewelled ornaments were never returned. Some that were returned had been robbed of priceless stones.

For many years a world-wide search was made to recover the Sword of Constantine, with rich rewards offered, all to no avail.

The sword which Constantine drew from its scabbard to defeat Maximian on the Tiber and crush the Diocletian persecution once and for all is gone, but the character of its ideals lives and burns as strongly as ever in the hearts of true Christians. No longer is the sword needed in spite of its historical importance. We possess a more potent power, a power that has never failed us as long as we held fast and true, the unconquerable spirit of Christ, the same that inspired Constantine the Great, the same imperishable spirit that spake through the lips of Jesus to all who believed in Him: 'Lo I am with you always.'

What more could we need?

While few may remember or know of the incidents herein related of Constantine the Great and his family as associated with Britain, a memorial still exists.

In the churchyard of the ancient parish church of St. Cuthbert, now in the city of York, stands near the main entrance a large stone cross on which is inscribed the following words:

'From this Parish Constantine the Great was declared Emperor, AD 306.'

Incontrovertible testimony to the astounding historic truth as stated by Cardinal Baronius, and to the glory of the great Christian achievement that stemmed from York, led by the great British Christian Constantine, and his British army that conquered Rome and proclaimed it Christian.

CHAPTER 19

THE MYSTERY OF THE CUP OF THE LAST SUPPER

W E are still intrigued with the mystery of the original Cup of the Last Supper, which we believe, from a study of the traditions, was preserved.

What was its ultimate fate?

The answer may lie in the ancient British tradition which associates the original Cup with Joseph of Arimathea at Avalon. Of the three Apostles most closely attached to Jesus it is generally assumed that Peter, the Rock, would be the one most likely to have accepted the dangerous assignment for its safety. On the other hand, Peter's commission was filled with danger to himself. The Edicts of Tiberius and Claudius had made it a capital offence for any person to embrace the teachings of the Way, and called for the destruction of anything pertaining to the Christian Cause. With the sword hanging over their heads the Apostles would most certainly have wished to place any sacred object where it would be safe. As the record proves, the church at Antioch could at the best be but a temporary haven for the treasured relic. As we know, John had previously transferred the safekeeping of Mary to the guardianship of her uncle, Joseph. All inference is that he took her, along with his other companions, to Britain, where she died and was buried. In this case it is logical to assume there would be no better haven for the Cup than in Joseph's possession at Avalon, presuming Peter was the temporary guardian. We know that Peter probably laboured in Britain three or four years before he went to Rome, and within ten years after the arrival of the Bethany group on the Sacred Isle of Avalon. Under the dangerous circumstances it is quite possible that Peter conveyed the original Cup with him to Britain, transferring it to the care of Joseph. The ancient British tradition has it that the sacred Cup was in Joseph's possession when he first arrived at Avalon, and when the first Christian persecution in Britain took place under the Claudian invasion, AD 42. After consulting with the elect Joseph secretly buried it so that it would be for ever safe from the touch of profane hands. If there is any merit to this persistent age-old tradition the original Cup of the Last Supper was buried within the cloaking earth of Chalice Hill.

It is quite significant that at the foot of the Tor where Joseph and his companions erected their wattle church is located a terraced garden known as Chalice Hill. Therein is a wonderful well of water that still bears the name of Chalice Well. From the earliest Christian times the hill and the well have been known by their particular name, with the well often referred to as the Holy Well. In the waters of this well King Lucius and countless other notable converts were baptized in the Christian faith. In this hill Joseph is claimed to have buried the Cup, and the springs flowing out of the hill to form the well gave the name to both Chalice Hill and Chalice Well. While the well was always known as the Chalice Well, and the Holy Well, centuries later Anglo-Saxon monks named it Blood Spring on account of the reddish stains that marked wherever its waters washed. They evolved the superstitious belief that the stains were the blood of Christ arising out of the buried Cup in Chalice Hill. The waters were never known as the Blood Spring by the early British Church. To them and to date it has always been the Chalice Well.

In 1883 the well was cleaned of the broken masonry and debris that had clogged it for centuries and the water analysed, which proved it to be fed by mineral springs of iron content; consequently wherever the mineral deposits of iron dried there was left the reddish stain that gave the appearance of blood, giving rise to the old monkish legend.

It is interesting to note that there is another well of famed antiquity near Padstow, in Cornwall, which from ancient times has been known as Jesus's Well.

That the Cup was buried by Joseph in Chalice Hill was firmly believed for over a thousand years, and was the theme of the search of King Arthur and the Knights of the Round Table for the Holy Grail.

How strongly the belief that Joseph buried the Holy Cup has persisted over the ages to modern times is shown in the many poems, songs and stories that abound. Tennyson immortalized the tradition of the Cup in the following verses he wrote:

'The cup, the cup itself from which our Lord
drank at the last sad supper with His own;
This from the blessed land of Amamat,
After the day of darkness, when the dead
went wandering over Moriah – the good Saint,
Arimathean Joseph, journeying brought to Glastonbury.'

Well might we ask, if there is no substance to the story of the Cup of the Last Supper, as herein related, how is it that the two places of interest were named Chalice Hill and Chalice Well nearly two thousand years ago by the founders of the first Christian church above ground in Britain? A place is never named without a reason. It is a label or an index to something plainly significant. Unlike some historic place names these two have never been challenged as to veracity. They have endured, endeared to the human heart as a living testimony to a sacred event. Today, in this astounding age of scientific materialism, to all Christians the Holy Communion is a hallowed ceremony. Jesus asked that it be done in lasting remembrance of Him. From time immemorial the communicants of the British Church have held steadfast by this lovely act of remembrance. In present times all Christian denominations stemming from the Mother Church at Avalon, no matter in what part of the world they may be, are most loyal in keeping faith with their Redeemer in practising the act of remembrance in devout reverence and in humility. Interesting as it may be to know and see the sacred Cup, it really does not matter; it is the significance of the memory that counts for the most and that lives fiercely in all true Christian hearts today, as it did nearly two thousand years ago.

CHAPTER 20

THE END OF THE GOLDEN TRAIL

JOSEPH, the Apostle of Britain, lived within four years of witnessing the second expulsion of the persecuting Romans from the Sceptred Isle. During those years the soil of Britain had become saturated with the blood of friend and foe in numerous battles and not once had the foot of the invader penetrated through the lines of the British warriors to set foot on the sacred Isle of Avalon, and none ever would. The desperate efforts of Imperial Rome to crush the power of the Word had succeeded in fanning the flame into an unquenchable fire that was then sweeping from Britain and Gaul into many other lands. The Christian spark Joseph had fostered was to be his enduring monument. The life of no Apostle, not even St. Paul, was more filled with high purpose, enterprise and achievement than was the life of the uncle of Jesus; therefore, there is no regret in stating that Joseph was not privileged to live to see the two memorable Christian conquests that were to follow his demise.

In spite of the many sorrows that had shadowed his life, his personal triumphs in spreading the teachings of 'The Way' from Britain far outweighed the tragedies he had shared and witnessed. He had viewed the first Christian army raised which shattered the Claudian Legions in the first pitched battle in defence of the new faith and the death on the field of the first Christian king, replaced by the noble Arviragus. Massed war continued under the dual leadership of the Pendragon Caradoc and Arviragus, in which the Flag of the Cross was first flown. The non-compromising armistice was between the Roman Emperor and the two dauntless British leaders. The British defeat at Brandon and the treacherous betrayal of Caractacus into captivity with all his royal family, followed by the Roman pardon of the British king, and the strange alliances between the scions of Rome with the royal British prince and princesses was unusual. The slaughter of the defenceless and the atrocious Menai massacre was avenged in the triumph and tragedy of the Boadicean campaign. Through it all there was an ever-flowing stream of converts aflame with the fire of the Gospel, spreading from Avalon into the land and camp of the enemy, valorously defiant. The martyrdom of Aristobulus and Simon Zelotes in Britain must have wrung his heart, but the founding of the first Christian church at Rome and the mission of St. Paul in Wales with the royal British must have soared his stalwart heart.

Joseph lived to see all but one of the original Apostles of Christ go to their immortal reward. The fate of most of them has been recited. James, brother of St. John, had been put to the sword by Herod, AD 64. And James, the brother of Jesus, was hurled from a pinnacle of the Temple to his death, AD 62.[134] On his monument is written: 'He hath been a true witness both to Jews and Greeks, that Jesus is the Christ.' St. John outlived Joseph. Apparently he was one of the very few apostles and disciples of Christ to die a natural death at the extreme age of 101 years.

Fifty years after Joseph had placed the body of Jesus in His tomb he laid down the sceptre of his mortal life on July 27th, AD 82. Loving hands and heart laid him to rest among the saintly company that had preceded him, close beside the grave of the Virgin Mary, near the little wattle church which he and his twelve companions had built over forty years before after setting foot on British soil.

Cressy, in *Church History of Brittany*, writes: 'Joseph was buried near the little wattle church he built.'

Across the stone lid of the sarcophagus on which his bones were later buried, under the initials of Joseph of Arimathea, are inscribed these immortal words: 'Ad Brittanos veni post Christum Sepelivi. Docui. Quievi.' (To the Britons I came after I buried the Christ. I taught, I have entered my rest.)

In these few simple words are contained more tragedy, romance, and drama than in any other inscription ever written; words so characteristic of all the faithful Apostles of Christ, seeking no self-justification, merely a simple record of a duty performed.

Maelgwyn of Avalon, who wrote about AD 450, describes the place of burial in these words:

'Joseph of Arimathea, the noble decurion, received his everlasting rest with his eleven associates in the Isle of Avalon. He lies in the southern angle of the bifurcated line of the Oratorium of the Adorable Virgin.'

Long before the time of Maelgwyn, a magnificent Abbey had risen over the original site, enclosing the wattle church encased in lead for its

---

[134] Eusebius, quoting Hegesippus.

preservation, and the relics of the sainted group. All the early and later authorities refer to the same resting-place of Joseph, as cited by Maelgwyn, and rarely do they fail to quote the inscription as it appeared on Joseph's tomb. Among the notable historians who make special reference to the inscription are John of Teignmouth, Leland, Hearne and Morgan.

Gildas the Wise, AD 425, whom modern historians refer to as the first British historian of reliable reportage, lived for quite a time at Glastonbury. He had access to all the records and original documents in the famous Abbey. His reference to the coming of Joseph to Britain, his life there and his death was written from examination of the old records.

William of Malmesbury is held in the highest esteem as an exacting, honest writer. His worthiness was so great that he was invited by the Abbot of Glastonbury to dwell among them and write a faithful history of the Abbey from a study of the ancient *MSS*. In AD 1121 he wrote his *Antiquity of Glastonbury*. In corroboration of his fine work he refers to the Eleutherian Mission at Glastonbury, AD 183, quoting from the record they had left. He writes:

'They also found the whole story in ancient writings how the holy apostles, having been scattered throughout the world, St. Philip the Apostle coming into France with a host of disciples, sent twelve of them into Britain to preach, and that – taught by revelation – constructed the said chapel which the Son of God afterwards dedicated to the honour of His Mother. Their leader, it is said, was Philip's dearest friend, Joseph of Arimathea, who buried our Lord.'

The learned Archbishop Ussher refers to William of Malmesbury as 'our chief historian'. Leland and others call him 'an elegant, learned, and faithful historian'. William dwelt twice at the famous Abbey in order to complete his splendid *MSS*. At that time, before the great fire, all the treasured records and manuscripts were in existence and at his disposal. He also confirms the time and place of Joseph's death and interment.

The original *MSS*. of William of Malmesbury's *Antiquity of Glastonbury* is in the Library of Trinity College, Cambridge. A translation from the original Latin was made from it by Thomas Hearn in 1727. Hearn adds to the record the death of William of Malmesbury in 1142, details of the great fire which destroyed the Abbey in 1184, with a listing of all the Abbots to the time of the Dissolution in 1539.

Archbishop Ussher, church historian, writes in his carefully detailed work of 'St. Joseph's burial in the bifurcated line next to the corner of St. Mary's Chapel and of the silver and white cruets containing the sweat and blood of Christ buried with him'. He recites the presentation by St. Joseph of the Flag of the Cross to Arviragus, 'for the insignia of the British race'. The Archbishop provides a copy of the licence, copied from the royal archives in the Tower of London, given by Edward III in 1345, to one John Bloom of London, with the right to excavate the body of St. Joseph beneath the enclosure of the monastery, and his finding of the body exactly where all had stated it rested. The document was signed by King Edward on June 8th, 1345. Ussher also quotes from the 'Record of the burial of St. Joseph and his companions', from *The Great Register of the Monks of Glaston.*

William Goode, the Jesuit, born at Glastonbury and educated there during the reign of Henry VIII, confirms the old records, further stating:

'There was in existence at Glastonia inscribed tablets to perpetuate St. Joseph's memory, chapels, crypts, crosses, arms, and the observance of the feast of St. Joseph for six days at the Kalends of August, as long as the Monks enjoyed most securely the King's charters.'

He also reports seeing the brass plate on an overturned cross in the reign of Queen Elizabeth I. He relates the arrival of Joseph with the Bethany group, the gifts of land to Joseph by King Arviragus, the silver cruets, size of the wattle church, and of the stone bearing the strange words 'Jesus-Maria', the arms of the abbey, the cross on the shield, and burial of Joseph at Glastonbury

For over one thousand years annual pilgrimages were made to the tomb of St. Joseph by pilgrims from all parts of the Christian world in the month of August.

The conversion of Britain by Joseph, and his establishment of the first Christian church above ground at Avalon, was not only the challenge of the British church in refuting the Papal claim to seniority as Christ's vice-regent on earth; it extended into the important matters of state when dealing with nations subject to Vatican control. British kings, queens and ambassadors defied Papal interference, refusing to treat with him or his emissaries. They would cite the record that Britain held seniority as being the first Christian nation, and that church was ruled by its Bishops, with Christ alone as the recognized Head of the Church. The kings and queens, by the terms of their Christian oath at coronation, gave allegiance to God, through Jesus Christ, and not to man or a church founded on a usurped authority. Strangely enough, the Vatican never denied British priority even when seeking to make alliances, or bring the British Church within the Roman Catholic fold. Royal and ambassadorial replies were pregnant with the Christian claim by Britain based on the life and death of Joseph in that country, St. Paul and others of Christ's elect who had dwelt among them. When controversy and antagonism was at its height between the Vatican and Britain during the reigns of Henry VIII and his daughter Queen Elizabeth I, Sir Robert Wingfield, English Ambassador to Spain, personally compiled the records of the Council of Constance in a book, proving that at the four great church councils British Bishops had been accorded seniority as head of the councils: Pisa 1409, Constance 1417, Sienna 1424 and Basle 1434, on the grounds that 'Joseph of Arimathea brought the faith to Britain immediately after the Passion of Christ'. Wingfield named the presiding British church dignitaries at Pisa: Robert Hallam, Bishop of Salisbury; Henry Chicele; and Thomas Chillenden, Prior of Christ Church, Canterbury. Hallam was the leader at Pisa and at Sienna. Others were Nicholas Bubwith, Bishop of Bath and Wells; the famed Cardinal Beaufort, Bishop of Winchester; and Nicholas Frome, Bishop of Glastonbury, who was chief delegate at Basle in 1434. This record was published at Louvain in 1517, a copy of which is in the Royal Library, and another in Sir Henry Wooton's. It was republished in the reign of Queen Elizabeth I and again under the Stuarts. The title of the work is '*A Briefe Abstract of the Question of Precedency Between England and Spain*', employed by Sir Henry Neville at the commission of the French king in an effort to bring peace between England and Spain, 1579.

It is of special notice that no book could be published without a royal licence. Charles I provided another licence for a printing in 1642. This book was entitled *Precedency of England in Respect to the Antiquity of Christian Religion immediately after the Passion of Christ in this Realm.* In 1651 Oliver Cromwell gave a licence substantiating the same claim.

In recent years Lord Queenborough discovered and purchased a copy of the 1642 edition, which he presented to the Royal Society of St. George.

Throughout the ages to present times such has been the power of the story of Joseph of Arimathea that kings, queens and people of Britain have defended the sovereignty of the Christian faith against all usurpers and aggressors.

What a triumphant history!

Every time I visited Glastonbury and stood before the Altar of St. Joseph amid the ruins of this glorious Abbey, my mind became crowded with the circumstances and incidents in the life of the Apostle of Britain. I seemed to sense the spirit of the noble decurio and his wonderful companions, and felt in my heart that the prophecy of Abraham, of Jacob, Isaiah, Jesus and St. Paul, had been fulfilled to the people of 'the Isles', through the medium of the uncle of Jesus.

Further reference to the tomb of St. Joseph of Arimathea at Glastonbury cannot be more fittingly presented than by reciting the words of the Rev. Lionel Smithett Lewis, former Vicar of Glastonbury, who devoted most of the eighty-six years of his life to searching the age-old archives, examining ancient tomes, official documents and yellowed manuscripts to substantiate the validity of the story of the life and death of St. Joseph and the Bethany family at Avalon, and in preserving the fascinating record of the most historic Christian church in the world. He writes:

'The body of St. Joseph, whose burial at the wattle church of St. Mary was recorded by Maelgwyn of Avalon, writing about AD 450, lay undisturbed till the year 1345, when Edward III gave his licence to John Bloom of London to dig for the body if the Abbot and monks permitted, and just as the discovery of the bones of King Arthur at Glastonbury in 1190 were recorded in far-away Essex by the monk Ralph de Coggeshall, so in a far-away monastery in 1367 we find a monk recording that "the bodies of Joseph of Arimathea and his companions were found at Glastonbury".

'The remains of St. Joseph were put in a silver casket which could be raised at will from a stone sarcophagus, the base of a shrine to which the frequent pilgrimage was made. This stone altar tomb, the base of the shrine, like the Holy Thorn, survived the Reformation.

'Holinshed, in his *"Chronicle"*, AD 1577, speaks of St. Joseph's sepulchre as being still at Glastonbury, and the learned John Ray in

238

his *"Itinerary"* records that on June 2nd, 1662, "We saw Joseph of Arimathea's tomb and chapel at the end of the church". As we have seen, the Holy Thorn was cut down in the Great Rebellion. The aftermath of the same period saw the altar tomb of St. Joseph leave its shrine. During the Commonwealth a Nonconformist divine was put in as incumbent of the Parish Church. In 1662 this interloper was turned out and a Churchman instituted. It was that very same year, in which by God's Providence John Ray came to Glastonbury and saw the tomb in the ruined chapel. Later in the year, tradition says, from fear of Puritanical fanaticism like that which destroyed the Holy Thorn, silently, hastily at night, the altar tomb was removed from the ruined shrine in St. Mary's Chapel at the Abbey, and placed in the churchyard of the Parish Church for protection outside of the East end of St. Mary's Chapel in that Church. There it remained till the autumn of 1928, when loving hands brought it reverently into the Church, and placed it in the ancient St. Katherine's Chapel, the North Transept.

'Moreover, there is a plinth inside to receive the silver ark with the Saint's remains. A glass top was put on the tomb that all generations might see what was found.'

As a matter of fact it was the Rev. Lewis who accidentally rediscovered the stone sarcophagus of Joseph. One autumn day, while walking by the ancient cemetery, he saw a large stone object, evidently lifted by the frosts, protruding from out of the earth. On examination, it was recognized as being the stone sarcophagus of St. Joseph. Willing hands helped to excavate the stone, and as the Rev. Lewis says in his report, it was re-enshrined in St. Katherine's Chapel, where it can be seen today.

It is indeed remarkable that it should be preserved undamaged from the rains, frost and snow, after reposing for two hundred and sixty-six years in its hastily constructed grave, where it had been placed in the dead of night to protect it from the desecrating hands of the fanatical Puritans.

Nearly two thousand years have passed since the uncle of Jesus was laid to his everlasting rest at Glastonbury, yet as recent as thirty years ago this sacred relic that contained his remains is almost miraculously raised from its centuries' old grave by an act of nature, to remind us, by the Will of God, of the trenchant drama of 'The Way', and our long Christian inheritance, out of which the most powerful democracies in history founded their constitutions – the Commonwealth of the British nations, and the great republic of the United States of America.

In many ancient histories describing the life of St. Joseph in Britain there is constant reference to the Holy Cruets. The story is that the two cruets contained the blood and sweat of Jesus and were brought by Joseph to Britain and were buried with him in a niche carved into his stone coffin. The old records indicate that the two cruets were held in the highest reverence by the Abbey throughout its existence. They are assigned as part of the coat of arms of Joseph. The cruets are shown imposed on a shield, one on each side of a thorny cross, with liquid droplets covering the rest of the space on the shield, symbolizing the blood and sweat of Jesus entering the cruets. They were the arms of the Abbey, and appeared in one of the large stained-glass windows of the church. The cruets and the Arthurian cross are much in evidence in the church records. King Arthur adopted the Cross of St. George as his kingly badge which can still be seen carved in the stone over one of the standing doorways.

The story of the search for the Holy Grail by the Knights of the Round Table carries a double meaning. It is generally believed that the search was for the Cup of the Last Supper, which Joseph is claimed to have concealed in Chalice Hill. On the other hand, the word Grail in old English means 'elements', which some writers indicate meant the lost cruets, in a few instances named vials. The record hardly bears out this belief, as all the early writings centuries prior to the time of King Arthur clearly state that the cruets, or vials, were placed within the sarcophagus of Joseph at his death and buried with him. The word Grail is also employed to mean a container, a chalice or a cup, which might better indicate that the search of the Knights of King Arthur was directed to find the Cup, which seems to be the most popular opinion. Mention of the Cup is shrouded in silence following the record of its concealment, but the cruets persist so strongly through the ritual of the old church, and as associated with Joseph, that there is no doubt that they represented an important memorial to the Bethany mission, perpetuated in tradition and ritual during those dramatic years.

In the report of Maelgwyn, reference is made to the fact that Joseph was buried with his eleven associates near to the Virgin Mary. Later records mention twelve associates and Leland,[135] who held a licence from Henry VIII to search the records of all the cathedrals, abbeys and places of learning in 1534, checked the library of Glastonbury Abbey. He reports thirteen associates laid to rest with Joseph, exclusive of the Mother of Jesus, and many records state that all the associates of Joseph and many other martyrs and saints were finally gathered together by his side and that of the gentle Virgin.

As we know, there were twelve companions who came to Britain with Joseph on his first arrival. If we add Marcella, the maid of the Bethany sisters, and Mary, we have fourteen members in the Bethany group. The last mention by Leland, the King's Antiquary, would indicate that all had been brought to Avalon, who had not died there, to be together as they had originally requested. We read of King Ina, AD 700, having a large number of martyrs re-interred at Avalon, and among them was the son of Joseph, who had laboured at Cor Eurgain and died at Glastonbury, over whom King Ina erected a church.

Not many years ago the church of King Ina was excavated at Glastonbury, but from lack of funds to maintain it has since become covered over again.

Roger of Hovedon, writing of the church at Marseilles, founded by Lazarus, states that after serving the church seven years, he died there and that his relics are at Marseilles. However, relics do not necessarily mean the body. Relics were associated with personal belongings which were preserved and treasured by the church. It is quite likely that the body of Lazarus was later transferred to Glastonbury. King Oswy, AD 840, was very active in transporting the bodies of martyrs and disciples from abroad to be reburied either at Glastonbury or Canterbury. Leland writes:

'The Isle of Avalon greedy of burials received thousands of sleepers among whom Joseph of Arimathea by name, entered his perpetual sleep. And he lies in a bifurcated line next the southern angle of the oratory by 13 inhabitants over the powerful adorable Virgin. Joseph had with him moreover in his sarcophagus, two white and silver cruets filled with the blood and sweat of Jesus. When his sarcophagus shall be opened it will be seen whole, and untouched in the future, and will be open to the whole world. From then neither

---

[135] Notes made as *King's Antiquary*.

water, nor dew from heaven, shall fail those inhabiting this most noble island. For much time before the Day of judgment these things shall be open in Josaphat and declared to the living.'

The statement by William of Malmesbury in *Acts of the Kings,* Book I, is also interesting and illuminating:

'The Church of which we are speaking – from its antiquity called by the Angles by way of distinction "Ealde Churche" that is "old Church" of wattle work at first, savoured somewhat of heavenly sanctity even from its foundation, and exhaled it over the whole country, claiming superior reverence though the structure was mean. Hence, here arrived whole tribes of the lower orders, thronging every path; here assembled the opulent of their pomp; and it became the crowded residence of the religious and the literary ... This church then is certainly the oldest I am acquainted with in England, and from this circumstance derives its name. In it are preserved the mortal remains of many saints, some of whom we shall notice in our progress, nor is there any corner of the church destitute of the ashes of the holy. The very floor, inlaid with polished stone, and the sides of the altar, and even the altar itself above and beneath, are laden with the multitude of relics. The antiquity and multitude of its saints have endued the place with so much sanctity that, at night, scarcely any one presumes to keep vigil there, or during the day spit upon its floor; he who is conscious of pollution shudders through his whole frame. No one ever brought hawk or horses within confines of the neighbouring cemetery who did not depart injured either in them or in himself. It is sufficiently evident that the men of that province had no oath more frequent or more sacred than to swear by The Old Church, fearing the swiftest vengeance on their perjury in this respect.

'In the meantime it is clear that the repository of so many saints may be deservedly called a heavenly sanctuary on earth. There are numbers of documents, though I abstain from mentioning them for fear of causing weariness, to prove how extremely venerable this place was held by the chief persons of the country, who there more especially chose to await the day of resurrection under the protection of the Mother of God.'

It is impossible to enumerate herein even a partial number of the thousands of illustrious names of kings, queens, apostles, disciples, saints and martyrs buried within the great Abbey and in its cemetery, in addition to St. Joseph and his twelve consecrated members of the Bethany band, and of Mary the Mother of Jesus. The illustrious host buried therein gave to this site the title of the most hallowed ground on earth. In addition it bears the name of the only royal cemetery dedicated in Christ.

We may mention in passing that King Coel, father of the famed Empress Helena, mother of Emperor Constantine the Great, is buried in the old cemetery at Glastonbury.

Queen Victoria had in her possession in the Royal Library a genealogical chart showing the kings and queens of Britain who were descended in direct line from the Shepherd King David. The genealogical chart prepared by the Rev. Milner[136] is considered to be the greatest masterpiece in proving the same fact. Through Joseph of Arimathea this strain was greatly strengthened. John of Glastonbury, historian and genealogist, shows that the children of Joseph married into the royal British families. For this reason King Arthur and the Tudor line claimed to be descended from Joseph. John of Glastonbury also asserts that the twelve Knights of the Round Table were descended from the line of Joseph, and their number of twelve was formed to perpetuate the existence of the original twelve companions who arrived in Britain with Joseph. The knights long ago passed into legend and folklore, but the famous Round Table is preserved today in Winchester County Hall, still wearing some of the green paint as decorated by Henry VIII when he entertained the French king. The original memories are still vivid of the chivalrous knights, the Quest for the Holy Grail, King Arthur and the beautiful Queen Guinevere, descendants of the Nobilis Decurio. The Thorn which Joseph planted on Weary All Hill grew to be a twin. The despoiler cut one down. The other part was saved because a splinter pierced the eye of the destroyer. He died from the wound. For thirty years it lived, long enough to see a new generation revolt against the hypocritical Puritans who had come to be hated for their desecrations, and displace them. Fortunately, a number of thorn trees had been budded from the surviving part of the original Holy Thorn, which botanists

---

[136] Milner, Rev. W.M.H. *Royal House of Britain An Enduring Dynasty +Chart* (London: The Covenant Publishing Company) 15th ed. 1991

agree was a Levantine thorn. Every Christmas the blossoms are gathered to decorate the altar of the Parish Church of St. John the Baptist, Glastonbury, keeping alive the significance of the ancient Josephian story.

St. Ninian, a British missionary out of Avalon, educated in Rome, founded Candida Casa, Whithorn, Scotland, AD 397. He was a great scholar, having served under St. Martin at Marmontier. In his travels he had found St. Jerome's original translations of the New Testament, the Psalms and Mosaic Laws. These, with many other important religious writings in the old British-Celto language, he took with him to Candida Casa, along with a copy of the Vulgate. Later, St. Columbanus, the great Celtic missionary, who died AD 615, with his Celtic co-worker St. Gall, went to Italy, where he founded Bobbio. He took with him a large quantity of the treasured *MSS.* from Candida Casa and from other Celtic church libraries. Remaining today are about seven hundred *MSS.* in the original British-Celtic language, which can be seen in the famed church libraries at Bobbio, Turin and Milan. On the margins of many appear notes made by St. Columbanus, in the same language, as readable today as when first written. At Bobbio are many beautiful illuminated works from Candida Casa, and *MSS.* of Irish Bangor. St. Gall left Bobbio to found the great monastery of St. Gall, Switzerland, and the monastery at Luxeuil in the Vosges, with their magnificent libraries containing numerous early British-Celtic manuscripts.

The famed library of St. Gallen was taken to Switzerland by the Irish disciples of St. Gallus. Among them is the religio-historical Irish *MS.* written AD 612 by St. Gallus, with considerable seventh-century Irish *MSS.* and other treasured ancient documents. In fact one finds more of these antique Irish treasures on the continent than in Ireland.

The chief data concerning the early Christian British missions are found in the British libraries, particularly in the Welsh Triads, the Psalter of Cashel, and *Chronicum Regum Pictorum.*

How deeply rooted were the lives and works of Joseph of Arimathea and the Bethany group in the early Christian workers is shown by the great wealth of documentation written by them during the six hundred years of the Golden Christian Era. The drama of the introduction of Christianity into Britain by Joseph was not confined to the British chroniclers. There are in existence many early works written by saints, scholars and church dignitaries who laboured on the continent during his lifetime and the years that followed. Some of the *MSS.*

produced in Gaul and Britanny make startling reading. All tell the same story in different form and the deep reverence in which Joseph was held by them is manifest in every word. The story never grew old. The first two books off the newly invented printing press, after the Bible, were on the Life of St. Joseph. The scholarly and historical works written of Joseph, the Apostle to the British, far outnumber the works written on the life of any one of the Apostles of Christ, St. Paul and Peter not excepted. Most of them were written by the best scholarly minds, historians and church authorities of those centuries. National disputes for over sixteen hundred years were settled on the validity of Joseph's existence in Britain with the Bethany Mission. Opposing nations recognized the validity of the claim. Disputists in the highest international church councils bowed to the belief, supported by the Popes and the Vatican into the twentieth century. Under such close scrutiny a myth, legend or tradition would have been disposed of in the first century AD. Instead, the keenest intellectuals over the centuries solidly propounded the historic fact that Joseph of Arimathea and the Bethany band did live, teach and die in Britain; that Joseph was the actual Apostle to the British, who founded the first Christian church above ground in Britain; that Britain was the first nation to accept the Christ Faith and from her shores stemmed the great army of missionaries that Christianized the world; and that the Covenant People are represented in Celto-Anglo-Saxondom.

How significant that everything appears to fall in line with prophecy!

The words of Isaiah as he addressed the people 'afar in the Isles of the West' become trenchant with positive meaning, as does the prophecy of Jeremiah. The prophets proclaimed that the Star of Jacob would spring from the line of David, the Shepherd King. Jesus, the Messiah, was descended from David, as also was His greatest banner-bearer, Joseph of Arimathea. Jesus, the Light of the World, directed His message to the 'lost sheep' whom He foretold would receive Him and His Word, and keep it. To Paul He gave His commission and the Apostle of the Gentiles went to the 'lost sheep of Israel', the Gentiles of the Isles. Joseph, the uncle of Jesus, went ahead under divine inspiration to prepare the way, converting and teaching the royal Gentiles, whom Paul established in Rome, to found the first Christian church by the uncircumcised. Joseph prepared the royal family in Britain, from whom Paul established his mission to Wales, after Joseph had laid the foundation. It was foretold that the redeemed lost sheep would keep the faith. They proved it as no other nation did by making the greatest blood sacrifice in history as they smashed the would-be destroyers of 'The Way'. They produced the man who conquered Rome with the Cross – Constantine the Great, who nationalized Rome in the faith. One hundred and fifty years before him his ancestors, the kings of Britain, were the first to nationalize their nation in the name of Christ, take their coronation oath and build their Parliamentary Constitution on the Christian platform. The sons and daughters of Manasseh founded from Britain the great republic of America, prophecy fulfilled by Britain and America, founding God's Commonwealth on which the sun never sets.

What a magnificent heritage and legacy the peoples of the Anglo-Saxon world possess and all because of one man who came to them in the beginning in the name of the Beloved One, as their Apostle. As such he remains today a successful instrument of divine guidance, Joseph of Arimathea, the Nobilis Decurio, uncle of Jesus and guardian of the Blessed Virgin, the Apostle of Christian Anglo-Saxondom in God's Commonwealth.

In striving toward the ultimate goal in His service, we can draw strength from the historic achievements of Joseph and his illustrious band, and the glorious company of the faithful who followed after making their supreme sacrifice, where necessary, in the name of Christ.

We may bow our hearts in humble appreciation of all they did for our sake to make us free men and women in the righteousness of the teachings of 'The Way'. May we arise in strength to hold aloft against His enemies the banner of the Cross Joseph first gave to Arviragus, as a sign and symbol of our race, to unite all mankind in the brotherhood of love.

The story of Joseph can never die. It is in the blood of our veins, immortalized. Joseph the Saint ended his glorious trail at Avalon, only to take up another more golden, in heaven.

Anyone who doubts the veracity of this majestic story does so in face of irrefutable evidence. As Sir Henry Spellman in *Concilia* truly writes: 'For anyone to longer doubt the historic authenticity of Glastonbury, and the Mission of Joseph, is ridiculous.'

APPENDIX

The Arrival and Establishment of Christianity in Britain

The date of the arrival of Christianity in Britain is very clearly stated in the illustrious *Historia Britannorum* compiled by Nennius in around AD 822. The compilation in the Harleian 3859 manuscript is believed to have been assembled between *circa* 650 and 822. The statement is that Christianity arrived in Britain – "in the last year of Tiberius". This would be AD 36-37 as the Roman year commenced on a date different from our present first of January. This is recorded in the Lives of the Saints and other sources.

Effectively Christianity arrived just three or four years after the crucifixion, and this is mirrored and echoed in a variety of ancient and traditional sources. The first three arrivals were St. Ilid (Joseph), St. Cyndaf (First chief-casting fisherman), and St. Mawon. With St. Ilid as the leading figure it is a simple matter to trace the Ilid place names in South East Wales. Ilid was said to be the chaplain of King Bran, great grandson of King Caradoc I, and at Trefran (Manor of Bran) there is the ancient Cor and church foundation named as Llanilid. Just west of Caer Caradoc – Castle of Caradoc ruins on Mynydd-y-Gaer = Fortress Mountain – Nant Ilid or the Stream of Ilid rises and flows down on the north side to yet another LlanIlid. Other Ilid sites are traceable and it appears that St. Ilid moved northwards towards Brecon, and the seven chapels around the site of the famous Llywel Stone would appear to mark his settlement.

The Llywel stone has three carved scenes,
1. a Pyramid and a Sphinx,
2. a man carrying a crook crossing waters,
3. the man with the shepherd's crook turning north.

Ancient Roman Maps were drawn with North turned ninety degrees to the left. When this orientation is applied to the Llywel Stone, the robed figure is travelling West from Egypt, and therefore through the Mediterranean. The figure then turns North travelling from the Gibraltar Straits to Britain. This Welsh Stone is in the British Museum in London where for 140 years it stood with these scenes to the wall and hidden, and modern protest has forced the "keepers" to move it so that the scenes are visible.

St. Ilid then appears to have moved on to the West Midlands to Glastenic – "Glastonbury" at Atherston, where the great ancient cemetery of the British still lies at Oldbury. Here he would have been under the patronage of King Gweirydd – George, the enemy feared by Nero and misnamed by the Romans as Arviragus. In British tradition Joseph – St. Ilid – gave Gweirydd "George" the white flag with the red cross emblazoned upon it.

The evidence points to St. Ilid arriving in Western Britain in AD 37 some five years before Claudius I invaded South East England. So King Caradoc I and his family, including the famous daughter St. Eurgain were Christian long before Caradoc I was treacherously betrayed and taken to Rome in AD 52 (15 years). St. Eurgain founded her well-known college monastery on the South-East Wales coast. There has been much confusion made by outsiders who have not investigated South-East Wales History. The Genealogies consistently show Bran was taken to Rome as a very young child, and he in turn later had a son named Caradoc II. The second Caradoc has been confused with the first, and Bran could not have been an old King when taken to Rome in AD 52.

Alan Wilson

BIBLIOGRAPHY

Abbott, L., *Evolution of Christianity*, Boston: Houghton, Mifflin and Co. 1893.
Alford, M., *Fides Regia Britannica sive Annales Ecclesiae Britannicae*, 1663, 4 vols.

Baronius, Cardinal C., *Annales Ecclesiastici (Ecclesiastical Annals)*, 12 volumes, 1588-1607.
Bede, *Historia ecclesiastica gentis Anglorum (The Ecclesiastical History of the English People) c. AD 731.*
Bumpus,T. F., *The Cathedrals of England and Wales*, (London: T.Werner Laurie) 1907.

Collier, *The Twelve Lessons of the Covenant Law.*
Cressy, Hugh Paulinus (1605 - 1674*), Church History of Brittany, or England* (1668).
Crossley, F.H., *The English Abbey.*
Cutts, *Turning Points in Church History.*

De Witt, *The History of France.*

Edwards, Archbishop, *Landmarks.*
Eichler, *The Customs of Mankind.*
*Elder, I. Hill, *Celt, Druid and Culdee*, The Covenant Publishing Company Ltd 1973.
Elliott, *Remarkable Characters and Places in the Holy Land.*

Froude, *Reign of Mary Tudor.*
Froude, *Edward VI.*

*Gayer, *The Heritage of the Anglo-Saxon Race - Chart,* The Covenant Publishing Company Ltd.
Gildas, *De Excidio et Conquestu Britanniae.*
Giraldus Cambrensis, *Topographia Hibernica (1188), Itinerarium Cambriae (1191), Descriptio Cambriae (1194).*
*Gordon, E. O., *Prehistoric London*, The Covenant Publishing Company Ltd. 1946.
Green, J. R., *Short History of the English People.*
Guizot, *The History of Gaul.*

Heath, Rev. Alban, *The Painted Savages of England,* The Covenant Publishing Co. Ltd.
Hewins, Prof. W.A.S., *The Royal Saints of Britain.*
Hughson, Rev., *Henry VII,*

Jones, Owen; Williams, Edward; Pughe, William Owen, (ed.), *Myvyrian Archaiology of Wales, collected out of ancient manuscripts.* 3 vols. 1801-7.

Kinnaman, Prof., *Diggers for Facts.*

Leatham, Diana, *They Built Upon Rock.*
Lewis, Rev. L. Smithett, *Glastonbury, the Mother of Saints.*
Lewis, Rev. L. Smithett, *The Holy Land of Britain.*
*Lewis, Rev. L. Smithett, *St. Joseph of Arimathea at Glastonbury,* (Cambridge: James Clarke & Co. Ltd.) 7th edn. 2nd imp. 1976.

MacKendrick, *God's Commonwealth,* The Covenant Publishing Company Ltd.
Marston, Sir Charles, *The Bible Comes Alive.*
Marston, Sir Charles, *The Bible is True.*
Milman, *The History of the Jews.*
Mommsen. Prof., *The History of Rome.*
Morgan, Rev. R.W., *The Churches of England and Rome.*
*Morgan, Rev. R. W., *St. Paul in Britain*, The Covenant Publishing Company Ltd 1978.
Morgan, Rev. R. W., *The Saints in Britain.*

Nicholson*, England's Greater Churches.*

O'Reilly, Rev. A. J., *The Martyrs of the Coliseum.*
O'Reilly, Rev. A. J., *The Victims of the Mamertine.*

Parsons, Rev. R., *Three Conversions of England.*
Prothero, Rev., *The Psalms in Human Life.*
Prydain, *Genealogies of the Saints in Britain.*

Rash, Rev. A. F., *This Sceptred Isle,* The Covenant Publishing Company Ltd.
Rees, Rev., *Welsh Saints.*
Ross, *The History of England.*

Simpson, *The Celtic Church of Britain, Gaul, Scotland, Ireland.*
Skeats, *Joseph of Arimathea.*
Smith, Dr. W., *Dictionary of Christian Biography.*
Smith, Dr. W., *Dictionary of the Bible.*
Spelman, Sir Henry, *Concilia.*
Stanley, Dean, *Historical Memorials of Canterbury.*

BIBLIOGRAPHY

Stokes, *Ireland and the Celtic Church.*
Strickland, Agnes, *Life of Queen Elizabeth I.*

Taylor, *Celtic Christianity in Cornwall.*
*Taylor, J.W., *The Coming of the Saints.*
Thierry's *'Norman Conquest'.*
Timbs & Gunn, *Abbeys, Castles and Ancient Halls of England and Wales.*
Trumper, *Historical Sites in Palestine.*

Winbolt, *Britain B.C.*

Young, *Analytical Concordance to the Bible.*

The Holy Bible (Scofield and King James versions).
The Oxford Biblical Dictionary and Concordance.
The Talmud.
The Anglo-Saxon Chronicle.
The Domesday Book.
Martyrologium Hieronymianum.
British Triads.
Classical references:
Works of Herodotus.
Virgil.
Martial.
Juvenal.
Julius Cæsar.

Valuable evidence and information in the form of ancient relics, documents and artefacts are to be found in the British Museum, London. Also in Edinburgh, Belfast, Dublin, and Cardiff.

Nearly all of the ancient abbeys and churches and cathedrals in Britain, particularly England, have a wealth of ancient historic documents, artefacts and numismatic collections bearing witness to the origin and development of the Christian Church in Britain as the original champion of the Christian faith.

Titles listed with an asterisk (*) are obtainable from The Covenant Publishing Co. Ltd., 121 Low Etherley, Bishop Auckland, County Durham, DL14 0HA, U.K. Tel: 01388 835753; email: admin@covpub.co.uk; www.covpub.co.uk.

INDEX

A

Abraham, 46, 50, 89, 238
Agricola, 96, 120, 148, 158, 202, 215
Agrippira, Queen, 105, 106
Alfred, King, 146, 207
Altars, stone, 46, 47, 81, 94, 110
Anglo-Saxon, 45, 51-54, 146, 231
Annas, High Priest, 11, 13, 21
Apostolic succession through St.
   Joseph, 72, 85, 164, 206, 227
Aquila, 113
Aricia, Queen of the Brigantes, 103,
   108, 109, 150, 215
Aristobulus, 38, 74, 78, 128, 161, 170,
   174, 185, 187-189, 190, 191, 193,
   233, *See also* Christian Martyrs:
   British
Ark of the Covenant, 43, 46
Arles, 31, 66, 167, 168, 196, 224
Arnobius, 80
Arthur, King, 207, 227, 231, 238, 240,
   243
Arviragus, 68, 71, 83, 86, 9-98, 101,
   108, 114, 127, 146, 150, 153, 154,
   158, 184, 192, 211, 216, 222, 236,
   248
Astronomy, druidical, 76
Augustus, Emperor Caesar, 18, 58,
   118
Aulus Plautius, 94, 97, 99-102, 107,
   114, 115, 117, 118, 120
Avalon, Sacred Isle, 71, 87, 97, 148,
   173, 202, 209, 246
Avilion, Isle of Departed Spirits, 148

B

Bangor Abbey, 7, 194, 195, 244;
   Mother of Monasteries, 194
Banner of the Cross, 86, 110, 233,
   236, 246

Baronius, Cardinal, 31, 62, 64, 65, 69,
   78, 122, 130, 140, 159, 160, 175,
   181, 191, 207, 213, 222, 229
Beatus, 170
Bede, the Venerable, 64, 122, 140,
   170, 183, 194, 207, 213
Belinus, 91
Bethany group, 38, 46, 62, 71, 140,
   146, 148, 165, 166, 169, 173, 199,
   230, 236, 241, 243, 244
Bethany Mission, 240
Blake, William, *Jerusalem*, 148, 149
Boadicea, Queen: attack on London,
   155; last battle and death, 156;
   place of last battle, 157; Queen of
   the Iceni, 153, 156; Statue, 157
Boniface III, first to accept title of
   Pope, 85, 206
Bran, King, 94, 120, 125, 186, 187-
   194, 203, 247, 248
Brennus, 91, 188
Brigantes, 94, 103, 108, 150, 215
Britain in AD 36, 33
Britain, naming of, 43
British Church antiquity, 76, 79, 84,
   85, 116, 125, 127, 128, 132, 164,
   172, 178, 182, 183, 190, 198, 205,
   206, 208, 210, 211, 217, 221, 236,
   241
British Church, different from Roman
   Catholic Church, 84
British Coins, 211
British Commonwealth, 53, 72, 214,
   218
British Freedom, 110
British language, 36, 48
British religion, 43
British Royal Family, genealogical
   chart, 243
Brittanic Isles, 45, 80
Brutus, 34
Byzantium, 224

252

C

Caiaphas, 10-13, 18, 19, 21, 22, 25, 82

Cairns, 47

Candida Casa, Whithorn Priory, 177, 244

Canute, King, 146

Capgrave, 67, 135, 140, 146, 165, 207

Caractacus, 68, 86, 87, 95-120, 125, 147, 150, 152, 153, 173, 176-204, 215, 218, 233

Caradoc, 68, 86, 94, 106, 118, 151, 177, 186-188, 198, 223, 233, 247, 248

Cassiterides, Tin Islands, 35, 39

Catacombs, 87

Celts, 34, 41-43, 45, 52, 94, 160

Chichester Stone, 118

Christian Church in Rome, 111

Christian Martyrs, 221; British, 87, 131, 220; Aristobulus, 189; Simon Zelotes, 161; Timotheus, Pudentiana, Praxedes, Novatus, 121

Christian names, 186

Christian persecution: Claudius, 88; Diocletian, 219; ended with Emperor Constantine, 222; Maximian, 220; Tiberius, 28

Christian, origins of the title, 37

Christianity, spread of, 201

Christians exiled from Holy Land, 29

Chrysostom, Patriarch of Constantinople, 64, 81, 83

Claudia, adopted daughter of Claudius, *see also* Gladys, 115-130, 171, 172, 176, 177, 182, 192, 193, 199, 201, 203, 216, 218

Claudian persecution, 58, 90-92, 96-109, 113-119, 142, 147, 151, 155, 159, 160, 171, 176, 177, 184, 220, 230, 233

Claudius, Emperor Caesar, 28, 88, 91, 94-107, 114, 115, 118, 122, 124, 128, 150-151, 176-177, 187, 193, 211, 230, 248

Clun, 102, 103, 110, 115, 150, 188

Coel, King, 216-219, 224, 243

Cogidubnus, King, 120

Cogidunus, King, 118

Colchester, 78, 154, 211, 212, 216-219, 222, 224

Constantine, Emperor, 85, 86, 93, 116, 163, 174, 182, 183, 211, 213, 217-218, 221-224, 226-229, 243, 246

Constantius Chlorus, Emperor, 215, 216, 218-221

Cor Eurgain, or Caer Urgan, 193, 198, 203, 218, 219, 241

Coraniaid, 108, 152, 153

Crescens, founded church in Gaul, 66

Crimea, 35, 47, 49

Cromwell, Oliver, 73, 147, 237

Cross, 77, 83, 97

Culdee, Culdees, 38, 193

Cyllinus, 107, 111, 120, 186, 187, 193, 194, 203

Cymric, 33-36, 43, 46, 48, 101, 112, 113, 121, 189, 192, 194, 197

Cynon, 111, 120, 186, 187, 193

D

Dammonia, Devon, 40

Danes, 45, 52, 147

Danites, 57

David, King, 17, 88, 245

Decianus, Catus, 151, 155, 160, 215

Decurio, Nobilis, *see also* Joseph of Arimathea, 15, 135

Defender of the Faith, 72, 203, 213

Diocese of London, 224

Diocletian, Emperor: Diocletian persecution, 58, 92, 93, 190, 203, 213, 219-222, 228

Divorce, 89

Domesday Book, 71, 145, 146

Domus Dei, the House of God, 145

T

Tabernacle, 75, 225
Taliesin, 81
Tarshish, 40, 57
Tax, paid by Jesus, 139
Tertullian of Carthage, 80
The Anglo-Saxon Chronicle, 146
The Mass, 164
Theanus, first Bishop of London, 208
Tiber, battle at, 221
Tiberius, Emperor Caesar, 18, 28, 58,
   81, 82, 118, 230, 247
Tin Mines of Britain, 15, 40, 41
Tithes, 225
Titus, 28, 102, 110
Torture, Roman, 92, 104, 179, 180
Tradition, meaning of, 37
Trajan, Emperor, 175
Tréves, or Trier, 217
Triads of Lazarus, 165
Triads of Paul, 195, 196
Trinobantes, 154
Tudors, 243
Tullian Keep, or Mamertine, 179

U

United States of America, 14, 53, 54,
   74, 76, 84, 112, 138, 162, 218, 240,
   246
Ussher, Archbishop, 64, 67, 72, 79,
   141, 158, 198, 213, 219, 235, 236

V

Veranius, 150
Vatican, The, 78, 129; Library, 31,
   34, 112

Venissa, *see also* Venus Julia, 114
Venus Julia, *see also* Venissa, 98,
   101, 114
Venusius, Pendragon of the Iceni,
   153, 158
Verulam, Verulamium, *see also* St.
   Albans, 121, 150, 154, 156, 221
Vespasian, Emperor, 28, 102, 110
Vicar of God, King Lucius, 210
Victoria, Queen, 243
Virgin Mary, 16, 70, 133, 136, 137,
   142, 143, 169, 234, 240
Vitalian, Pope, 182, 183
Vortigern, 51

W

Warwickshire, 156
Wattle Chapel, 74-76, 141, 231, 234,
   236, 238
Weary All Hill, 73, 243
Whitby, Council of, 164
Whithorn Priory, *see* Candida Casa,
   244
Whiting, Abbot, 147
William, King, 146, 204, 227
Winchester, 72, 79, 127, 178, 203,
   204, 207, 209, 211, 214, 226, 243
Worship of Images and Relics, 198

Y

Yesu, 77
Yiddish, 36
York, seat of Emperors, 215
Yorkshire Britons, 109

BOOKS FOR FURTHER READING

The Stone of Destiny by F.Wallace Connon
A substantially revised and updated version of this classic text about the history and mystery of the Stone of Destiny: the British Coronation Stone. Includes a new chapter by Michael A. Clark on the return of the Stone to Scotland in 1996.

Celt, Druid and Culdee by I. Hill Elder
Which is the first Christian Church outside Jerusalem? Who brought Christianity to the British Isles? Who were the Druids and what did they teach?
All these and many other questions are answered in this remarkable book.

Did Our Lord Visit Britain as they say in Cornwall and Somerset? by the Revd C.C. Dobson, M.A.
Now in a new revised edition, this booklet keeps alive the traditions and legends of the early Christian church, long before Augustine. It shows that the Protestant Faith is built upon "The Rock" of our Lord Jesus and not the "shifting sands" of any one ordinary man.

Our Neglected Heritage by Gladys Taylor
A series of five booklets tracing the establishment and growth of the early British Church. "For many centuries the people of Britain and England in particular have been kept in ignorance of their true history."
Read these books and find out the truth as "this applies to both Christian and pre-Christian times."
Volume 1: The Early Church
Volume 2: The Hidden Centuries
Volume 3: The Magnet of the Isles
Volume 4: The Celtic Influence
Volume 5: Division and Dispersion

Our National Liturgy: The Book of Common Prayer by A.W. Faith
The Book of Common Prayer is, next to the Bible, the most important literary monument of the Christian reformation of the Faith. Second only to the Bible, it has been the greatest force in the development of the Anglo-Saxon character.

The Royal House of Britain: An Enduring Dynasty by Rev W.H.M. Milner
A hardback presentation of the genealogy of our Royal Family. It includes a detailed chart tracing our throne back to King David of Israel.

These books and many others are obtainable from:

The Covenant Publishing Company Limited
121 Low Etherley
Bishop Auckland
Co Durham
DL14 0HA
United Kingdom
Telephone: +44 (0) 1388 835 753
Email: admin@covpub.co.uk